4636 9046

THE **DOPER**
NEXT
DOOR

THE DOPER NEXT DOOR

MY STRANGE AND SCANDALOUS YEAR ON PERFORMANCE ENHANCING DRUGS

ANDREW TILIN

COUNTERPOINT

BERKELEY

Copyright © 2011 by Andrew Tilin. All rights reserved under International
and Pan-American Copyright Conventions.

Library of Congress Cataloging-in-Publication Data

Tilin, Andrew.
The doper next door : my strange and scandalous year on performance-enhancing drugs /
Andrew Tilin.
p. cm.
ISBN-13: 978-1-58243-715-6 (hardback)
ISBN-10: 1-58243-715-7 (hardback)
1. Drug abuse—Social aspects—California—San Francisco. 2. Tilin, Andrew—Drug use—
Biography. 3. Body image. 4. Testosterone. 5. Hormones. I. Title.
HV5833.S25T55 2011
362.290973—dc23
2011012718

Cover design by Michael Fusco
Interior design by meganjonesdesign.com

COUNTERPOINT
1919 Fifth Street
Berkeley, CA 94710
www.counterpointpress.com

Distributed by Publishers Group West
Printed in the United States of America

10 9 8 7 6 5 4 3 2 1

for mom, dad, and tracy
If only the four of us could go out for Chinese. Boy.

for michael
Pull me, I'll push you, forever.

for my beautiful wife and children
The love one heart can hold.

contents

note from the author

Heck yes, I changed some names in this book. Not mine, nor the names of my expert sources. But I felt that certain participating friends, family members, and professionals deserved protection and privacy in the wake of my unconventional acts. However, this is a work of nonfiction. Everyone in it is a real person (or cat, or hormone). All the events in this book occurred, although I occasionally resequenced them, and sometimes I altered details in order to make a person or people less identifiable. Some conversations, particularly those from my distant past, have been re-created to the best of my abilities.

prologue

say hi to dad

The syringes aren't cooperating. There are two of them next to my bathroom sink, each about the size of a ballpoint pen. One contains testosterone, the other a hormone known as DHEA. Together, I've been told, they will make my middle-aged body leaner, stronger, and sexier . . . turn me into the Adonis I've never been. I've spent months getting my hands on these drugs, and by now I have a reasonable grasp on an elaborate doping protocol. Yet on this first morning as a doper, I realize that nobody has ever said anything about how to remove the syringe caps. Do the little plastic knobs unscrew? Even with plenty of nervous energy at my disposal, the suckers are on tight. I grab one of the syringes off the counter to try again. Sweat trickles down my back.

My kids aren't helping. Having finished their morning routines, they're standing outside the bathroom door. It's a Tuesday—my turn to drive them to school.

"Daddy!" Sophie hollers, turning the bathroom's doorknob.

I anticipated my five-year-old's attempts at barging in on me. My pants and underpants hang around my ankles, but I have wedged my left knee up against the door. Sophie can't open it.

"When are we going?" she pleads. Sophie isn't as quiet and shy as she was just a year earlier in preschool. She already has convictions.

"Just a minute," I say. Did doping superstar athletes like Jose Canseco ever have such mornings? "I'm almost done," I lie.

I'm at the beginning of a journey that already feels long. So far, I've endlessly contemplated why I want to get involved with perfor-mance-enhancing drugs. Reassured my worried wife that steroids would turn me into a young man instead of a hormone-fueled fury. Guaranteed her that our sex life would reach new heights. Weighed the legality and ethics of entering—and perhaps unfairly dominat-ing—my beloved amateur bicycle races. Worried about how my drug use might affect my kids. Wondered if the drugs would open some Pandora's box that holds both myths and truths about virility. Performed exhaustive research just to find someone I could trust to recommend a doping protocol that won't kill me. Endured batteries of blood tests.

And then I had to get the stuff.

A little twist and a strong pull, I finally discover, and the syringe cap comes unstuck.

A fist pounds on the bathroom door. "Dad, where's my Paul Frank sweater?"

It's Benjamin, my seven-year-old. He's sweet and has a soft demeanor, that is when he's not being a punky little boy. He's also, already, a style king.

Benjamin turns the doorknob now. I press my knee harder against the door.

"I don't know. Pick out something else, buddy," I say, and decide to start with the DHEA. The hormone is delivered through a topical cream that's packaged in a syringe for precision dosing. I press the tube's blue plunger slowly with my right thumb, carefully watching it inch past seven hash marks until a dime-sized lump wiggles out onto the tip of my left index finger. The cream is white and cool, a bit thicker than hand lotion. I reach around and rub it onto my lower back, introducing a hormone that's supposed to act like a physiological pump-primer for the rocket fuel that is testosterone.

I grab the other syringe, squeezing out the testosterone, which I apply to my inner thighs. This white lotion is gummier than the DHEA cream—I rub it vigorously into my skin, but little white specks remain around my pores and leg hair.

"Dad, what are you doing?" Benjamin asks impatiently. He'd apparently found his sweater. Then I hear the kids launch into a pillow fight on my bed.

"Just getting off the toilet," I announce, fanning my crotch with one hand. I use the other to flush, even though there's nothing to flush.

I still see some white specks, but we're running late for school. I pull up my pants and then wash my hands. Washing is important: "Contaminating" others with supplemental testosterone, I've been warned, can have serious repercussions, especially for children. The partner of a testosterone user told me that her two-year-old sprouted pubic hair.

Benjamin gives another twist of the doorknob and a push. To his and Sophie's surprise, the door swings open. And with all the drama of a curtain being raised, a different father appears before them. Here, my little ones, for better or worse, is your forty-two-year-old drugged up dad, a guy with a wife, a cat, a mortgage, two therapists, multiple bicycles, a career, and now enough foreign substances in his body to get him thrown out of the Tour de France. Call him the parent with an asterisk, the everyman's cheater.

Call him the doper next door.

"Now," I ask the two bright faces staring up at me, "are we ready for the day?"

here's your citizen doper

The drugs found me.

I know, that sounds a lot like the lame excuses served up by pro athletes busted for doping. "I needed to keep up with the competition," they protest. Or, "Everyone else was doing it." *Everyone else was doing it*—the classic, pathetic argument that's never weaker than when you're deploying it to justify dumping chemicals into your body that influence your muscles, mind, relationships, and *cojones*. Not that my reason for getting on the stuff was any better. In fact, my path to doping—the complicated and wild world of doping—really did start with someone else who was doing it. My wife, Juliana. My sweet, grounded, yoga-teaching, family-portrait-shooting wife. While Juliana acknowledges and confronts life's infinite strains, she routinely aspires to smile and be happy. And when she became a doper, I watched her doping do incredible things for her. Because of Juliana, I became a doper, too.

The story starts on an unremarkable workday morning in the middle of 2007, about six months before I introduce my body to supplemental testosterone. Juliana stands opposite me, on the other side of our unmade, king-size bed. She's brushing her teeth.

"Will you straighten the sheet?" I ask.

Juliana and I, together or separately, have made our shared bed every morning for the better part of seventeen years, which is how long we've been a couple. We both can live with growing piles of mail or unfolded laundry—Juliana even better than me. In fact a basket full of the latter, jammed full of clean and colorful workout and cycling clothes, has been sitting in our small bedroom for the last couple days. It's right next to our dresser, pushed against a rolled up yoga mat and a cylinder of foam that I sometimes use to iron out the tightness in my muscles. I swear, my body gets stiffer with each passing week.

Juliana shakes her head *no* but since she has a mouth full of toothpaste foam, she can't say why she's not cooperating. I give her a look, one that says *Come on already. I want to leave for work.* Juliana responds only as she can: Her full cheeks lift the corners of her mouth into a broad, warm, tolerant smile, toothpaste and all. This woman knows my quick temper, how even little things can make me anxious. She's patient with my moods, and I know I'm lucky. She's my easygoing girl.

I laugh. We count on each other a lot to laugh.

Her mouth still full of toothpaste, Juliana pulls back the blanket to expose the bottom sheet. It's wet. The damp spot on the sheet is considerable, easily the size of her torso.

"Oh," I say, and I let the sheet float back down to the mattress. For a while now, Juliana has had these crazy-bad night sweats. They can be so intense that her nightgown gets drenched. Sometimes I wake up in the early morning hours and catch her silhouette moving across the room in search of something dry to wear. Other times I wake up at daylight only to find Juliana naked and conked out under damp sheets.

"Strip the bed," she manages to say without spilling any of the toothpaste foam in her mouth. "Seeing doctor today."

I pull the bedding off the mattress while Juliana steps inside our bathroom to spit.

"What do you think is the matter?" I ask. I hear Juliana rinsing her mouth in the sink. We can easily converse between the two rooms—our "master bath," so to speak, is ridiculously small, no bigger than a tiny closet. We bought our aging, fixer-upper of a house in the Bay Area's Oakland Hills largely because it's close to open space that's filled with trails for running, biking, and hiking. We tolerate the outdated bathrooms.

"I'm getting older. It's a big drag," says Juliana, using two fingers on her left hand to stretch the skin on her forehead while looking at herself in the bathroom mirror. We're both conscious of the deepening lines in our faces.

"You know, I'm just exhausted again," she says, the brightness quickly leaving her voice. I've noticed more and more mood swings in Juliana. She'll be cheery as usual, then suddenly become irritable. It's not like her.

"I don't really want to hear what the doctor has to say," she continues. "I'm probably perimenopausal."

I'm not totally clear on what "perimenopausal" means, but I'm sure it has something to do with aging, and that it's not a laughing matter for women. I decide, for once, to keep my mouth shut. There's no way to playfully ask if perimenopause turns women like Juliana

from happy, quirky, vibrant forty-one-year-olds into sleepless, sometimes surly, low-libido Ms. Hydes. Also not funny.

"I'm sure the doctor will help," I say, gathering the bed sheets into
my arms. "There's medicine for perimenopause, right?"

"Well, there are hormones," says Juliana, opening the door to the
shower and turning on the water.

"Like what?"

"Estrogen and progesterone," she says. "I've heard that some
women use testosterone and human growth hormone, too.

"I'm getting in the shower. Have a good day," Juliana adds, and
waves blankly before closing the glass door behind her. She then raises
her voice over the noise of the running water to tell me to wake up
Benjamin and Sophie on my way out. They have school.

Testosterone and human growth hormone, I think. Any sports nut
has heard of that stuff, which through the years I'd also seen called
"T" and "HGH." I've loved baseball since I was a kid, and of course
I'm aware that Barry Bonds, the famous, muscle-bound slugger for
my beloved San Francisco Giants, is accused of using T and HGH to
improve his athletic performance.

Then I think about aging women using similar drugs, and wonder
if it makes them all bulgy and imposing too.

Old lady dopers, I think while walking down our hallway, holding
the bundle of damp sheets. *Maybe they could hit homers on testosterone and HGH.*

Now that's a funny thought.

I ASK MY PAL MICHAEL what he thinks of when he hears the word
"hormone." I'm still tickled and intrigued by the conversation I'd had

with Juliana a couple days earlier about the T and HGH. I'd never thought of those drugs as some sort of *medicine*.

"I think of what dopers use to cheat in sports. Stuff like testosterone," says Michael over his mobile phone. "How about you?"

"Same," I say.

I'm on my mobile phone too. We're both stuck in morning rush-hour traffic in different parts of the Bay Area. I'm on the way to my small Berkeley office from where I report and write stories as a free-lance journalist. He's headed to the high school where he teaches.

I've known Michael Piesco since 1975, when we were both ten years old. He's one of my closest friends. There's nothing I can't tell him, and we think similarly about many things—food, sports, fitness, and humor. Interacting with Mike, however, isn't all backslaps. My buddy strongly defends the truth in this world as he perceives it, even if his views sometimes put him at odds with people—his family, or me, or even everyone who loves fast food.

Over my cell phone, I mention what's been going on lately with Juliana, and how her body may be changing with age.

"I don't want to hear that. The way you and Juliana and I take care of ourselves, we deserve to be twenty-five and strong for a long time," he says. "The people who line up for Burger King and could care less about their bodies should grow old for us."

"Juliana said that some women take testosterone and HGH as they age," I say. "Bizarre."

"I guess if Juliana ever decides to race a bike," says Michael, "she'll be right at home with all the other cheaters."

That's a good one. Michael and I are both cycling nuts, and if there's any sport that's synonymous with hormones, steroids, and performance-enhancing drugs, it's professional bike racing. But Mike's response reflects what plenty of people—really, plenty of men—think about supplemental hormones. Performance enhancement, however, is only part of the story of hormone use.

"I don't think Juliana could be found guilty of doping," I say. "Her doctor only gave her prescriptions for estrogen and progesterone. They don't boost athletic performance. I looked it up."

In doing my research I'd also discovered that Juliana's experience is hardly unique. Supplemental hormone consumption figures vary widely (the industry isn't uniformly regulated), but in 2007 American women received well over 10 million prescriptions for such hormones. The drugs are designed to counter the physiological and chemical changes that occur in their maturing (middle age and beyond) bodies. Specifically, these women battle perimenopause and menopause, which are the stretches of their lives when menstruation becomes irregular and ultimately stops altogether. Menopause thus causes a loss of fertility, and for some women the changes to their bodies also bring on mood swings, hot flashes and/or night sweats, and a decreased sexual appetite, among other symptoms. In search of relief, some women take synthetic versions of estrogen and progesterone, two naturally occurring hormones in women's bodies that are depleted during perimenopause and menopause. As for testosterone and human growth hormone, Juliana was right: Occasionally, I read, older women also take synthetic versions of those hormones—testosterone for added libido, HGH for improved sleep and vitality—to fight the effects of aging.

"They don't take them to hit mammoth home runs," I tell Michael.

"At least not in the Major Leagues," he says. "Who knows what goes on in the dugouts of women's softball games. Let's just say I've seen girls with Bonds-like power."

Mike's comments are snarky, but I confess: I identify with his thinking. Men, especially those who watch as much late-night ESPN as Mike and I do, often react differently to the idea of hormone use than women. While women have learned about the role of hormones in their bodies since puberty, men often remain ignorant of their own natural hormones. In short, say "testosterone" or "human growth hormone," and most men think bad thoughts. They think performance enhancement, doping, cheating.

And yes, I credit our collective dubiousness in part to the media, which for over two decades has educated us and shaped our views about substances like T and HGH. Sports journalists have focused on the ways these hormones promote the enhancement of muscle and athletic ability. Testosterone is a hormone. Specifically, it's a hormone as well as a steroid, which is really a particular kind of molecule that's made inside our bodies as well as in laboratories. HGH isn't a steroid but a protein-based hormone, and it's also made naturally as well as synthetically. They both trigger muscle growth, but also serve a number of other functions in adult bodies that sports journalists largely ignore.

That same press has also repeatedly vilified testosterone and growth hormone, and for a justifiable reason: Despite being frowned upon in essentially all competition, such hormones are frequently taken by athletes to gain an unfair advantage. So Canadian sprinter Ben Johnson, who introduced many sports fans to steroids when he was caught doping with testosterone-derived drugs at the 1988 Summer Olympics, was portrayed in newspapers and magazines as a monster. Slugger Jose Canseco did nothing for his bad boy image when he wrote the 2005 book *Juiced*, a tell-all about drug abuse in Major League Baseball. Cynical reporters felt that American cyclist Floyd Landis, who tested positive for using testosterone in the 2006 Tour de France, was lying about his proclaimed innocence—and they turned out to be right.

As for baseball's Barry Bonds, it's unlikely that he'll ever be found guilty of using substances like T and HGH. But in the 2007 baseball season, which was underway when I began learning about hormones, Bonds was en route to capturing the nearly mythical title of Major League Baseball's all-time home run leader. Yet media and fans across the country regularly booed him. Maybe he deserved it—even longtime Giants fans like Michael and me have our misgivings about the insufferable superstar.

"Bonds has already been hung in the court of public opinion," I tell Mike as I drive. "The same can be said for hormones like testosterone and human growth hormone."

Mike interjects. "Okay, fine, so there are middle-aged women who take hormones. Some of us have jobs waiting for us, Mr. Drug Detective. What's your point?"

"Wait. It's coming," I say.

I tell Michael that, sure enough, a test from Sweden found that women who take supplemental testosterone have more sex drive. The National Institute on Aging admitted that older women on growth hormone shed body fat. And, I say, these drugs aren't only being administered to aging women: Teenagers, horses, dwarves, dogs, and the diseased have all been administered hormones and performance-enhancing drugs for a variety of reasons. Finally, I mention that I dug up some news distributed by the Massachusetts Institute of Technology. It said older men could benefit from the use of supplemental testosterone.

The phone line is silent. I can tell that Michael thinks I'm bullshitting him. He wants to hear more before he says anything. Testosterone, to his thinking, is just for athletes trying to gain an edge.

Get to the stuff about guys like us being twenty-five forever.

"Older men are already taking it," I tell him. "Middle-aged men like you or me, and older. Not to earn pro contracts. Just to hold off decline."

I explain how I read about doctors who believe that relatively healthy middle-aged men enter their own type of menopause, and that these men might want to take steroids and additional hormones that we've come to know as performance-enhancing drugs not to win home-run titles but to rev up their fading bodies. I describe Web pages dedicated to the rejuvenating benefits of testosterone, and whether it's best taken via cream or a hypodermic needle. I found odes to growth hormone's abilities to reshape older physiques, and tales of Joe Schmoes dosing up on erythropoietin, or "EPO," a blood-enhancement drug that's been widely used by cheating endurance athletes. I add that I saw some memorable images, too. The heads of gray-haired men with wrinkled faces set atop incredibly muscular bodies. The images seemed laughable and wacky, like the most amateurish of Photoshopped pictures. But the captions insisted that the photographs hadn't been doctored.

"I kept visiting the same Web pages because I couldn't believe what I saw," I explain. "Maybe it's proven medicine and I just haven't heard about it. But when I read about regular guys taking drugs like testosterone, HGH, and EPO, I kept thinking that this was doping. That maybe we're living among doping dads, doping neighbors, doping accountants, and that somehow they're slimy, like Canseco and Floyd Landis. I don't know, citizen dopers. Somehow they're cheating. Like, time. Age."

I would later discover that AndroGel, which is a leading testosterone supplement made by Solvay Pharmaceuticals, was prescribed 1.6 million times in one year alone. Small compared to the women's hormone market. Still, that's a lot of T.

Michael hasn't said anything for a while now.

"Mike?" I add.

"I'm still here," he says.

I know why else he's quiet. Michael and I are both deep into our careers, and I'm raising a family, too. But some things haven't changed much since we were fifth graders at San Francisco's Town School for Boys. At Town we'd come up with conspiracy theories about our strict teachers, and pretend to act out the heroic feats of our favorite pro athletes on Town's blacktop play yard. Thirty-two years later, Michael and I are both recreational bike racers, living fifty miles from each other in the Bay Area and doing our best imitations of Lance Armstrong, the seven-time winner of the Tour de France. And just like the olden days, we can fall into conversations that pit us against the world.

After every bike race where Michael and I get trounced, which is to say just about every race we enter, the two of us make each other feel better by assuring one another that we face a lot of dubious competition. We swear that some of the cyclists we ride against, with their cut bodies, powerful sprinting abilities, and endless endurance, must be on the kinds of performance-enhancing drugs that have also been used by the many pro riders who have been busted over the years. We're half-joking, but then again, we're half-serious. Who can hold down a job, let alone have a significant other or a family, or even have time to tackle mundane chores like oil changes or taking out the trash, and ride the way some of these guys ride? Dopers! Scumbags! Our suspicions make us feel better about finishing well behind the winners, even if we have no evidence to back up our claims.

"You really think guys are doping in our races?" he finally says. Mike has always been serious about his racing. He's more dedicated to the sport than I am. Cycling clothes and bikes play the roles of decorations and furniture in his apartment.

"I'm not sure. I guess it depends how easy it is to get the drugs, or medicine, or whatever it's called," I say. "I bet there's a whole black market for it.

"It could be anybody," I go on. "How do I know it's not you? Are you a doper?" I joke.

"Yeah, right, I'm a doper," he chuckles. "That is the most ridiculous thing I've ever heard."

I'VE SPENT A LOT of my career as a magazine journalist writing about sports, and following around hardbodies with my pad and pen. The endless stream of backpackers, yogis, and triathletes as well as elite runners, skiers, mountaineers, and pro cyclists that I've interviewed all have had one thing in common: youth. Which is why, for days after my discussion with Michael, I can't keep the Internet images of those men with wrinkled faces and young bodies out of my head.

They look like aliens. Just wrong. Why would anyone do that to himself?

I've gone from being interested in hormone-using, menopausal women like Juliana to preoccupied by men who aren't much different than me—at least, I'd imagine, not to begin with—save for the fact that they're apparently turning back the clock. In my mind, I start to envision a story about citizen doping.

A friend of a friend who's written about hormones tells me that I should start my research by contacting citizen doping's gatekeepers—medical professionals who have access to the goods. He gives me the phone number for a small Southern California medical clinic, and one day in July 2007 I call. My expectations are low.

Hormones carry a stigma. Anyone involved with these drugs will be secretive and weird.

I'm supposed to ask for someone named Randy Ice. The name sounds like it belongs to a drug dealer.

A fellow with a deep voice answers. I ask for Ice.

"This is Randy," he says cheerfully.

I ease into a discussion about hormones. Ice couldn't be friendlier and more forthcoming.

"Sure, we put some middle-aged men on testosterone," says Ice, a chirpy physical therapist and cycling enthusiast who helps run the Temecula-based clinic. He answers my questions patiently and with authority, as if he's a gardener and I'm asking him if plants might benefit from soil, sunlight, and water.

"The hormones are safe and effective," Ice says. "They work."

"Work at doing what?" I ask.

"At making patients feel and function a lot better as the years go by," Ice says. "What if, at sixty years old, a man could be 200 pounds and have just two percent body fat?"

I know that four or five percent body fat is quite low, and in healthy males is usually only found among highly trained athletes. "Two" sounds crazy.

"Uh," I respond, trying to wrap my brain around such a notion. "He'd have aged better than Superman?"

Ice tells me I'm not far off. He says that steroids and other performance-enhancing drugs are legally available to make even a grandpa feel stronger, hornier, and more confident. Ice adds that there's a growing demand for the goods and services that his clinic provides. "This isn't about me or a few people on the Internet," he says. "It's going on all over the country."

Before we hang up, Ice tells me that he belongs to a fraternity called the anti-aging industry. Soon I turn again to the Web and peel back the curtain on a subculture that's oriented toward the hormone-seeking everyman. There are huge anti-aging conferences dedicated to the exploration and popularization of, among other things, hormone science. The Web gives me the sense that thousands of doctors and health-care professionals are ready to make assessments and write prescriptions. I find hormone protocols with registered trademarks and neighborhood pharmacies that prepare the drugs.

I discover that the anti-aging industry approaches growing old as a problem if not a disease, and that the industry's mission is to prevent illness and improve one's quality of life as he or she ages. Anti-agers say that their treatments can be about as safe as Corn Flakes, and that certain drugs have the potential to deliver strength, confidence, and libido. Anti-agers disagree with the many critics who insist that their industry turns its back on scientific rigor, and have no intention for their drug protocols to be exploited for legalized doping. Just the opposite! On the Web, anti-agers argue that if it's okay to chase health and vitality through hip replacements, Botox, and Lasik surgery, then why not through hormones? They assert that big, established pharmaceutical companies, gynecologists, and urologists often serve up similar messages. Links take Internet users to pages where Hollywood stars—*of course Hollywood, eternally vain Hollywood, is in on this anti-aging world*—endorse the industry. There's the permanently blonde and busty Suzanne Somers, pitching her anti-aging book. Here's Sylvester Stallone, still flaunting a boxer's biceps thirty years after Rocky first played on the big screen. I click on a video featuring Sly, who delivers nothing short of an anti-aging call to arms:

"I'm all for aging, but let someone else do it," Stallone says casually on a promotional clip for an anti-aging clinic. "So you figure, what's it going to take?" he continues, staring into the camera. "Men like yourself. Forward thinking. Who have a different perspective on life. Who realize that what nature takes away, maybe it's up to us to supply it."

With signature manly Ramboness, Stallone tells guys like me—aging but still young, at least in our minds—that we're in control of a greater destiny.

I replay the video.

"Men like yourself. Forward thinking. Who have a different perspective on life."

I smirk. *What a schtick! Everything, Stallone says, is better on the juice!*

Right then, I decide I want to write a story about a regular guy, a face in the crowd who isn't impossibly over the hill or out of shape and gets pulled into anti-aging's promises, Stallone's reassurances, and the visions of having the strength of a Barry Bonds and the endurance of a Floyd Landis. Are the glamorous guarantees thoroughly bogus, and the products placebos for a softening modern-day man? Or am I just being reactive and cynical, as my soulful wife often gently reminds me. Could there be science that really moves the chronological needle?

This guy that I'll look for, he lives the doping life, but unlike some spoiled and physically gifted super-jock, he has to deal with everyday demands. Kids. Wife. Job. Oil changes. Do steroids make his world a better place? Might he show me—and Michael and Juliana and our friends and thousands of others straddling the fulcrum between youth and love handles—that life is better on the 'roids? That we can all be twenty-and-change again? Sitting in front of my computer, I imagine the gym workouts that cause this person's muscles to inflate like balloons, the purring wife who swears that her husband has been reinvented, and the Sly-style swagger that informs all of his decisions. Will I feel envy? Pity? There has to be an ugly underbelly, too. Has to be.

I'm in for the whole glorious, virility-boosting, time-reversing, clichéd, surprising, disappointing, dangerous, hyperbolic hormone-taking experience.

Now all I have to do is find my man.

YES, I'M HOPING FOR A LOT. It's the rare individual who readily admits to leaning hard on a pharmaceutical crutch. Conversations around water coolers don't revolve around who's popping Zoloft. Singles meeting at bars refrain from raising their glasses to Viagra. Suggest performance-enhancing drugs and public exposure and men's minds turn to shamed athletes. They remember Major League Baseball player Mark McGwire, a big, strong man who in 2005 fidgeted and stumbled over his words like a ninety-eight-pound weakling as members of Congress interrogated him on Capitol Hill about his steroid use. There would be another ugly and memorable moment, too, during my search for a story subject: In the fall of 2007, American track star and five-time Olympic medalist Marion Jones will weep in front of the national press while admitting to cheating, and ultimately go to prison on perjury charges. Apparently I need to find someone who's willing to bare his doping soul and live with public embarrassment.

Shortly after speaking with Randy Ice, I embark on a legitimate manhunt. I'm thinking that I need a weekend-warrior type, someone who likes to get outside and push himself. I have a hunch that sports-related institutions and governing bodies will be good places to find names—there has to be some character who doped and might recount his tale. Or secretly lead me to other dopers.

I call every big sports organization that I think might help, including the World Anti-Doping and United States Anti-Doping agencies, the American College of Sports Medicine, and USA Cycling. But since 2000, USADA has focused on busting elite and professional athletes, frequently via drug tests. Those guilty parties wouldn't fit the "everyman" bill, nor would they be doping any longer, or likely to rat on their buddies. Historically, high-level athletes who cheat have been a tight-lipped bunch.

I reach out to coaches in both track and field and bike racing, and contact Gary Wadler, a New York–based internist specializing in drugs and sports and an advisor to the White House Office of National Drug Control Policy.

Wadler says he has no names for me and tells me to try a guy named Nick Evans. Evans, a Southern California–based bodybuilder and orthopedic surgeon, has published medical papers on the behavior of admitted, amateur steroid users.

"Unfortunately I have no experience with the endurance athlete," Evans writes me in an email, and then refers me to studies that concern weightlifters. I don't need to find a marathon runner, but I'm uninterested in working with a gym rat. Plenty of weightlifters and bodybuilders think it's weird *not* to be on drugs.

I inquire with a physician who occasionally advises doping bike racers on staying off the drugs. She responds in an email that her clients are pros, and that some of them are really sad cases. She knows one former doper who's bipolar, and wonders if his condition is due in part to substance abuse. She adds that he'd really flourish if only "he went on antipsychotic meds."

I look locally. Northern California is home to one of the largest pools of amateur bike racers in the nation. Surely someone would trust me to tell his story with care.

I contact everyone that I know, including chiropractors, athletes, coaches, bike-store owners, and physical therapists. Nobody has any names for me, although plenty of bike racers swear that their competition uses drugs. I make a connection with one fifty-three-year-old male bike racer who turns out to be even more suspicious and disgusted with his peers than Michael or me. In fact, he claims, doping drove him from the sport.

"I was going up Mt. Hamilton"—a 4,000-foot-plus mountain in the southern Bay Area—"in this old fart masters race, and these yuppies, they were doped to the gills. I could see it in their faces, in the way they were sweating profusely. They had this look," he tells me over the phone. "I watched them for a while and then I said fuck this. I turned around, went back to my car, and tore up my bike-racing license. That was that."

Too bad he didn't have names to go with the sweaty faces.

Another day, I'm at work and tune into National Public Radio's *Talk of the Nation* call-in show while host Neal Conan discusses doping in sports. I nearly fall out of my seat when a caller identifies herself as from the Bay Area, and then says that she knows a middle-of-the-pack bike racer on steroids.

I Google the woman's name—*Talk of the Nation* announces first names only—and the town where she says she's from. No dice. I call NPR's offices in Washington, DC and make a preoccupied producer promise that she'll call me back and perhaps give me the caller's contact information. She doesn't, but a female racer I know miraculously tracks down the caller, who's also a competitive cyclist. Three weeks later the caller and I have coffee. For an hour, the conversation bounces around—moving, jobs, kids, great places to ride bikes. She's a perfectly nice person. I keep waiting for her to bring up the subject that's brought us together: a citizen doper. I hope that she'll volunteer some information before I try to pry it out of her.

She drops the subject almost as quickly as it comes up. "You know, I won't give you the name of the person I referred to on NPR," she says coyly, and then takes a sip of her tea. But when the caller and I go for a long bike ride together in Berkeley a couple weeks later, the supposed doper's identity slips from her lips. Now what do I do?

I find the man's contact information easily enough and do nothing for days. I can't decide if reaching out to him will betray the woman's trust in me. And I'm afraid if I ask for permission she'll shoot me down.

Hey, maybe she dropped the guy's name on purpose! I'm so close—a doper in my sights!

Finally I succumb to temptation. Without my informant's knowledge, I write the man a snail-mail letter, explaining that his identity need never be revealed. Will he tell me his story? Days later, I hear back—from her. The man is her ex-boyfriend. I've just contributed to their crumbling relationship.

"My existing defenses are down and have left me talking too much, too soon, to the wrong people," she writes me in an email, adding that in the wake of my snail-mail letter, she and her ex have agreed to cease speaking for an entire year. "You have your lead, and it will or will not get you on the road you are seeking."

I never hear from him. Perhaps that's the outcome I deserve.

I take a different approach to a challenge that increasingly feels like searching for a hypodermic needle in a haystack. *Outside* magazine assigns me a profile of an ex-pro cyclist named Joe Papp. Even among his peers, the thirty-two-year-old Papp is an exception because he took dozens and dozens of different illegal substances, and because he's willing to talk freely about many of his experiences. Papp won't name names, and he isn't the right person for my citizen doper story. But he knows lots of people. People know Papp, too—cycling fans in particular, many of whom are amateur racers angered by Papp's drug-related exploits. They regularly disparage the former pro on cycling blogs and Internet chat rooms.

I send out dozens of emails and make lots of calls, dropping Papp's name and explaining that I'm casting a wide net, researching stories about doping pros and amateurs. One afternoon I open an email containing a forwarded note from an amateur bike racer in the eastern United States.

I read it and immediately call Juliana. She's with Benjamin and Sophie, who are home from school.

"I'm psyched!" I say. "Found my man!"

"What man?" says Juliana. I can hear Benjamin in the background, asking her for a cookie.

"The doper person," I say. "You know, the guy I'm looking for who takes hormones or steroids or whatever."

Ever since kids came into our lives, Juliana hasn't kept up with all my stories. She used to know a lot more about my assignments and the people that I interviewed. We'd talk about my work. Now we discuss groceries, playground locations, and soccer practices, when there's a free moment at all.

"Apparently this guy is sagging under the burden of taking something that boosts his performance," I explain. "Listen to what he wrote in this email."

I read her the letter:

"'Fuck it, I'm willing to do it, because this is a story that NEEDS to be told,'" it says. "'I'll spill all the details—I just can't keep it to myself any longer and look myself in the mirror, you know?'"

"Yessss!!!" I say over the phone.

"That's great, Andrew!" says Juliana. "Hey, can I call you back in a little while?"

So much for a celebration.

Through email, I immediately reach out to the apparent doper, introducing myself and telling him about my years of experience as a journalist. I write that I think he's brave for stepping forward and potentially addressing touchy issues like aging, drug use, and performance enhancement. I explain that if he's feeling badly about having taken steroids, the story may provide some redemption by scaring others straight. Maybe doping isn't all it's cracked up to be—that added strength and stamina come with unforeseen drawbacks. I offer to maintain his anonymity in anything that I may write about him.

Four days later, I haven't heard back. I worry that that the guy is getting cold feet. I write him another polite and encouraging note.

This time he responds.

"If this is some kind of a joke," he writes in a short email, "just know that this is a very serious personal matter."

I write back again, highly concerned that I could lose this guy. I tend to him about as carefully as I would a withering seedling. I offer the man references and story clips. I send him digital pictures of myself: *Here I am at a Giants game. That's me in a bike race. That's another one of my story subjects standing next to me.*

In the wake of the mess I helped create with that other potential doper and his ex-girlfriend, I badly want to win this person's faith. *Trust me!*

Three days later he writes me an email. He states that he'd be insane to talk.

"I don't need 'redemption' or 'closure,'" he explains. "What I need is for nobody to ever find out what I've done."

I respond with reassurances, one more time. I never hear from him again.

AROUND THE SAME TIME that my communications end with the drug-user from back east, I make my first foray into the world of anti-aging medicine. I contact a couple of local doctors. Might any of their patients, I ask, be willing to work with me on an honest story about taking hormones like testosterone or HGH? I tell the doctors that their practices may also receive attention in the story.

I make an appointment to see one physician, who's located about ninety minutes from my home. Her tidy waiting room is an altar to vitality, with cheerful, red walls and serious endocrinology magazines spread out on a table. A flat-screen TV offers patient testimonials. The doctor greets me—a middle-aged woman who looks like she's been built by medicine, or maybe a mason. Her broad shoulders and straight torso exhibit the hard-edged shape of a castle wall. Her face has fewer wrinkles than her pressed suit.

I follow the doctor into an office.

"So you're a writer, hmmm?" she says, slowly rubbing her oddly muscular hands together. The doctor's voice is also curious. A little too deep.

"Yes. As I told you over the phone, I'm interested in writing a magazine story or even a book about someone who takes supplemental hormones," I say. "I'd like to chronicle a slice of someone's life while they take their medications."

The doctor launches into a story, but unfortunately it's her own. She's a former flight surgeon in the United States Air Force, and a member of the International Hormone Society. She's versed in both nutrigenomics, whatever that is, and hormone-replacement therapy.

She says that she works with many patients that already have had cosmetic surgery. "They look well," she says, her taut face barely moving as she speaks, "and now they want to feel the same way." The doctor tells me that, when it comes to hormones, she practices what she preaches.

You don't say . . .

I ask her if I might be able to work with one of her patients.

Straight-backed, she reclines in her chair. "I'm really interested in finding a writer to help me get down *my* life story," she says. "Does that opportunity sound interesting to you?"

It doesn't, and I politely decline the offer. I explain that I want to profile a run-of-the-mill, doe-eyed hormone-taking patient, not a physician. This is not the answer she wants to hear, and she soon asks me if I'm interested in becoming a patient. I politely tell her I'll consider the offer and show myself out.

I visit another anti-aging doctor, this one in San Francisco, who ultimately tells me that he, with his lawyer at his side, wants to cowrite a book with me about hormone supplementation. Again I pass. I want to work with a patient, not a doctor, let alone a lawyer who might want to cut out the controversial anecdotes that I like best.

Finally I put in another call to Randy Ice, the physical therapist who only months earlier had introduced me to the anti-aging industry. I ask him about interviewing his patients. He says he'll get back to me. His partner isn't enthused about asking patients if they want to share their stories.

By fall 2007 I am officially discouraged. The near misses, the no's, the uncooperative doctors. I consider dropping the whole manhunt, giving up on the story. I realize that, even if I were to find a willing doper, I'd face problems. I'm unsure that such a subject will tell me the truth. And probably nobody will let me watch as he medicates himself with testosterone or gets into bed with his wife. Nor can I envision shadowing this person in a public gym with my pad and pen.

It seems like finding the right doper and the right situation is all but impossible.

Or is it?

ONE NIGHT IN NOVEMBER 2007, with the kids already asleep, Juliana and I pull back the covers on our bed. There they are: The same sheets we've slept on for about the last seven nights. They're fine. Juliana hasn't had night sweats for weeks. She's been in a consistently good mood, and her sex drive is better. As she climbs into bed, her nightshirt inches up just enough so that I spot the tiny patch on her lower abdomen. It looks something like a rectangular Band-Aid, and isn't much bigger than a fingernail.

"There's the trusty estrogen patch," I say.

"Wouldn't be without it," says Juliana, putting on her reading glasses and fluffing her pillows. "I feel so much better."

For Juliana, taking the hormones estrogen and progesterone has made a difference bordering on the miraculous. The tiny pills and patches have altered her physiology and outlook on life. She's sleeping through the night and behaving more like her old, happy-go-lucky self. I've watched the transformation, which from my viewpoint is akin to a fairy waving her magic wand.

"I want to talk to you about something," I say, next to her in bed. Juliana lowers the issue of *Yoga Journal* that she's paging through, guides a lock of her shoulder-length, brown hair behind her right ear, and slowly turns her head toward me. It's a turn I've seen many, many times—Juliana's equivalent of a deep breath. That turn says *Okay, something big is on Andrew's mind.*

"You know I've been looking for this citizen doper type, a doper next door who I could write about," I say, sitting upright on the bed. I have too much energy to lie down.

"Uh-huh," she says.

"And I haven't found anyone who's willing to talk to me," I continue.

"Right."

"I've been giving this a lot of thought," I say. "The doper next door doesn't have to be someone that I find," I say, crossing my arms. "The doper next door could be me."

For a moment she sits very still.

"So you want to take drugs like testosterone or whatever else those football players use. Put them in your body," she finally says, evenly. "Seriously? Do you have any idea what you'd be in for?"

I consider pointing to her estrogen patch and saying, *You're already on the stuff!* But I don't do that. I have better, more mature arguments.

"I've done a lot of research," I say. "I think there's a sane approach to this. I don't need to go hog-wild like some pro athlete."

I tell Juliana that I've been reading about the anti-aging industry, and that I'd become less critical of it. The lines between traditional and anti-aging medicine, I explain, sometimes blur. Nowadays, a urologist will prescribe testosterone to a middle-aged man, and anti-aging doctors generally recommend that their patients take relatively small amounts of the same steroids that elite athletes might take by the fistful. Meanwhile, I've learned that the medical establishment can't definitively prove that these limited dosages will hurt you, and also can't deny that they might help. Scientific research has shown that healthy test subjects have sometimes benefited from taking supplemental hormones like testosterone and human growth hormone.

"The science is complicated," I say to Juliana, extending my arms toward the ceiling to stretch out my back. "The research on these hormones and steroids isn't conclusive."

"*Not* conclusive?" says Juliana. She's still listening, patient as I explain my crazy idea to her, but I notice that now her arms are crossed. "What's the best possible scenario?"

"That these drugs work as those cheesy, online anti-aging websites promise. I'll have bigger muscles and more erections and sex drive. More energy and confidence," I say. "Plus I'll have a really wild story. There's no better way to write an intimate portrayal of a regular guy's experience on steroids."

"But taking this stuff just for a story," Juliana says, sitting up and grabbing another pillow to put behind her head. "I don't know. What's the *worst*-case scenario?"

It's my turn to take a deep breath. "If I take testosterone, my testicles could shrink, although they'd likely return to normal size after I stop taking the T," I say. "I could lose my hair, my blood could become a little thicker, and I could suffer from breast enlargement."

Juliana's eyes widen.

"Man cans. Bitch tits," I say. She snorts. I grin.

"Those are the only dangers?" she says.

"No," I say, "there are more."

I recite some other side effects. Rashes, body acne, high blood pressure, and altered moods.

Juliana says she's heard that guys who take hormones have mood swings—*'roid rage.*

"Yes. But plenty of doctors think that supplemental testosterone, even in huge doses, isn't responsible for unpredictable behavior."

"Okay. Go on," she says. "What else? What other risks?"

"Well . . . there's currently a lot of debate in the scientific community over whether or not supplemental testosterone contributes to the occurrence of prostate cancer," I say. "There are also reasons to believe that supplemental growth hormone causes bones to thicken and joints to swell. It may also cause cancer. EPO can cause heart failure—"

Juliana interrupts. "And you want to take these drugs for *a story*? Is your life worth it?"

"Remember when we took Lariam years ago in India?" I ask. Lariam is a malaria preventative. That glorious trip to the subcontinent feels like it happened a lifetime ago. "Remember all the potential side effects? The list was crazy and long. Seizures, violent behavior, thoughts of suicide. We still took it, and we were fine."

"I remember before we took those pills for the first time, I looked into your eyes and told you that I loved you," she says. "I was scared then, and I'm scared now. You know, it's not just about you, either. Or the two of us," she adds, and then grabs one of the pillows from behind her and hugs it. "We have kids."

I clench my jaw. I don't have a response. I want to trot out the I-could-get-hit-by-a-crashing-airplane argument, because, through all of my research on the Web and phone interviews for my magazine story on doping, I know that most of these drugs' horrific side effects are rare, and seem to come from irresponsible and excessive use of the substances. I'm all but convinced that I'm going to pursue becoming the doper next door. I have to convince Juliana that I should do this.

But for now we agree to resume the conversation again later. Then we both stare at the ceiling for a while before going to sleep.

OVER THE NEXT COUPLE OF DAYS, I tell a small number of people about my idea. Very small. Three people.

"Don't do it. Keep looking for someone else," pronounces my older sister, Tracy. She's had an opinion ever since we were both kids and she'd infuriate babysitters who, like many people young and old, were my sister's intellectual inferiors. Tracy also loves me, a lot—as the only children of our parents, we've both already endured a disproportionate amount of family drama and tragedy. Of course she'd have a strong response.

"Do not take it so lightly that you're letting in the fountain of youth," warns my therapist, speaking in a strange, prophetic, Yoda-like tone.

I tell Michael next. "I don't care what anyone says. I'm going forward with it," I say. "I'll be fine. I won't let this thing spin out of control."

"Okay, I hear you. Just tell me one thing," he responds. "Are you doping to write a book? Or is the idea of a book your excuse to become a doper?"

He's got me there. I do think that taking the drugs would allow me to write something far different from ye olde condemnation of a cheating athlete, or the gobble-everything-in-the-medicine-cabinet-while-desperately-trying-to-be-Hunter-S.-Thompson drug adventure. My recollections would be more thoughtful and balanced, and written at a time when 38 million male Baby Boomers are keen on defying old age.

Mike, however, has me nailed. The doping means more to me than just the writing. My life is half over. I perpetually carry concerns about my wife, children, and house payments. I am fit and blessed with good health, but I don't walk with the lightness that I once did. I see my shrinking muscles in the mirror. I feel my age in the way I pedal a bike, or throw a baseball with Benjamin. I acknowledge my envy—or resignation—every time I interview yet another hard-bodied, elite athlete for a story. *That's not me,* I think. *That'll never be me again.*

But the anti-aging industry allows me to think differently, and over the past few months, I'd stared at enough images of older people with oddly strong bodies to become covetous. Increasingly, I could picture myself walking in step with the movement: Exploring a new life through hormonal science, and not complaining if I could reform my body until it resembled something worthy of the pages of *Men's Health* magazine (at least from the neck down).

The truth is that by the time I confessed to Juliana that I wanted to be the doper next door, I was already eager to find out for myself if youth really can come in a syringe.

FOR A WEEK AFTER proposing my idea to Juliana, we conduct nightly negotiations. She finally consents to the project, provided that I proceed as cautiously as possible. I tell her that I will, and that I think good times lie ahead. One day soon, I tell her, a more energetic husband could very well walk through the front door. He might be carrying a trophy from a bike race, or flowers. Or sweep his wife off her feet and carry *her*, straight to the bedroom. Clichés or not, in the middle of an old relationship, of an increasingly old life, those images seem pretty dang magnificent to me.

But in the back of my mind, I also know that I'm about to enroll myself in a thoroughly modern experiment, courtesy of endocrine science that's on the edge of going mainstream. However, nobody knows whether or not 'roid rage exists. I have no idea which doctor to call, or what drugs to take. Plus, sometimes the anti-aging industry's science seems so terribly flimsy. I interview one anti-aging doctor who argues that the rate of cancer occurrence in the general population is higher than the rate of cancer occurrence among those taking supplemental growth hormone. "Therefore a higher level of growth hormone in people shows a reduced occurrence of cancer," he says without hesitation. Proof by deduction. Concerning.

I worry about more than health. I wonder about my many relationships. Juliana and I agree to keep the doping a secret from everyone except a small circle of friends and family members. I'm not sure how they'll react to my undertaking. I also fear others finding out without me telling them. I'm not too much bigger than a jockey— small boned and sinewy, with size eight feet. I imagine sprouting muscles and pimples, turning into a cross between Bonds and Beavis, and then having to answer probing questions at my book club meetings. Or having awkward conversations with other parents at my children's school.

Except for Michael and a couple other buddies, I don't feel like I can trust anyone in cycling to know about my doping. Even in amateur races, taking steroids is against the rules. I can only hope that nobody raises an eyebrow if I start to race freakishly well, or win.

Of course, as Juliana had said, I'm most concerned with how doping will affect my family. I'll have to keep the secret of my drug use from my children. I can't explain a world that I see as gray, where these drugs aren't necessarily the scourge of society and sports, to children who only perceive the world in black and white.

"Do all the home runs that Barry Bonds hit count?" Benjamin says to me one day in mid-November. We're in our kitchen having breakfast, and Benjamin, with his warm head of thick brown hair hovering under my nose, sits on my lap. He still has a Giants jersey sporting Bonds's name and number, but now that my boy can read I'm no longer sure that he wants to wear it. The headline on the front page of the day's *San Francisco Chronicle* sports section, which lies flat on the table in front of us, reads LEGACY IN PERIL. The story describes how Bonds, following the season where he'd just become baseball's all-time home-run leader, has been accused of perjury in connection with accusations of him taking performance-enhancing drugs.

As I'd discover during what would become my year of doping, the questions—Why? What? How? When?—would often outpace the answers. The truth is, I'd often underestimate the drugs. They would change my interactions with my children. Color my friends' perceptions of me. Dramatically alter my cycling abilities. Make me wonder exactly who I was looking at in the mirror. And perhaps most significantly, play a leading role as both threat and savior to my then thirteen-year marriage. In the end, my doping experiment didn't just affect me. It confused and wowed me. It overshadowed my entire life.

seeking ageless advice

here are two ways to become a doper. One of them is easy, even
if it's not confidence-inspiring or ethical. You can buy hormones,
steroids, and other performance-enhancing substances via a black market that exists around the globe, in countries like Australia, Thailand,
China, India, and the United States.

The well-worn route into the black market is to find a drug dealer.
That's what Barry Bonds apparently did. Bonds used some mysterious
substances courtesy of an old pal who was a weightlifting nut. Trusty
friend that this guy was, he allegedly purchased growth hormone for
Bonds from folks who had tested HIV-positive and needed cash more
than the drugs prescribed to them. Another drug dealer was Joe Papp,
the doping, ex–pro cyclist who I wrote about for *Outside* magazine.
Federal prosecutors say that Papp made $80,000 selling Chinese-made,
synthetic versions of growth hormone and EPO from September 2006
to September 2007. In fact, Drug Enforcement Administration agents

raided Papp's home in a Pittsburgh suburb only weeks after I'd interviewed him in the same house. To think what Joe could have sent me home with!

You can also opt to skip the "connection" and head over to the gym yourself. Pick a venue that attracts serious bodybuilders, and hang out around the dumbbells or squat racks. Listen for conversations that include words like *juice, cut, gear, jacked,* and *dart.* You'll know to approach someone if you overhear him say, "Dude, this gear won't give you bitch tits. You'll get cut." (Translation: "Pal, these drugs won't cause breast enlargement. You'll become lean.") If one is to believe the steroid websites, prices in this sales channel go up when demand is high, like before spring break and summer vacation.

Another choice is buying drugs from the comfort of your own home, via the Internet. Purchasing performance-enhancing drugs on the Web seems as challenging as picking up a Danielle Steel book on Amazon. One night toward the end of November 2007, only a few weeks after Juliana has consented to let me pursue a doping regimen, I'm at home, working late on the computer. I surf sites like roidstore.com, pharmaeurope.com, and domesticgear.com, among many others. They appear to do business with all the subtlety of used car salesmen. "We have the best prices by far on items including Tren, Clenbuterol, Anadrol tabs, Sustanon 250, and Dbol," guarantees domesticgear.com. "We also blow the competition out of the water with our prices on Winstrol Depot and Winstrol tabs. No one even comes close."

I have no idea what half this stuff is.

As I click from page to page, I hear Juliana walk down the flight of stairs off the living room. Soon she appears in our home office.

"Are you coming to bed soon?" she asks, the tips of her hair wet from her evening bath. Juliana always takes a hot bath before going to bed, part of her nighttime ritual for winding down. The heat also helps her to warm up the sheets, which she often slides between alone. I frequently work late.

"I'll shut down the computer in a minute," I say. Juliana smells good, like coconut moisturizer. Her hand is on my shoulder. A decade ago I would've thought of coming toward her. Maybe even just five years ago. But life has changed, and now, even with Juliana on hormones, we're often too tired for sex. Or business comes before pleasure. Or one person or the other is inevitably not in the mood. Sometimes rejection hurts someone's feelings, and then there might be a cooling-off period before Juliana and I have sex again. It's a vicious cycle. Simply put, intimacy can be more trouble than it's worth.

My eyes quickly turn from her to the computer screen.

"Hey, look at this crazy world," I say.

She leans over and tilts the screen on my laptop so that the picture is clear to her. She looks at the Internet site. Domesticgear.com has pictures of bodybuilders who make superheroes look skinny. Plus there are product photos of bottles that supposedly contain steroids.

"It's like a doper's department store," I say with a laugh. "Incredible."

Juliana takes her hand off my shoulder and straightens.

"You promised me you'd be cautious," she says, crossing her arms. "Buying drugs off the Web seems reckless."

"I'm not, I'm just seeing the extent to which—"

"This freak parade isn't very funny to me," she interrupts, and then extends her right arm toward my laptop and uses her fingers to scroll down the page. "You could get sucked into these drugs and take them forever," she says, while the images from my computer monitor reflect off her glasses. "A little more muscle and suddenly you'll want bigger muscles. Next thing you know you're buying a lot of drugs off the Internet and looking like these people."

I swivel in my chair, turning my back on the computer. "I'm sorry Juliana," I say. "I don't mean to scare you. I'm just looking around so I can soak in the subculture. I don't think I'll ever want to become a bodybuilder. And I know enough not to take these websites seriously."

Still seated, I lean over and hug Juliana while she's standing. My arms wrap around her waist, and my cheek rests against her stomach, and I can feel its warmth even from the other side of her shirt. The hug somehow feels more intimate than if our embrace brought us face to face. Her belly against my cheek feels mortal and human. She is flesh, heat, bone.

I don't want to hurt this person.

Juliana runs her fingers through my short hair. I again reassure her that I'll soon turn off the computer and come to bed. She turns around to go upstairs.

I flip through a couple more steroid-selling websites and marvel that they even exist. Steroids aren't on store shelves at Wal-Mart, or available via Amazon, for a reason: They're illegal to purchase without a prescription. The federal Anabolic Steroids Control Act of 1990 (which was expanded in 2004) categorizes steroids like testosterone alongside barbiturates and some narcotics. Unlawful possession can earn first offenders one year in prison and/or a minimum $1,000 fine. Illegally acquire steroids and you can end up with a criminal record.

There are multiple ways to get caught, too. U.S. Customs officials increasingly watch for the illegal importation of performance-enhancing drugs. Meanwhile, federal and state agencies that upend online distributors and pharmacies for illegal sales have been known to follow paper trails back to customers' doorsteps. As for drug dealers and related "friends," they can turn on you. When they're busted, authorities sometimes reward snitching. Dealers, or even those just intending to sell steroids, can go to federal prison for up to ten years for a first-time offense. Or dealers can expose their clients and hope for leniency from a sentencing judge.

If such potential discipline doesn't scare your average steroid-buying customer, the drug-selling sites should. They can't be trusted. Some take your money and send you nothing, or bogus drugs that contain either none of the advertised substance, too much, or too little. You might also receive veterinary-grade drugs, which are made under more lax production guidelines than steroids meant for human consumption. Other performance-enhancing drugs come from underground labs, or "UGLs," which can be medieval setups—tangles of plastic hoses, beakers, and baggies full of raw materials in grimy kitchens. According to a Reuters story, some of this home-delivered dope has been found to contain metals like arsenic, lead, and tin. How about this marketing slogan for a doping ecommerce site: *From our filthy sinks to your precious veins!*

I close my Web browser. Juliana had nothing to worry about. I'd never buy the stuff illegally. I cringed at the vision of some plainclothes cop handcuffing me in a local gym, or having no clue as to what I was putting into my own body. My decision was also a matter of ethics. Breaking federal law may be an effective literary device, but not the most admirable. The whole idea of black-market drugs repulsed me.

Then again, the whole idea of doping once repulsed me.

Earlier I mentioned that there are two ways to become a doper. The alternative approach to the black market is to obtain drugs via prescription, which means to dope under the care of a doctor. Such a choice involves a lot more time, trouble, and expense. But the idea of doping under someone's watch also gives me—and Juliana—more peace of mind.

I turn off my computer and write a big message to myself on a sticky note: "Call family doctor."

"IS THIS VISIT of an urgent nature?" my doctor's receptionist asks on the phone.

How does one briefly—dare I say, gracefully—enter into complex issues surrounding his virility?

Perhaps I should get your feedback. You see, I want to take steroids . . .

"I guess not," I say.

The receptionist gives me my doctor's first available "well" appointment—in about two weeks. I begin what seems like a long wait by passing the time constructively. That is, I further research the anti-aging industry.

Many anti-aging clinic websites are off-putting. There are clichéd "before" and "after" photos, 1-800 numbers, and schmaltzy slogans such as, "Turning back the hands of time." The sites invite you to make an appointment, which is a level of salesmanship that a lot of people—myself included—don't generally associate with medicine. In general, the clinics call their steroid/hormone treatments "hormone-replacement therapy."

I pick up several of the anti-aging movement's bibles to see if I'm even a candidate for the clinics' form of therapy. Books like *Forever Ageless, The Testosterone Syndrome,* and Suzanne Somers's *Ageless* tell me exactly what I hope to find. My forty-something malaise, creaks, and aches are precisely what anti-aging doctors identify as treatable symptoms of a medical condition called "andropause," which is a decline in the production of hormones like testosterone as men age ("andro-" is the Greek prefix meaning "male"). Andropause, the anti-aging doctors say, is nothing short of a men's menopause—and aging women aren't the only people that might benefit from taking supplemental hormones. Hormone-replacement therapy, the books maintain, help men battle bone density loss, eroding muscle mass, listlessness, mild depression, anxiety, lack of focus, and—the apparent sign that a man's physiological apocalypse is upon him—a declining sex drive. ("Most guys think that as long as they can 'get it up,' all is well," Somers writes in *Ageless.* "[But] for most men the erection is the last thing to go.").

The books offer a lot of basic information about hormones. Hormones are naturally occurring chemical messengers released by cells in one part of your body that move via the bloodstream and trigger responses elsewhere in your body. Hormones influence myriad functions like metabolism, immune system reaction, and sex drive, and play a role in everything from eyesight to body temperature. The hormone adrenaline, for example, is secreted by the adrenal glands just above the kidneys, and it binds to cellular "receptors" in the liver and muscles with the goal of, among other things, triggering the release of additional glucose (fuel) into the bloodstream. That glorious burst of energy you feel when you're jaywalking ahead of oncoming traffic and can suddenly explode into an Olympian's sprint? Give some credit to your adept hormones.

As men grow older, our hormone levels can decline, courtesy of illness, stress, aging, and, some even argue, exposure to overhead power lines (due to life-sapping electromagnetic fields). This depletion, according to the anti-aging industry, is where steroids and their ilk come in. Supplemental doses of testosterone and growth hormone (and estrogen and progesterone for women) replenish hormone levels, which then jump-start processes inside a body that might encourage muscles to grow, or libido to rise. "The assumption is that we'll bring you back to the levels you had in your twenties," one anti-aging doctor tells me over the phone.

Such grand promises often chafe members of America's esteemed medical institutions, who don't embrace a lot of anti-aging thinking—like the argument that a seventy-year-old man, courtesy of a long and steady decline in his body's ability to produce hormones, typically has half the testosterone that he did at about thirty years of age.

"There's no final word on whether or not inherent change in male hormone levels comes with age. There is evidence that some older, healthy men are relatively similar to where they were while young," says Dr. Richard Sherins, a former senior investigator in endocrinology at the National Institutes of Health and president of the American Society of Andrology. "Many men don't need male-hormone replacement."

Meanwhile the mainstream media regularly takes shots at the anti-aging industry. The press has especially targeted two of the industry's highest profile practitioners, osteopaths Ron Klatz and Robert Goldman, claiming that because they received their medical degrees in Belize, they should never have used the designation "MD" after their names. In 1992, Klatz and Goldman founded the industry's largest professional group, the American Academy of Anti-Aging Medicine (A4M), a nonprofit scientific, medical, and educational society that in April 2007 *The New York Times* portrayed as "a consistent focus of criticism, derided by [a mainstream medical] establishment that calls anti-aging medicine quackery or hype . . . and labels the academy's promotions as medically and legally specious." The A4M says the story in the *Times,* titled "Aging: Disease or Business Opportunity," was riddled with factual errors and that they were not given sufficient opportunity for rebuttal.

What's an aspiring doper to do? I don't want to put drugs meant for a horse, along with arsenic and tin, in my body. I don't want to ignore the criticisms of anti-aging medicine, either. But I have to imagine that a significant number of the many millions of steroid users in the U.S. turn to people in white lab coats, and not the black market, for advice and recommendations. I trust that, between the Internet, further research, and a journalist's healthy streak of cynicism, I won't leave decisions about my body to some Dr. Frankenstein. Besides, if the anti-aging books are any indication, many anti-aging doctors are fairly conservative with their prescription pads.

The more I read about andropause, the more I'm convinced that it describes me. I often drag myself outside to ride my bike, and then there's the lack of nooky in my relationship. Other symptoms of middle age are appearing as well. One day early in my quest to dope, while driving my car, I reach back with my right arm to grab Sophie's lower leg and give her a quick tickle. My daughter and I both know the routine: My squeeze of her calf begets Sophie's unexpectedly hearty laugh, and a big smile full of baby-sized Chiclet teeth, which I can enjoy in my rearview mirror. Yet as I rotate my right shoulder, I hear a mysterious and loud pop come from somewhere near my neck. Sophie hears it too. *What was that?* I brace myself for some disabling pain, and thankfully it doesn't come. But the freaky noise makes me wonder if I'm living inside a physiological time bomb, and that when it detonates I'll turn into a bag of cricks and flab.

Whether I'm enduring a real physiological decline or just sliding into life as a calcifying soccer dad, in my mind I make andropause my own, to the point that I go ahead and re-christen it *Andrewpause*. Convinced that life could be much better, and still well over a week away from the appointment with my family doctor, I call an anti-aging clinic. I briefly mention my Andrewpausal symptoms over the phone to an administrative assistant. She asks if I can come in this Thursday. Today is Tuesday. I say yes. Performance-enhancing drugs, I believe, are only an office visit away.

I CHOOSE TO SEE a doctor who's located way out of town. I'm already heavily invested in this project, and I'm not ready for anyone I know to interfere with my objectives by spotting me walking into an anti-aging clinic. It's one thing to admit to yourself that your testosterone tank might require topping off. Explaining that need—on the spur of the moment—to a friend or competitive cyclist might be awkward. I could come off as a cheater, a wimp, or both.

You know, I'd say with a wobbly smile while standing with a hand on the door to the doctor's office, *you can't be too masculine.*

What if this someone that I run into then tells his wife about our crossing paths, and soon she, her friends, and all of their children start steering clear of me, like I'm some sort of hormone-happy leper? What if I'm outed on Facebook? If the tweets start flying? My mind runs wild with a long list of bizarre social repercussions. Men wanting to arm-wrestle. Kids asking me if I'll turn into the Incredible Hulk.

I pick a doctor in another state, not far from the California border. Unlike others I considered, including a Harvard Medical School grad, he's a onetime bike racer. He's also formally trained in both internal and homeopathic medicine. I assume that his shift into the specialty was for many of the same practical reasons as other anti-aging doctors: the low barrier to enter the field, sane working hours, and patients who often must pay out of pocket. On the down side, I'd learned that this doctor had lost his license to practice medicine in California for repeated negligent acts, like treating a wheezing asthmatic in part with a regimen of "visualization." I tried not to dwell on those discoveries, and vowed not to mention them to him. Still, after meeting him I come to think of this physician as Dr. Iffy.

On the morning-long drive to Iffy's small-town clinic, my emotions swing wildly. One minute I feel downright listless and Andrewpausal, and the next I'm manic, repeatedly glancing into my rearview mirror to see if the cops are on my tail. My rendezvous with a doping doc makes me feel like I'm about to steal from a cookie jar. The sinister pleasure of seeking something forbidden!

Joe Papp, the drug-using, ex-pro cyclist whom I'd profiled, previously had admitted to me that doping gave him a thrill beyond making him faster on a bike.

"Part of doping's excitement is having access to secret weapons. You belong to a private society, like the mafia," Papp had said. "It's almost an intoxicating feeling."

When I arrive at Iffy's address, I'm slightly disappointed. His low-slung building doesn't look foreboding. It's clean and new, a brightly painted, one-story structure fronted by the kind of perfectly paved parking lot you'd find at the grand opening of a suburban Pottery Barn. One side of the building faces a golf course.

Before arriving, I had filled out a standard medical history, and was instructed to show up in my workout clothes. Preceding my visit with the doctor himself, Iffy's assistant gives me a physical stress test, which largely involves riding a stationary bicycle. Iffy wants to gauge my abilities in terms of oxygen consumption and carbon dioxide production because they're one way to quantify my energy levels. Indeed, the testing, his promotional literature claims, helps him to better understand my holistic health and abilities to produce certain hormones. I've come to understand that hormone levels are generally measured by blood or saliva tests. But I do what's asked of me.

Unfortunately I ace the test—or would that be fail—as the fidgety assistant pulls me off the stationary bike before I reach some critical level of tiredness. Soon I towel off, change clothes, and meet the white-haired, sixty-something Iffy in his office. His space is standard fare, with a cluttered desk, a microscope to one side, and a poster spelling out the Hippocratic oath.

Iffy doesn't say much at first, settling into the chair behind his desk and paging through the results of my stress test. The silence becomes uncomfortable. I get anxious.

You've driven all this way to convince a doctor that a healthy and thin nonsmoker with a twenty-five-year history of endurance training needs medical assistance. This guy sees right through you.

"You're either souped up on something or an exerciser or both," Iffy finally comments with a little grunt. "Your heart factor on our test was 149 percent. We don't see numbers like this."

Think fast, bud.

"I knew that test would put me in a curious light," I say, sitting up in my chair.

Be honest without spilling all the beans. Don't make it obvious that you want Iffy to write you a prescription.

"I am healthy, yes." I add. "But sometimes I still don't feel great."

You can do better than that.

"Do you have specific symptoms?" says Iffy, putting his forearms on his chair's armrests and reclining his seatback. Iffy looks every bit as fit as me—tall and thin, with a lab coat that hangs off his shoulders.

He probably never touches steroids. He thinks they're crap, just a revenue stream courtesy of couch-potato patients hoping to be delivered from their fading bodies.

"It's not one certain problem," I say. "Sort of a general, overall feeling of heaviness."

He nods but says nothing, as if I'm only partway through my explanation.

More!

I ramble for a while, saying the same kinds of things—my energy is low, I don't feel as strong as I used to—and then finally I tell him the truth: that I'm an aging journalist wondering what it's like to take supplemental hormones.

"Ah," Iffy says, and writes something down in his notebook.

"Are you on hormone therapy?" I ask him.

"Started twelve years ago, when I went from a heavy workout schedule to basically none. In about six months I put on fifteen pounds and my sex drive went down the tubes," he says. "But when you exercise like you do, it tends to pump up your hormone levels."

There go my chances. Buh-bye, prescription pad.

But Iffy gives me an opening.

"So are you truly losing your drive for things?" he asks.

I go on and on about Andrewpause. I tell Iffy that, despite my impressive fitness, I'm not what I used to be, which is not a lie. I drag myself through life on a regular basis. I'm not very horny.

Iffy smiles.

"Sounds to me like you're someone who can use some testosterone," he says. "If you don't need it and you take it, you're hurting yourself. But if you need testosterone and don't get it," he adds, "you're really hurting yourself."

T for me!

Iffy explains that he wants to elevate my testosterone high into "physiologic"—or what are considered normal—adult male levels, which range anywhere from approximately 250 to 1,100 nanograms per deciliter (ng/dl) of blood. Under no circumstances, he says, will he give me over-the-top, "supraphysiologic" amounts like those that pro athletes use to become muscle-bound giants. He'd start me on 100 milligrams of testosterone daily, or one-twentieth of the extreme dosages that crazed bodybuilders say they've taken. Gym rats consider weekly dosages of 600 milligrams to be utterly sane. Iffy's prescription is right in the ballpark.

"You're going to be a happy guy," he says. "It'll all be coming back to you."

I'm about to become bionic!

Iffy gives me more details. The testosterone comes in a cream form. A pharmacy will mix a powder version of high quality, manmade testosterone ("United States Pharmacopeia grade") into a lotion-like base that helps with the absorption of the hormone into my bloodstream. I must rub it on daily and look for a few signs of hormonal excess.

"If you're losing hair on your head, get acne, or notice your skin is especially oily, you could be getting too much. Then we'll make a nice adjustment," he says.

Iffy also cautions me. Supplemental testosterone can cause my levels of dihydrotestosterone, or DHT, to rise. DHT is a byproduct of testosterone, and he says that it can stimulate growth of the prostate gland. Other doctors and scientists, I'll later discover, think differently, and over the coming months I'll realize that the relationships between supplemental testosterone, prostate growth, and prostate cancer are complicated and not fully known. But at the time, Iffy's warning grabs me. The doctor wants me to schedule four "prostate-specific antigen" (PSA) tests a year as part of some regular blood analysis. Levels of PSA, which is a chemical created by the prostate, elevate in the presence of, among other things, prostate cancer.

Iffy then waves his hand. He implies that I shouldn't worry too much.

"Truth is, incidence of all these diseases goes up when testosterone levels go *down*," he says with an enthusiastic nod. "If anything, lack of the T causes disease."

The comment doesn't make me feel better. In fact it raises a red flag. Even in my limited knowledge of hormones, I know that the established medical community doesn't uniformly hail testosterone treatment as a preventative or cure for any sort of cancer. The doctor can only be referring to isolated scientific findings.

Something else bothers me, too. Iffy doesn't require a record of my testosterone levels before I start dosing. For all he knows, I could already be a doper—a doper with testosterone levels that are through the roof. My PSA levels could also be dangerously high.

Why isn't he taking every precaution?

Iffy seems well intentioned but not thorough. I'm not feeling so great about this anymore.

Before I leave, we shake hands and agree to talk again in three months. I pay $450 for the test and appointment, and a woman at the front desk tells me that a pharmacy will contact me soon about filling my first prescription for T. But by the time I reach the Pottery Barn–perfect parking lot, I've decided I won't be back. The drugs may be dangling right in front of me, but I don't want the testosterone this way.

I don't see Iffy again.

IN EARLY DECEMBER 2007, I show up for my appointment with my family doctor, Regina Vu. A week earlier I'd had some blood work done. Vu, unlike Iffy, demanded it.

We meet in an examination room in her offices, and she puts me through a routine checkup. Soon after she slides her stethoscope back into a coat pocket, she declares me to be in good health.

I proceed to explain my potential doping odyssey to her. Vu silently taps her fingers on a counter as she looks again at the results of my blood work. She looks up at me. She doesn't look intrigued or amused.

"First of all, for someone your age, your testosterone levels are normal," she says. "And when it comes to adults, true growth hormone deficiency occurs in a very small percentage of the population."

The disappointment regarding my testosterone scores washes over me. T therapy, I'd decided while talking to Dr. Iffy, was the logical place to begin my doping program. Human growth hormone, he had said, is expensive and harder to legitimately prescribe. Its benefits aren't entirely known. But testosterone is relatively cheap, regularly prescribed, potent, and easy to track through blood tests.

I ask Vu to see my T numbers. She gives me the printouts.

"They're low," I say, scanning the page. At 327 nanograms per deciliter, I continue, I'm near the bottom of the normal reference range for testosterone levels in an adult male. My score, according to some reference ranges, is less than one-third what it could be. And, I continue, according to experts, my testosterone could very well be dropping as we speak. (I don't dare say that it could also very well be stable.) While I can't argue that 327 is off the charts, I'm probably not enjoying Jean-Claude Van Damme–levels of testosterone.

"Why shouldn't I go higher?" I continue. "Is it unhealthy?"

"It's not unhealthy to be where you are," Vu replies as she stands up from a stool. "It's not like you're considering whether or not to take Pez," she adds with a shake of her head.

Vu advises me against getting on the juice, and tells me that anti-aging medicine isn't her line of work. Before leaving the examination room, she emphasizes that, should I go through with my experiment, to proceed cautiously. She makes me promise to schedule regular blood tests.

Walking out of Vu's downtown Oakland office, I'm undeterred. My testosterone may be normal. I may be healthy. But I might be missing a lot by not living at testosterone's *upper* ranges of normal. I could be healthier. Erasing my Andrewpause.

Man, you are already in this anti-aging thing deep.

I need to find the right doping doc, and I start the search after my appointment with Vu by calling Juliana's women's health doctor. She's well versed in hormones. "Only females," she tells me. "But I know a good men's urologist. They own Viagra and testosterone."

The next day I'm sitting in front of the urologist that she'd recommended. While testosterone isn't only about men's urinary tracts and male reproductive systems, a urologist is the closest thing that men have to a "men's health doctor." Urologists diagnose low-level testosterone, and prescribe testosterone gels or adhesive patches that are manufactured by big pharmaceutical companies.

"I'll bring up your levels," says the doctor, looking over my blood-test results. The urologist has a head of thick black hair that would've done Samson proud. "I prescribe it, and you can pick it up at Walgreens."

Tempting. But the knock on urologists is that, when it comes to doling out testosterone, they can be conservative. They often recommend 50-milligram daily dosages, and Iffy had already offered to prescribe me twice that amount. I want to explore other options.

I call the strangely deep-voiced anti-aging doctor whom I'd visited months earlier during my search for citizen dopers. She asks for a whopping $500 for additional blood testing, and as much as $1,250 per month to oversee my program. Too expensive. I contact the Life Extension Institute in Palm Springs, and discover that the

Institute's head doctor is on probation courtesy of the Medical Board of California. Too sketchy. A San Francisco–based physician wants me to complete a twenty-three-page medical history. Too involved. A Los Angeles–based anti-aging doctor is opening a practice in China. Too distracted. A registered nurse practices anti-aging medicine on the side in nearby Marin County. Too unqualified for me.

Almost half a year after I first imagine shadowing a citizen doper, I'm still practically at square one. I don't have a subject, let alone a doctor, a doping regimen, or drugs. I can't even turn *myself* into a doper.

But over the course of my research, I've learned about an opportunity that gives me hope. Every year near Christmastime, anti-aging's largest membership organization, the American Academy of Anti-Aging Medicine, holds its big annual gathering in Las Vegas. The A4M says it's a 20,000-plus-member organization, and I've been told that everyone who's anyone in the anti-aging community shows up for the event.

I receive the okay from Juliana to go and secure a press pass. Then I quickly book a flight for Sin City.

THE 2007 INTERNATIONAL CONGRESS on Anti-Aging Medicine and the adjoining commercial "expo"—held in carpeted conference rooms in Las Vegas's Venetian Hotel—border on the exotic. Men on stages speak to large audiences about the keys to unlocking good health. ("Do not consume foods of animal origin before saliva sampling!") Aisles fill with strange and fascinating—that is, enhanced, tanned, ripped, and/or tautened—browsers. Barkers call for attention ("Grow your own growth hormone, or your money back!"). A Japanese woman hands me a small packet of "antioxidant" drinking water called H₄O, and I receive literature on "feminine rejuvenation surgery," which involves fixing what's "worn out down there." I also encounter keynote speaker Suzanne Somers, the *Three's Company* actress and author of diet and health books that have reached bestesller lists for nearly fifteen years. ("I've been *pregnenoloned* and *growth-hormoned* and *testosteroned*. You can choose fifty-year-old medicine or you can jump on this fast-moving train!")

I'm lost among the attendees—approximately five thousand doctors, nurses, entrepreneurs, homeopaths, and pharmacists—and not sure how to find the anti-aging guru who will guide me. Seeking enlightenment would've felt slightly less daunting at the A4M's debut conference. In 1992, the organization's Ron Klatz and Robert Goldman hosted an event that boasted only sixty scientific delegates and twelve exhibitors. In those days, the idea of battling aging was in its infancy, and in at least one way, Klatz and Goldman were the trend's unlikely champions: Several years earlier, they had co-written the first of two books critical of steroids in sports. But knowing that drugs like growth hormone might help athletes meant the substances could also have the potential to benefit average, healthy folks, whether they were young or old. Klatz and Goldman soon began promoting the apparent age-reversing effects of HGH, and ultimately developed a following among people who paid good money for muscles and the promise of pep. The supporting science, traditional doctors would argue, wasn't conclusive, and there was no research that spoke to the long-term effects of relatively healthy populations taking modest amounts of steroids and other hormones for the purposes of feeling better. But Goldman himself was a compelling, brawny billboard for vitality. Broad-chested, a student of fitness and steroid biochemistry, and a fixture in bodybuilding circles,

Goldman established world records for a slew of feats. He's performed 13,500 consecutive sit-ups, and 321 consecutive handstand pushups. His imposing presence alone could convince many a potential patient to try a new approach to personal healthcare.

Fifteen years later, traditional medicine still cries that plenty of anti-aging's science remains inconclusive, stating that there's a shortage of the clinical research, such as double-blind testing, to back up industry claims. Nonetheless, Klatz and Goldman enjoy celebrity status, walking into the spotlight at many of the A4M programs that have been held around the globe, in cities like Dusseldorf, Tokyo, and Dubai. At the 2007 Vegas expo, many of the hundreds of vendors paid $1,000 or more for a single unit of space (the 2007 Shanghai anti-aging expo featured approximately three thousand booths). Access to all three days of the conference ran attendees as much as $1,100, and sitting in on certain lectures required people to pay more. Overall, the global anti-aging industry is currently worth an estimated $115.5 billion, and that number supposedly grows about nine percent annually. Vetting all of these facts is difficult, however. For one thing, Klatz and Goldman are inherently private about their histories and business dealings.

I sensed the A4M's wariness even before arriving at the show. Klatz and Goldman, I'd been told by fellow writers, don't love journalists. Too many stories have called the anti-aging industry's science suspicious, and its motivations unscrupulous, for them to want to talk. When I wrote the co-founders with my request for a rarely awarded press pass, I emphasized that I wanted to put myself on an anti-aging "program." I explained that I had faith in their industry and wanted to make a lab rat out of myself. When I did gain access, I still had to promise the A4M's marketing director that I wouldn't chronicle my visit with a tape recorder or camera. I also couldn't push for interviews with either Goldman or Klatz. I was told that their schedules were impenetrable.

Funnily enough, I bump into Klatz soon after the expo opens. He turns out to be chatty.

"I'm not afraid to speak to the press, as long as the press is going to be fair," he says, gesticulating with his hands. Klatz is solid and dark-haired with thick flanks. "Who knows what the next big breakthrough is?" he adds, sweeping his left arm in front of the expo booths behind him. "Who is anyone to say what's promising and what's not?"

Not unreasonable questions, I think, though in the wake of meeting Klatz it's hard for me to to feel completely secure in taking medicine that's "promising" instead of utterly proven. At the event I attend nearly a dozen presentations, and listen to a variety of doctors and self-titled experts suggest anti-aging protocols that are all over the map. Take testosterone dosing, for instance. One presenting physician says that men should take no more than 25 milligrams per day. Another recommends a range between 0.5 and 10 milligrams, and a third says the range should be between 50 and 200 milligrams. The presenters themselves aren't always reassuring, either. One doctor wearing a peach-tinted suit is ready to prescribe growth hormone at the sight of the smallest wrinkle on a body. A second doctor proclaims that growth hormone has been sufficiently studied because an Internet search of the substance returned 55,000 hits inside of medical citations.

After digesting the umpteenth lecture about growth hormone, I walk into one of the Venetian's lobbies and call Juliana on my cell phone.

"These people think pretty highly of HGH," I say as a platinum blond woman walks up and asks me if I know where the "neuro-integration therapy" booth is.

"I wonder if anyone in here will ever die," I say to Juliana. "Or if their bodies will decompose when they do."

I sit down in another presentation about growth hormone. I make eye contact with the woman sitting next to me. We both sit and listen for another five minutes, and then she leans toward me. "These people do an awful lot of HGH," she whispers, her eyes looking straight ahead.

Her name is Renee Rassid, and she's a middle-aged internist and anti-aging specialist from the Chicago area. Rassid is refreshing. She's dark-featured and pretty in a chemical-free-looking way. I like her all the much better when, after the presentation ends, she encourages me to think through my options before starting a program.

I tell her I feel like the little lost bird in the children's book *Are You My Mother?* and ask Rassid if there's an anti-aging protocol for men that she recommends.

"I want to talk to someone who will make me feel very safe," I explain.

"Have you heard of Susie Wiley and the Wiley Protocol?" she asks. "I discovered Wiley only because some woman called my office, begging me to prescribe the hormone therapy to her. At first I hesitated, because it's different. But then I put her on it. Suddenly I was her hero."

Rassid stands up to leave the meeting room. "Wiley is an interesting woman," she adds. "I'll introduce you."

LATER THAT DAY WE MEET at Wiley's small booth. It features a green and purple sign that's designed to look like a block from the periodic table of the elements. It has the letters "Wp"—for Wiley Protocol—printed inside.

Rassid introduces me to T. S. "Susie" Wiley—a short, dark-haired, fifty-five-year-old, Buddha-shaped woman. She's not unattractive, but looks even less enhanced than Rassid. Wiley explains that she's walking around the space shoeless because, as she says, "I'd rather be comfortable than taller." I like her immediately.

Now here's a real person.

I'm upfront with Wiley.

"I'm a writer looking to chronicle my experiences while taking hormones," I say. "But frankly, a lot of the people here give me pause. I don't know who to believe."

"Oh, this industry. It's fraught with a lack of authenticity," she says, walking over to a stack of books that all display the name "T. S. Wiley" on the white and purple spine. She grabs one, and holds it up. "The book I wrote about hormone-replacement therapy has hundreds of references. None of them are bogus."

She opens the book and flips to the back where there are dozens of pages of footnotes. She looks at me and smiles. Wrinkles form around her mouth.

"Go ahead and look at the notes," she says. "There's nothing funky. You're not going to find that my science is based on weird or fictitious sources. Nothing in here comes from that famous scientific work, 'Jump-Start My Car with Crystals.'"

"Jump-start my what?" I say.

"That's a joke. No such paper," she says, laughing. "Not to my knowledge anyway."

Okay, I like her a lot. Someone I can talk to.

Wiley continues. Without hesitating, she explains that she's not an MD, or for that matter an osteopath, naturopath, or chiropractor. Instead she's a tireless researcher—a "citizen scientist," she likes to say—who has a decade-long history of studying hormones with the likes of an oncologist and a molecular biologist.

Unorthodox background: minus. Honesty: plus.

"Last time I checked, one doesn't need a license to think," she says.

Wiley tells me that she recently testified in front of the U.S. Senate in defense of hormone-replacement therapy, and that her novel approach to hormone replacement commands an entire chapter in Suzanne Somers's best-selling anti-aging book. She mentions a pilot study involving the Wiley Protocol to be performed at the University of Texas at Tyler.

This is only getting better.

With her pale and plump hands, Wiley gives me her book, *Sex, Lies, and Menopause: The Shocking Truth About Hormone Replacement Therapy*. In it, Wiley says, she argues that women need a hormone-replacement protocol that's unlike most others. In the Wiley Protocol, the amount of supplemental hormones used throughout the month changes a la the ebb and flow of a woman's natural hormones.

"It's what I call rhythmic dosing, as opposed to static dosing," Wiley says.

Then she crosses her arms. "You know, men run on rhythms too."

Wiley explains that there are already thousands of females on her protocol, and attracting men is all part of a master plan to bring standardized hormone-replacement therapy to a vast audience. She has approximately one hundred of doctors all over the United States prescribing her protocol, and has trained nearly two dozen pharmacists across the country to create hormone creams made exactly to her specifications. "The packaging for my men's products will be ready January 1," she assures me. Then she points straight at me and lowers her voice, mocking the hype that inevitably pops up on the expo floor. "Yes, you too could be on the Wiley Protocol in no time flat," she says.

Wiley shakes my hand and excuses herself to talk to some happy-looking older women who have arrived at her expo space.

I walk around the show for a few minutes, relieved and paging through Wiley's book. I've found my guru in a persuasive and wise-cracking mother of five and "citizen scientist" from Santa Barbara, California. Wiley seems sane and intelligent, has surrounded herself with MDs, and claims to have a systematized approach to hormone therapy treatment. I'm hardly kidding myself—I know that she's some-where on a huge continuum between Marcus Welby and Jonas Salk. I'll have to remain vigilant in terms of the care and drugs that I receive, and during my long doping experience I'll discover that, indeed, there's good reason to question both Wiley and her protocol. But in a world that feels as foreign as the anti-aging community, I'm all for someone who has some healthy perspective and a big desire to systematize what could ultimately be perceived as cutting-edge medicine. If Wiley's mak-ing "McHormones" for all, with predictable dosing and results, than I'm ready to stand in line.

3

arriving at the moment

"**T**he drugs could turn me into Alice Cooper! A wild-eyed, chicken-tossing terror." I'm on the phone with Michael, talking big as I drive home from the Oakland airport after meeting Susie Wiley at the anti-aging conference. "Occupational hazards, you know."

"Must've been free samples at the show. Baby syringes. You're already amped," he says. "Call me back in a year. We'll see if you're still jolly."

Mike is notably ambivalent about my experiment—to his thinking the substances are creepy and corrupting, and yet he realizes that the story is potentially juicy. But he's decided to humor me, for the time being anyway, and during our phone conversation he lets me enjoy some giddiness over landing a doping guru. Besides, Mike knows me well enough to know that I'll be sufficiently sobered when I take aim with the syringes, morning and night, and wipe on the substances. I'm not, at my essence, a freewheeling guy. I insist that my clean socks be folded instead of balled up (less stress on the elastic), and after three decades, I still cook pasta with a timer. So being meticulous about every last aspect of this doping experiment isn't just practical. It's somewhere in my neurotic life-script.

I soon find flaws with my plan to go on the Wiley Protocol. While I had envisioned Wiley herself guiding me with reassuring precision and professionalism, it turns out she won't be my on-the-ground doping guru. Instead, as with virtually all of her clients, she appoints such duties to "Wiley Protocol Providers." Back in Vegas, Wiley had assured me that medical practitioners are given "Provider" status only after understanding the protocol (its doctor's manual is nearly four hundred pages) and consenting to work with one of the dozens of pharmacies across the country that make and distribute her hormone creams. She'd said many of her providers had taken her two-day educational seminar, too. Wiley also guarantees that she and I wouldn't lose touch while I'm on the program.

I'm more resigned than reassured. I look through the directory of providers on Wiley's website for a good match. I find, to my mind, some Doc Iffy–caliber medicos. A physician with a degree from some Hungarian university. A nurse who swears by flower essence remedies. Wiley had suggested that I work with a Dr. Jasmine Patil, an internist who practices in a coastal town within a couple hours of my Oakland home. I call and make an appointment.

In mid-January 2008, I pull up to an office complex consisting of one-story, weathered-wood buildings that look like grounded tree houses and are dotted across a generous parking lot. There are a lot of empty spaces, and no signs of life. When I walk inside one of the buildings, my eyes have to adjust to a dark space. A skylight in the open interior, which features doors at the far end that presumably lead to offices and examination rooms, funnels sunshine onto reading materials like *Life Extension* magazine.

I check in at a desk with a young office-administrative type who wears the kind of flowery, hand-stitched blouse I'd last seen on concertgoers at Grateful Dead shows in the early 1980s.

I half expect her to break into "Shakedown Street." Instead she's efficient, and asks me to have a seat and help myself to the reading material.

Minutes later a door opens and a small woman moves toward me with the sturdy stride of a beat cop. She extends a hand to shake mine. "Andrew?"

Dr. Patil barely introduces herself before turning around to lead me into an examination room. I'm intrigued. There's the businesslike, heel-toe stride. Thick, dark hair rests on her shoulders with the smooth perfection of a holiday tablecloth. She wears black, knit, pressed slacks and a matching vest. Patil, an East Indian with eyebrows that are as straight and defined as a bottom line, looks more like an Ernst & Young executive than a doctor.

We enter and sit down in a surprisingly welcoming room. It's paneled in decorative, rough-sawn wood. Gathered, dried branches lean just so in a vase. I relax, for a sec.

"You've driven quite a ways," she says, looking me up and down with her big brown eyes. "Tell me. What brings you here? What are you feeling?" she asks.

I thought Wiley would've talked to this physician before I showed up. I thought I was in. I'm supposed to be vetting her.

Having already played this meet-the-doc game, and at the risk of walking away from the visit with nothing, I immediately come clean. I don't want to lie to someone in charge of overseeing my health care.

I'm a middle-aged journalist, I say. I've come for two reasons. I want to write about what life is like on Wiley's hormone-replacement therapy. Plus I want to feel better.

"I'm often tired," I explain, palms up. "The kids, the wife, the career. I'm worn down."

"Let's start with basics. Like sleep. Are you getting enough sleep? Deep sleep?" asks Patil, crossing her arms and shifting her weight so that she leans forward and toward me, like an interrogator. Her questions roll off a one-note voice that's as seamless as a conveyor belt. Patil's perfect hair remains undisturbed.

"Sleep can do you wonders. Without it, you'll have obvious problems," she continues. "You can have issues with cortisol, for one. What about supplements?" she adds. "What herbs do you take? How are your SHBG levels?"

The pop quiz stumped me back at "cortisol." I don't know what "SHBG" stands for. Up to this point, I'd been focused on one thing: securing treatment. I thought that I'd wade deeper into the science later, after I go on the drugs.

That is if Dr. Gatekeeper here prescribes me anything. Maybe we need to get Wiley on the horn.

I review my Andrewpausal symptoms for Patil. I tell her that I've lost some of my mental sharpness. I admit having experienced some depression.

"Honestly, I'm afraid of looking and acting old. I'm middle-aged. Am I already on life's long, sucky, uninterrupted descent?" I ask.

Sucky?

"I notice an absence of the . . . morning erections of my twenty-something past," I add, with a self-conscious cough.

Dr. Patil doesn't react.

Well, you've found the no-bullshit physician. Three cheers for that. Now give her the dang blood-test data.

I fish the results of my month-old blood work out of my shoulder bag and hand them to her. She crosses a leg and rests her chin on her left thumb.

"SHBG is okay," says Dr. Patil. "That's a protein," she adds. "Sex hormone-binding globulin."

I nod an "Ah."

"Free testosterone . . . total testosterone . . . free and weakly bound testosterone," she says after flipping to the test's second page. "All in the normal range. Although these figures are on the very low end," she says.

"A urologist recently told me the same thing," I say, mounting an argument.

"The urologist thought I might benefit from supplemental tes-tosterone. He offered to put me on hormone-replacement therapy," I say. "But Wiley's protocol seems particularly detailed and thought through. I believe it might be the smarter choice."

Dr. Patil has me lie down on the examination table. She pinches and pokes, listening to my breathing with her stethoscope, feeling around my abdomen, looking at my ears, nose, and throat. Even with the documented blood work and the urologist's recent suggestions, she conducts a full exam.

"Your blood pressure is fine, too," she says, after letting the air out of the inflatable arm cuff of the old-fashioned blood-pressure meter. "But I'm sure Susie would agree. Your hormone numbers could come up," she says. "I've witnessed the improvements in hormone-replacement therapy many times. In lots of women, and some men, too," she adds.

She pauses, reviewing my chart.

Then, without looking up, she says, "I'll put you on Wiley."

Perfecto! Competent doctor joins Team Andrewpause.

"But I want to know more specifics," she continues. "We need more comprehensive lab-work done before you start. I want to see additional baselines."

I nod.

"No argument from me," I say, rolling down my shirtsleeve after she removes the inflatable cuff. "I'll keep the data coming."

PATIL AND I TALK a while longer. She hardly turns chummy, but I receive additional insight and reassurance as to why any physician, especially one as persnickety and accomplished as Dr. Patil, would be drawn to an anti-aging field that many doctors call quackery.

First Patil tells me that she believes medicine is all turned around.

"I used to see twenty-five patients a day," she says, sitting across from where I sit on the examination table. She grabs a glass of water set near her clipboard. Fresh lemon slices bob at the top.

"I'd have fifteen minutes to spend with every patient. I believe there are places where doctors have about half that amount of time," she says. Above her on the exam-room wall is a framed graduation certificate from a highly regarded American university. "I became a doctor to provide people with real health care. But with the clock ticking, you can't possibly deal with much more than a cold."

Patil practiced medicine on a stopwatch, far away from the lazy, salty air of her current ocean-side home, for years. In her mid-forties and a U.S. citizen for over three decades, Patil is a wife and mother of two who was a high school valedictorian in Texas and graduated top of her class from an esteemed eastern college. She received her medical degree in the Southwest and performed her residency at the University of Michigan. She did not receive a formal education in flower essence.

As an internist working near the Rust Belt, Patil saw clients for myriad setbacks—heart attacks, strokes, busted bones. Back in the day, the fast-paced work brought her satisfaction. For years, she returned the broken and sick to work, play, and their families. Practicing conventional, evidence-based medicine—treatment derived from scientific method, or measurable proof of its effectiveness—she reflexively prescribed drugs for every pain. Lipitor for cholesterol. Actos for diabetes. Aspirin for the heart. Pills for all! If patients' parts needed further attention, Patil referred her clients to specialists like cardiologists and neurologists.

Tired of the Midwestern climate, in 2001 Patil, along with her husband and children, moved to California and its mild weather. She resumed her internal medicine practice with a local physicians' group. But her patient population, and the citizenry in general, were a surprise. Patil and her family had landed in a spot that could be characterized as definitive counter-thinking California. Folks were preoccupied with air quality, composting, vegan restaurant menus, commuting by bicycle, and alternative health care. One patient asked Patil to weigh in on the herbs he'd been recommended by a homeopath. Another wanted to seek out a chiropractor for a second opinion.

"Someone came to me saying that they were treating their HIV with acupuncture," says Patil, drawing her shoulders back and straightening her spine. "I thought that was crazy."

Where, Patil thought, were the double-blind tests proving the efficacy of Chinese herbs? What about the empirical evidence that chiropractic work relieved arthritis?

But her patients' consistent reluctance to accept Western medicine as doctrine ultimately gave Patil pause. She began to read the books and information about alternative thinking and therapies that her clients had given her. Patil devoured *The Truth About the Drug Companies*, a damning book about corruption and manipulation inside the pharmaceutical industry, and dwelled on the potential ripple effects of prescription drugs. Patil questioned, for instance, how the Lipitor she prescribed might influence cholesterol levels in a patient's brain or adrenals. She grew increasingly resentful of treating clients as if they were racecars coming in for pit stops. Just as an elderly patient would set aside his walker and sit down to be examined, it was time for Patil to diagnose him and move on. Get up, Pops! The waiting room is full!

Then, in 2002, unexpected results emerged from a huge and now famous medical study conducted by the National Institutes of Health. The eleven-year-old Women's Health Initiative—which followed over 160,000 menopausal, hormone-taking women nationwide—was halted early because investigators questioned the prudence of allowing the subjects to continue with hormone-replacement therapy (HRT). The study reported that, in certain combinations, supplemental doses of estrogen and progesterone taken specifically to battle menopause could pose increased risk of heart attack, stroke, blood clots, and breast cancer. Like many physicians, Patil took her menopausal patients off HRT. However, some of them returned in tortured states. They complained of sleeplessness, chest pains, and panic attacks. The women told Patil that if she didn't put them back on HRT, they'd find someone else who would.

Patil also discovered that, in the absence of hormone replacement therapy, some women complaining of hot flashes were receiving prescriptions from doctors for anti-depressants. She fumed. Anti-depressants aren't designed to address menopause; they don't target problems around sleeplessness, weight gain, and diminishing sex drive. They're for clinical depression. Even if doctors pass them out like Halloween treats, Patil knew that anti-depressants wouldn't cure women of their menopausal symptoms. The meds might also cause side effects including headaches, anxiety, nausea, and higher blood pressure.

"For hot flashes," Patil says, shaking her head. "Anti-depressants."

Patil sought something different for her patients. She didn't mothball her medical license, or cancel her subscription to the *Journal of the American Medical Association*. But she opened her own internal-medicine office, saw fewer clients, paused long enough during her day to add lemon slices to her water, and took a holistic approach to medicine that incorporated nutrition and lifestyle advice.

On her own, Patil continued to prescribe hormone therapies that she'd first prescribed in the wake of the WHI findings, when she dove into hormone research and became something of a self-taught expert. She studied the Women's Health Initiative findings and found what she believed were shortfalls and oversights. She began prescribing "bioidentical" hormones. "Bioidenticals," while manmade, have the same chemical composition as naturally occurring hormones. Bioidenticals are derived from plants, and many doctors and scientists in the anti-aging community argued that these hormones were superior to the pharmaceutical-industry engineered (and patented) "synthetic" hormones that were used by stricken WHI subjects. Patil wasn't completely confident that the bioidenticals were better, so she carefully dosed her patients and, especially in the absence of thorough scientific testing, watched them—and their blood work—closely for any signs of distress.

Then, in 2005, Patil read Susie Wiley's book, *Sex, Lies, and Menopause*. Soon afterward she began prescribing the Wiley Protocol, which emulated the ebb-and-flow hormone cycles that women experience when they're in their twenties and in peak health. Patil collected tales of how her patients were walking wrecks until the protocol transformed them. The turnarounds were gratifying.

"I must have about one hundred female patients on Wiley," Patil says to me, removing her stethoscope and standing up. "I like to think that those patients are in a better place now than when they first arrived," she adds.

We walk slowly through the doorway of the examination room, seventy-five minutes after we'd entered it.

"But understand that when it comes to the Wiley Protocol for Men, we have a fraction of the information on guys than we do on women. You're one of the early adopters," she adds, putting her clipboard under her arm. "You're something of a guinea pig."

Not the animal reference I was hoping for. I'd rather: You're gonna be a tiger.

I clench my jaw. Patil notices my concern.

"I'll monitor you," she says with a nod. "We'll check your blood every three months, and closely observe how you're absorbing the hormone creams."

I'm still unsure, but Patil's smarts, healthy skepticism, and experience with hormones makes the guinea-pig reference better slide through my consciousness. She's the most competent anti-aging doctor I've encountered.

The next day I have my blood work done, and confirm that results will be sent straight to Patil's office. Then I wait for the drugs to arrive in the mail.

"THIS SIDE WILL BE for my towels," I tell Juliana late on a Tuesday night, days after meeting Patil. I'm highly conscious of how anal-retentive I sound and appear, folding and re-folding a bath towel in attempts to create a noticeable gap between it and the towel already hanging on the small towel rack. Juliana, who's sitting up in bed and reading, gives me a quick smile and an "Okay" before turning back to her book. I continue. "Never drape your towels over mine. I'll need to keep the testosterone to myself."

In preparation for the arrival of the drugs, I'm busily separating toiletries and towels in our small bathroom. Patil had told me more than once that the Wiley Protocol hormone creams are quite potent, and in the wake of some of her female patients "contaminating" their husbands with supplemental female hormones, that I should do what I can to keep my 'roids to myself. (Wiley, for the record, disagrees with Patil, and thinks contamination via her products occurs quite rarely.) In order to avoid contaminating my family with testosterone, Patil wants me to wait two hours after applying the creams before my affected areas might come in contact with Juliana or the children. I go one step further. I want to keep my clothes and towels separate, too. Who knows what hormones might lurk on the corner of a washcloth, or a pair of jeans lying inside-out on the bedroom floor. Better neurotic than sorry.

I carefully fold the towel again, this time into thirds. I discover that if I fold the towel next to it exactly the same way, they don't touch on the rack. It's a tight fit.

The kids are asleep. Juliana and I are, as usual, knackered. Earlier tonight we finished helping Benjamin piece together a school assignment—a last-minute poster-board project that featured one-time Alcatraz celebrity prisoner Al Capone. I was amazed at how much Benjamin had taken to the braggadocio that seeps out of every Capone image we printed from the Web, and how he spoke reverently of the gangster no matter how many times I reminded him that the guy was nasty. But Benjamin is eight years old, and between the machine-gun noises coming from my son's pursed lips and the pretend bullets emerging from his fingers, it was obvious that he's already drunk on the mythology of the rogue American male: Capone wielded big weapons, talked tough, and dominated lots of people—the thug is a little boy's version of a high achiever. In truth, the original Scarface was probably one part gunpowder and two parts testosterone.

"Here's where I'll store the syringes," I say to Juliana, my eyes remaining on the messy contents of the under-sink cabinet while my arm extends out of the bathroom, lifting up a small, black toiletry travel bag so that she can see it from bed. "Don't touch the bag."

Juliana doesn't respond.

"Juliana?" I ask, my eyes still trained on the old shampoo bottles and an electric hairdryer lying askew under the sink.

She still doesn't answer me.

"*Juliana*," I repeat, and this time I get up off the floor to look straight at her. She's asleep, her book still open and torso propped up by pillows, atop our slab of a Tempur-Pedic mattress. Juliana is pretty when she's asleep—the smooth skin around her eyes is relaxed and soft. Her lips are full and a gentle red.

"Juliana," I say, softer now, approaching the bed and resting my left hand gently on her left shoulder. Her eyelids flap open.

"Can we go over a couple more things about my hormone creams before you go to sleep?"

"I *am* asleep," she says, licking her lips and leaning forward to remove a couple of the pillows from behind her. "I was."

"Juliana, you promised me that I could go over these precautions with you tonight," I say, trying not to sigh. "They won't take long to explain."

"Can it wait until tomorrow?" she says, and slaps at the mushy pillow she likes to sleep on before lying flat on her back.

"That's what you said last night," I say, hands on my hips, knowing I sound childish.

"What's the big urgency?" she asks, her eyes closed.

"The creams will show up any day, and I want to start using them right away," I say. "I don't want to have this conversation after I've started rubbing on the testosterone. We can't have it with the children around."

"Let's do it tomorrow. I'm exhausted," she says, briefly sitting up to grab a silk eye bag. She lies back down on her back and carefully rests the eye bag over her eyes. Juliana likes to sleep in black-hole dark.

"Blame your picky son," she says, chuckling and centering the eye bag. "I thought we'd never get that project done."

"Dammit Juliana," I snap, the tone of my voice completely altered, right along with my level of irritation. "Don't blow me off. You can't keep this measly commitment," I moan, lecturing her. "You never make time for us to talk."

"Please don't use that tone of voice," she says, now awake but still under the eye bag. The dang eye bag might as well be as big as the Great Wall of China, or Fenway Park's Green Monster. There's suddenly plenty of distance between us. "You're not improving the situation," she adds.

How I love being middle-aged! Kids, carpools, bills, pets, flab, conflict, and "partners."

Yes, when Juliana and I decided to have children we shed the designation of *Couple*. Now we're *Partners*, or perhaps a *Couple of Cooperators*, each attempting to make it through our busy days, trying to be good parents as well as supportive of each other. Too often, unfortunately, we fail to have each other's back.

I try to calm down, return to a pleasant tone.

Easy there, Fire Boy. Think before you speak again. Listen to what your partner is saying.

They're mantras that I learned in couples therapy, which we'd been attending every Tuesday for the better part of a year. Today's ninety-minute session had been dismal. After nearly fourteen years of marriage and eighteen years of relationship, the divisiveness between us was high. With our round-headed, gray-haired, bespectacled owl of a therapist in front of us and books like *For Each Other* and *The Guide to Getting it On* facing us in overstuffed bookshelves, Juliana and I attempted to air out and hopefully soothe some crappy feelings. Juliana talked about how she had called me on the phone, eighteen months earlier, from a yoga/spiritual retreat after having epiphanies about her feelings of loneliness in our relationship. I had surfed the Web during part of the conversation. Then we talked about how I had picked up Juliana at the airport last fall after playing Daddy and Mommy for over a week while she visited family and friends in her adopted hometown of Austin, Texas only for her to inform me that life in the Bay Area had become intolerably mundane and she wanted to move. Then our owl-like therapist had stood up and mechanically enunciated words like "empathy" and "compassion" while writing them on a white board.

Minutes later, I said *screw this* and Juliana said *I am light and you are darkness*, and we both seethed and cried. Then, when the session was over, we walked out holding hands because of our collective fear for the future.

Nowadays it seems like we can argue about money, sex, who last cleaned the litter box, and, apparently, the way we arrange bath towels. How about bath towels as metaphors: I am the responsible and nitpicky worrier, and my towel is folded into perfect thirds. Juliana, who is spontaneous, far less in her head, and mostly interested in life's pleasures, doesn't care how her bath towel hangs. It's a towel! Are its folds more important than sleep? Dreams? How had towels fallen directly on the paths walked by our parents, all of whom fought endlessly and ended up divorced?

You learned to listen today, Andrew. The therapist reminded you that true listening is a gift of "incomprehensible magnitude," both to offer and to receive. Ask for that gift.

"Juliana," I say, looking at her lying behind the eye bag, using (*fucking!*) ridiculous amounts of restraint to speak (*goddamn!*) evenly and almost mechanically, "what I've asked of you is really important to me. For everyone's well being, I want to show you how to treat anything that might come in contact with my hormone creams with the utmost caution. For your safety."

Juliana slowly pulls the eye bag off her face and sits up. She is no longer sleepy. She also seems less angry.

"Thank you," she says with a smile. "That was nice. Even if you did sound like a robot."

I laugh. She laughs. The tension dissipates. She gets out of bed, and I show her how to fold the towels so that hers won't come in contact with mine. I point out the toiletry bag where I'll store the syringes, and how it should remain untouched by her, and far enough back in the messy under-sink cabinet that Benjamin and Sophie won't likely reach for it. I explain that I'll use the left pocket in the three-pocket hamper in our garage for my dirty clothes, and and we walk into the garage for a look.

"Nothing else should go into the left pocket," I say, pointing at the hamper. Juliana smiles softly, and flexes her toes inside of her slippers.

She's listening to me.

"Meanwhile I'll keep my clothes out of the hallway hamper," I add.

We walk away from the garage and back toward our bedroom. "Okay," says Juliana, playfully grabbing my pajama shirt and pulling me closer. "It's us versus Andrewpause."

I SO KNOW WHAT'S COMING. I'm about to get grief for turning into one very anal cyclist.

"Ohhhhh, something's different today," says Michael, standing on a paved bike path and straddling his bicycle. He leans the upper half of his six-foot-four frame over his handlebars, and with his right hand removes his wraparound sunglasses from his face and threads them into the vent slots of his cycling helmet. He looks over my bike and me. "There are changes," he says with a wry grin. Mike's long, dark, handsome face is unshaven, which is not new. His grooming has always run a distant sixth to eating, sleeping, teaching, relaxing, cycling—the things that matter in the World According to Michael. Mike wouldn't be unhappy if his clothes closet contained little more than exercise duds and sweatpants. He finds the latter to be excellent for lounging, as well as almost all pre- and post-workout activities. To my friend, outside of his work wear, there isn't much time or necessity for other clothing.

This morning I spot some specks of gray in Mike's three-day stubble. But I don't make fun of his aging mug, not yet anyway. I'll let him abuse me first.

"Speak up, man," says Michael, as we pedal our racing bikes out of the bayside town of Sausalito. "Explain yourself."

Earlier in the week, Michael had convinced me to join him today—a late January Saturday morning—in Marin County for a weekend training ride. We don't share these experiences often enough, and we know if we rode together more that the training would feel like less of a grind. But I'm constantly attempting to squeeze in hours worth of weekend workouts in the hills right around my house so that I can hang out with the family. Michael often rides with other racers near his place fifty miles south of Oakland, although he doesn't consider those cyclists great friends. Great friends who he can hassle.

"Why are you prodding me? No doping to confess of," I say, sounding sweetly innocent while zipping up my windbreaker vest.

We're both dressed, ankles to Adam's apples, in logoed cycling clothing. We're those aging, racer-guy fitness types, drawn not to midlife distractions involving poker chips, golf clubs, or pole dancers, but rather Lycra. "Still waiting for the drugs."

"Come on," he says, looking straight ahead. We're riding toward the town of Mill Valley, and 2,500-foot tall Mt. Tamalpais. "Don't pretend, LeMond."

Through the years, Mike and I have nicknamed each other with the names of acclaimed pro cyclists, many of them past Tour de France champions. I've called him *Delgado* (Pedro Delgado, 1988 victor) and *Big Mig* (Miguel Indurain, 1991–1995). He's called me *Hinault* (Bernard Hinault, a bunch of wins) and *Simoni* (Gilberto Simoni, never prevailed at the Tour). But the one name we both return to is "LeMond." Greg LeMond won the Tour de France three times, and his first victory came when Michael and I were barely beyond our teens, and still in search of heroes. Back in 1986, when LeMond became the first American ever to win the Tour, he rolled into our souls and never left.

"What, this?" I say, pointing to the bike computer that's anchored to my handlebar. It's only a little smaller than a smartphone, which makes it notably bigger than most other, far simpler bike computers. It's a new addition to my two-wheeled steed.

"*You'll never see me with a power meter,*" singsongs Mike, imitating me, while reaching over to my bike and dragging one of his gloved fingers across the red, white, black, and yellow face of the super-duper computer. "*Too obsessive.* Weren't those your words, LeMond?"

I expect nothing less from Michael after buying a German-made "power meter," arguably the most precise instrument available to track a cyclist's abilities, and standard issue for the sport's best professional teams. Power meters measure and record the power (in watts) that a cyclist generates with each pedal stroke. The recorded data can then be downloaded from the bike computer to a PC or laptop, and studied, as numbers or in graphs, for further analysis and training strategies. My power meter, from the German manufacturer SRM, is a truly elaborate and geeky device. I sold both myself and Juliana on the ridiculously steep, $3,000 purchase—enough money to buy a decent racing bike, or probably feed five hundred starving children into their adulthood, yet it only lands me a used unit—because I thought that the power meter might help me track my freakish progress as a doping bike racer.

Please. You coveted that thing. Technology plus cycling plus a way to monitor and maximize your every movement. A bike-riding, control freak's dream machine!

"Business purchase," I say, as we start to ascend a narrow, wooded road deep in Mill Valley that will take us up a shoulder of Mt. Tam. I try not to smirk. "It's for the book."

Mike surges ahead. Because of constantly changing speeds, surrounding traffic, and even which way the wind blows, road riders out for a spin together often drift out of each other's earshot, which is why cycling is often sprinkled with choppy conversations. I'm content to ride behind Michael for a while anyway, enjoying the rhythms of pedaling and the slight side to side motion of the bike underneath me as we climb, as well as the view of Mike's lean and thin legs. They bend, extend, and move round and round with fluidity, like they were built for the task, like they were bathed in oil.

Behind Michael, I can also duck more potential abuse. Road riding and racing are involved, detail-oriented endeavors, and over the last couple years I've reversed each vow I've ever made about not falling prey to the sport's fuss and demands. I said I'd never shave my legs (done for myriad reasons, including tradition, easier application of lotions and creams, less chance of dirt finding its way into scrapes, and, without a doubt, aesthetics), hire a cycling coach (like the pros), or travel all over Northern California to race against other dedicated amateur cyclists. Then I did all of those things. Michael has been road racing longer than me, and he was the one who ultimately convinced me that the sum of the sport's many elements is a healthier, more disciplined, and happier life. Backing him up are the many bike-racing training books arguing that road racing, while time-consuming, can be compartmentalized. A block of time when you ride. Another when you work. Another when you sleep, and another when you spend time with the family. Mike, the rhetoric, and the schedules all make sense, even though I struggle endlessly to stick to the itineraries. Whether or not I'll find happiness in highly structured workouts and tight schedules still remains to be seen.

Michael and I ride down a particularly sinuous stretch of Highway 1 and toward the tiny coastal community of Muir Beach, and I steal glances at my new power meter and its multiple rows of numerical feedback. It will help me track my fitness gains; allow my coach, whom I recently hired, to download my workout data and be apprised of my fitness; and guide me, via data including power, heart rate, and the number of revolutions pedaled per minute (cadence), to train as effectively and efficiently possible.

This gizmo isn't a $3,000 boy toy. It's a dope-o-meter. It's a time-saving, fitness-building device. It'll prove its worth.

Mike and I pedal easily over the flat roads in Muir Beach and then back up another hill. Highway 1 plateaus and, on what is a gloriously sunny and still, nearly traffic-free morning, we can see the swaying Pacific Ocean to our left, just a few hundred feet down a green hillside. The water sparkles fresh blue, without a whitecap in sight. It's the uninterrupted blue of seamless life and calm, and the picture is enhanced by the sounds of the ocean's softly breaking waves. Not too far from the Golden Gate Bridge and San Francisco to our south, and to the broad sands of Stinson Beach to our north, we share a great moment: Two best friends, atop their sleek and light machines, taking in a mild California winter day.

I look down at my power meter and see that we have already been cycling for about forty-five minutes, and that I'm frequently generating more than 230 watts during the ride. My coach instructed me to ride for two hours max, and to average 200 watts.

"Let's turn around," I say to Mike after reaching down to grab the water bottle out of a lightweight carbon-fiber cage bolted to my bike frame. I gulp down some fluid.

"Why?" he says. "Let's at least go to Stinson. Or ride Bolinas Fairfax Road." Mike pushes his arm warmers, the stretchy sleeves designed to extend over a cyclist's arms for added weather protection, down until they're gathered at his wrists.

"It's gorgeous out," he says, pedaling softly. "Are you tired?"

"No. It's early season. I don't need to be out here all day," I say. "Let's head back."

Mike nearly stops in the middle of the empty, two-lane road. He stands up off his saddle to better balance on his pedals.

"Is your contraption telling you that it's time to turn around?" he asks. We both stop, each unclipping a cycling shoe out of our ski-binding style pedals to put a foot down on the pavement. Mike looks at me with an emotionless face, which for years has telegraphed his patience for my obsessive behavior. I think I first saw that face when we were eleven years old, and Mike waited while I kept re-buckling my ski boots in search of the right mix of comfort and tightness. Mike can get obsessive, too. But he's better than me at turning that mode off.

"I think I've created a monster," he says.

"Listen old man," I say. "You could probably use some more rest, anyway."

"This is not about me. The power meter's telling us to go home on an incredible morning," he says, wagging his right index finger, in a nasally, dweebish, gently mocking voice that I've heard him dip into for thirty years, "and we're going to heed it."

"You'll have one soon," I taunt.

"You're deep into the data now, LeMond," says Michael, pushing forward his right pedal and balancing again on his moving bike. "My friend the science experiment."

Mike shakes his head. He makes a U-turn to go back the way we came, and I follow.

I TEACH MYSELF TO HUNT, first squirrels and then wild boar and buffalo. I sew my own clothes, join a gang, and stare at the stars and crawl inside of waterfalls until, almost simultaneously, I comprehend the universe and fear absolutely nothing.

Hardly. But I am a city kid, born and largely raised in San Francisco, and like most of my privileged pals, by the time I'm ten years old I am testosterone-y in mind if not in body: I'm street-savvy and aware enough to take public transportation everywhere. I navigate traffic while skateboarding down some of the city's steep hills, and fend for myself all weekend long, playing football or basketball in city parks that are miles from home. In the winters I take a bus with other kids to the mountains, and ski without adults. In the summers I attend a camp near Yosemite for a month at a time. No doubt, my mother and father care a lot, and worry about me. By giving me a lot of independence, they also teach me to lean on them less and less.

Sometimes I leave my home in San Francisco's Marina district before dawn. I am twelve when I begin to jog, first with my dad, who lives in a nearby apartment, and then by myself or with Michael. I plunge into San Francisco's summertime fog, and seldom see other runners my age. I love my flat, four-mile outings toward the Golden Gate Bridge and Fort Point, where the bay waters thump giant, wave-breaking stones that send salty mist into the air and across my face. I never tire of the bridge's amber lights, red paint, and arching lines, nor the steady rhythm and quiet, the only noise coming from my breath, the foghorns, and my shoes skidding on the gravel along Crissy Field and then slapping the pavement as I approach the old fort. I like team sports, too, but I'm drawn to running because to me it is its own drug, almost always energizing instead of tiring. By the time I'm a teenager, the walls of my room are decorated with posters of famous runners. My friends idolize football, tennis, and basketball players, and my teenage heroes are relatively unknown endurance athletes—lean, seemingly steroid-free, top American distance runners like Craig Virgin, Bill Rodgers, and the late Steve Prefontaine. I am a passionate if only decent high school cross-country runner, but I identify with my heroes' challenges: *Always on the edge of exhaustion. Constantly short of breath. Forever holding a one-person dialogue about how much effort to put forth.* To my thinking, there is a certain maturity demanded of the endurance athlete—a long-distance runner, I believe, is often an old soul. Your performances result from great introspection in that they are often what you make them to be. Nobody catches your pass, or screens your defender.

By the time I'm a teenager my parents are already divorced, adding another layer to my independence. I live with my mom most of the time, and she's great. In some ways, anyway. She stocks the refrigerator with killer foods like salami, sugary yogurt, and huge dill pickles, and keeps the house full of chocolate. Mom has been known to follow me down water slides, and she turns me into the San Francisco Giants fan that I am today. On more than one occasion, Mom pulls me out of school for opening-day ballgames. She regularly tunes into the Giants on the television or radio. She's fun to be around. She's a mom-kid.

Mom also buys me—and herself, and others—lots of nice things, and bad spending habits are one of her faults. She constantly spends money that isn't to be found in a piggy bank, or any other type of bank. Sometimes she tells me not to answer the phone, and I quickly figure out why: Collection agencies call us. I notice that one of her favorite grocery stores, Cal-Mart, occasionally accepts only cash from her. She bounces too many checks. When she and my father were married, they fought over mounting credit card debt. And when I'm sixteen and Mom tells me we have to move out of the house I grew up in, the house that had been my grandmother's, I know why—she needs the cash. Our beautiful flats are owned outright—Mom inherited them, as well as money, from her mother, who had made a good living owning a clothing manufacturing business. We have a tenant upstairs. But apparently living mortgage-free and enjoying rental-property income aren't enough.

A year and change later, my entire family is at a wedding when I learn a stunning truth about my father. It's an occasion that again starts my internal clock moving at the speed of dog years, and has me attempting to put a leash on a confusing existence that I hope will someday turn youthful. But not on this day.

I am looking down our row during the wedding ceremony, in a small room at a family friend's wedding. There's Dad, straightening his tie and sitting next to Mom, who's sitting next to her date, whatever his name is. Mom and Dad have remained great friends, but something about them sitting together strikes me as strange.

How many women go to a wedding with two guys—an ex-husband and a date?

Suddenly a realization comes to me, something that I know to be true so clearly that I wonder why I didn't see it sooner.

"Yes," Tracy says when I confront her after the ceremony. "Dad is gay."

Tracy—outspoken, full of convictions, more imposing than her five-foot-two body, and seldom fooled. Her thick, wavy, brown hair provides worthy shade for all the thinking power that propelled my sister into a New England college, and ultimately studies in Jerusalem, a graduate degree, and a career in sales. I consider our savviness to be shared and genetic, but Tracy is a cut above, and she'd picked up on my dad's sexuality before my mother had, and five years before I did. Maybe it was the absence of girlfriends in my dad's life, or his many male friends, his salmon-colored suit, the white loafers, or the sudden appearance of a thick mustache. Those characterizations sound hopelessly clichéd now, but back in 1977 my dad's personal choices and décor were a combined badge of honor, a sign of belonging to a small but fast-emerging brotherhood.

Inside of that Victorian house, Tracy tells me that my parents worried about how I'd respond to my dad's homosexuality. They decided to wait until I figured it out on my own.

My dad and mom walk up to us. They both have Champagne in their hands.

"Andrew figured it out," says Tracy, looking at the two of them. She's never been one for subtlety. "About Dad."

My father and I look at each other. His mustachioed face seems uncertain of committing to an expression. He's got half a foot on me, but he looks down at me submissively. I don't know what to think either, or how to tell him that everything's okay. I don't know if it is. I'm only seventeen.

This is my dad. He is gay. This is, like, wow. Huge.

Dad finally puts his arms around me. He smells like cologne. His embrace is warm, and I'm happy to be in his arms.

"I'm still the same," he says, keeping his arms around me. "Nothing changes how much I love you, Andrew," he says. "But you need time to understand your feelings."

I hug him back, assure him that I'm fine, that I don't.

But I do. I'm seventeen and on the T! Syringes, no. Puberty and manly impulses, you betcha! All my friends and I can talk about, in our cracking voices, is girls.

And my dad is gay!

In an ideal and open-minded world—and in the mid 1980s, gay scenes in San Francisco's bathhouses and the Castro district made the city about as open-minded as many folks could ever imagine—the

young son of a gay man doesn't care about his dad's sexual prefer-
ences. That is, if that young son is an open-minded kid.

Apparently I am not.

Being so progressive, at that age, in an era when sodomy is still
outlawed in plenty of states and White House press secretary Larry
Speakes cracks jokes about AIDS, is a lot to expect.

For a time after my dad admits to me that he's homosexual, my
buddies and I carry on as usual, slinging "homo" and "fag" insults
around about as often as we toss a football. Any one of us whose
behavior isn't sufficiently aggressive or macho might be met with ridi-
culers armed with limp wrists, or abuse followed by effeminate, lisp-
ing voices.

I'm tho thorry I thpilled my drink on your thlackth. Excuthe me!
We are so funny! Fags are faggy!

But after a while I really tune into the conversations that I have
with friends from my informed and progressive, private high school
and my own hypocrisy dawns on me. My father is a *poofter*, and he is
also my dad. Whom I love.

I can't tolerate the insults much longer. We are racists, bigots,
complete jerks. I tell some of my oldest friends about my father: Dave,
Andy, and Doug. Stephen, Peter, and Adam. Michael, of course.
Michael's response to my news is confused, like mine. Like the others'.

"Man," he says one morning while we stretch on the expanse of
grass known as the Marina Green before running to Fort Point and
back. "When did you find that out?"

"Maybe a month ago," I say.

"Your dad is still your dad," says Michael. "He's still totally cool
with me. I mean, yeah."

Yeah. Increasingly, I stick close to my friends who know about my father and are sensitive to the issue. The other guys just seem so immature.

Grow up!

Fortunately, my relationship with my father doesn't change much. I'm still a huge part of what I believe is his simple existence (at least he leaves me with that impression, and I don't inquire about his life beyond what I already know). My dad, extremely anxious by nature, doesn't like to stray far from San Francisco, especially after spending a few years institutionalized for debilitating clinical depression that we all probably should have seen coming but didn't. He and I are often content to sit at a tiny table in his Marina apartment kitchen, eating culotte steaks with baked potatoes, and large blocks of barely defrosted Pepperidge Farm chocolate cake. Sometimes Michael joins us. His family lives only blocks from my dad's place.

I do wonder for a while, because my father is gay, if I'm gay too.

Did I inherit his homosexuality? Could it be passed on? Is there something funny in the Tilin . . . testosterone?

I look at the posters of the runners on my bedroom walls. I appreciate their physiques. I like their sinew, and streamlined muscles. If I find a man attractive, what does that mean? If I'm gay, so what. Right? Michael's handsome, with a lot of muscular definition. Is that a bad thing to confess? My teenage brain can't wrap around it all.

IN THE FALL OF 1983 I attend college at the University of California, have short and long and super-short relationships with women, and confirm to myself that I'm drawn to the opposite sex. Berkeley is less than thirty minutes from my mom's and dad's homes, and yet

I often—happily—feel like I'm thousands of miles away. No gold-finished-shower-handled reminders of my mother's insane excess. None of my dad's Donna Summer albums ringing in my ears. Except for the tuition checks that my mom consistently bounces, I am lucky in that I can be a carefree, beer-drinking, bicycle-riding, girl-scamming college student. I am young in body and spirit and on the four-and-a-half-year graduation plan.

The call from my father comes in the summer of 1987, on the eve of my twenty-second birthday, at the offices of a Bay Area magazine where I have a summer internship.

"I'm sick," he says.

I say nothing.

"Did you hear me?" he asks.

"Oh no," I say.

I know what's coming, right this moment and for months or years, and then for the rest of my life: a suffering family, and my father's death. The tears form quickly. My forehead gets hot. I stare deep into the nothingness of an empty, white bulletin board.

"Pneumocystis pneumonia," he says.

That's the form of pneumonia especially found in people with AIDS. In 1987, an AIDS diagnosis meant about two years to live.

My mother, sister, paternal grandparents, and I wear ourselves out for a good portion of the next eighteen months. My father, always vulnerable emotionally, is now increasingly of a like way physically, and needs us frequently. He has fevers, chills, and night sweats. We treat his rashes and canker sores. We make sure he has the right pills—round ones at night, capsules in the morning. We research new and experimental drugs. Unfortunately, some of the most effective medications to help prevent AIDS patients from wasting away aren't yet available to my dad. Two of them are the synthetic hormones erythropoietin (EPO) and human growth hormone (HGH), which even prior to my dad's demise were used by doping athletes. That's a crazy thought: My dad's death might have been postponed and certainly would've been less agonizing if we could've accessed drugs that were already within reach of athletes trying to win. That is, to make men and women better at *playing games*. Barry Bond's drug dealer apparently bought some of his goods from men with AIDS, all so that athletes could better *play their stinking games*.

My father dies on April 17, 1989, at forty-nine years of age. I'm twenty-four, going on fifty. For decades I have done what I can to make his life—and my life within his—safe and navigable. I am profoundly sad. I miss my dad, not my *gay* dad, or my *helpless* dad. The one who made me steaks, ate ice cream only after it melted (like me), and bought me my first tape recorder to use in my story reporting.

Dad's passing, however, is also an unburdening. In my mid-twenties, I discover that dying and death, for those loved ones who keep living, is miserable and an absolute ton of work. But when my father passes, the logistics around him die too. I inherit some money, and have a chance to feel footloose. Seizing my opportunity takes me a year, but when a friend who's an editor in Boulder, Colorado promises to help me find work, for once in my life I don't think twice. I see a life as a writer, runner, and cyclist. Boulder is a fitness town that has exactly what I crave: vitality. I say yes, and I leave the Bay Area and my puffy-eyed family behind.

I RIDE MY ROAD BIKE up Flagstaff. Take my mountain bike on the St. Vrain trail. Walk amongst the ice-smooth Flatirons. Eat ice cream on the Pearl Street Mall, and have long talks about life and sports with my new roommate, a bright ex-pro tennis player. Boulder is clear-skied and straightforward, and in my first weeks everything feels so beautifully simple. To spin! To breathe! To set up a desk and go at the QWERTY keyboard! Freedom with every blink and inhale of that Rocky Mountain air.

Life gets even better. Juliana washes over me like a deliciously soothing breeze. Falling for her has everything to do with lust, friendship, doing youthful things together and, in due time, love.

It is August 1990. Juliana is a cute graphic designer for the local sports magazine where my friend works. My friend asks if I want to go over to Juliana's place—her two roommates are throwing Juliana a birthday party. Soon after I arrive, the birthday girl and I dance to Lyle Lovett, and shovel up homemade guacamole with vegetables grown in her home's garden. There is a cake. Juliana's twenty-fifth birthday is seven weeks after mine.

"You're going to fit right in here," she says on the house's back patio. Juliana wears a colorful, Aztec-pattern, burgundy and gold tank top, and a pair of silver, elaborate, dangly earrings.

"A lot of us have come here to start again, and become people we've always wanted to be," says Juliana, her smile widening as she hoists a giant zucchini off the table. "Like squash farmers."

There's a brightness about her, a wit and intelligence blended with levity rather than intensity. I think I could get used to those qualities.

I'm also drawn to Juliana's exotic aesthetic, and her humor. Juliana's eyes are the color of trust—a warm and sincere greenish brown. Her cheeks are soft and joyous, with gentle, rounded lines. Her long, pretty arms and legs—permanently shaded brown by the

West Texas sun of her childhood, and her Mexican roots—move in a deliberate and sexy way.

We enter into a relationship. Juliana and I go to a bluegrass concert in the tiny hill town of Nederland and eat spicy Thai food in some unremarkable Boulder restaurant that leaves us both laughing and crying over the fiery meal. We go mountain biking and camping together, and in the fall of 1990 wake up to a funky smell after pitching our tent the night before, in darkness, on the gritty and pervasive sandstone outside the tiny town of Moab, Utah.

"What is that terrible stink? It seems like it's coming from inside the tent," I say that morning, still zipped up in my sleeping bag. I curl into a tight ball, pushing my nose deep into my bag's nylon skin, as if the material and the feathers insulating my bag will somehow block the odor. It doesn't work.

"We have to figure this out," I insist, trying to breathe only through my mouth. "Like, now." I feel my tension rise.

Juliana is still in her sleeping bag, too. She starts to giggle, at first a little and then in great, guttural, uncontrollable waves of laughter.

"What?" I say impatiently.

She stops laughing long enough to speak.

"We pitched the tent on top of cow shit," she finally pronounces.

She unzips her sleeping bag enough to extend an arm. She starts patting the nylon tent floor around her, probing. Then Juliana stops the mine-sweep style search and keeps patting down on the same spot, which is between my bag and hers. She starts laughing hard again— enough to make me start laughing, too. She's right. It's cow shit.

Juliana shrugs off so much of life's crap. She doesn't fret over deadlines. She lives frugally, and doesn't mind. She laughs about the dysfunctions in her upbringing, and refuses to obsess over a father who's rarely been in her life. Meanwhile, deadlines, my parents, and money twist me up. My mother sometimes calls to tell me that she's low on funds, knowing full well of my inheritance. I apologize and tell her that I won't loan her money. When I tell a therapist about how awful that makes me feel, she reminds me that giving my mother money won't solve her overspending problems. Handouts, she says, will forever alter the dynamic between us.

As if it hasn't been permanently altered already.

Over and over, endurance sports, similar to all things Juliana-related, return me to equanimity, and to life inside the body and mind of a young man. Beautiful Boulder frequently attracts world-class runners, triathletes, and cyclists, who come to train in the thin air that makes their bodies better able to process the oxygen that's fuel for their muscles.

I am far from world-class, but while living in Boulder I race triathlons. I also land a job editing a magazine for hard-core amateur triathletes, and I get into my editing and writing, too. My life is finally humming when, in the fall of 1991, I receive a call from the editor of *Outside* magazine. At the time, *Outside* was a Chicago-based outdoor-lifestyle publication that I'd long enjoyed. He asks me if I'm interested in applying for an editorial job. *Outside*, which champions endurance athletes, depicting them in smart sentences and four-color, fabulous 8.5-by-11-inch glossiness, delivers its great messages to endurance-sports aficionados across the nation. Of course I want to work there. What better place for a journalist, endurance-athlete, and life-force-seeker to connect with the rock stars of youth, strength, and stamina?

On a pretty Colorado day in October 1991, Juliana and I kiss passionately, and afterwards remain in a standing embrace. We are inside of the shingled, two-story home that I rent with a new housemate on Boulder's Mapleton Avenue, but I won't be living here much longer. *Outside* has offered me a job. I've asked Juliana to come with me to Chicago. The two of us will go: It's a huge decision and a big commitment to one another. We're both twenty-six and talking like adults. Even though we both still love our youth.

"We'll make a nice home. Lots of cooking, videos on those cold winter nights, and summer strolls on Lake Michigan," I say to her.

"Blues music," she says. "I'm excited. The big city."

A life together.

An energizing, turbocharged existence!

I find *Outside* to be a great magazine, with very smart editors who demand a whole lot of thinking and work performed behind a desk. Juliana and I also discover that Chicago is truly a big city. A big, bruising, urban city, with a lot of gray snow and concrete that's too much for a West Texas girl like Juliana, who misses the handsome evergreens and simplicity of immaculate Boulder. I work increasingly more hours, and run and ride less. Juliana and I both know that I've made an intelligent career move. A grown-up move that begets increasingly grown-up lives, with more and more grown-up complications.

"When are you coming home?" Juliana asks me over the phone one night when I'm working late, a few months after I start the job. As I work more and more evenings, and the weeks turn into months and years, the questions change and indeed flow both ways, but the essences of such questions remain the same: Love. Dedication. Control. Maturity.

And for Juliana and me, there are moves to other places, and nicer apartments, and new dining room tables, and small mortgages and pets, and bigger mortgages and children, and bigger mortgages still and living room furniture and more moves, and different jobs, and kids that want to go skiing and need the exact right back-to-school supplies and wardrobes. And then, one day, I find myself standing on the driveway of my nearly jumbo-mortgage house, opening the locking mailbox because in this day and age I have to guard against nagging crap like identity theft. I ignore all the credit card offers and instead open the anonymous, brown, padded envelope by pulling on the convenient little tab, and I see syringes. Syringes that promise to help me forget growing up too fast and keeping everything under control, and to help me remember my youth and strength, when I ran and rode a bike effortlessly and had fantasies about devouring my mate and occasionally almost made them come true. And I look at the syringes again and think that maybe I've been given a second chance. Then I smile and turn around, and suddenly the weight of the too expensive house and hopelessly complicated life seem profoundly less burdensome.

alien urges

S omething is in bed with us. I wake up before daylight and sense an additional presence. It's not unwelcome like a nightmare, really it could be considered more like a dream. I wouldn't call it an out of body experience. More like an extended-body experience. What I don't know is that I should become used to having it around.

On this sunny winter morning in February 2008, Juliana and I are under the sheets with a body part that's been shaped by a phenomenon called *nocturnal penile tumescence*. In my youth, I called it *morning wood*. Others call it *BEMHO*, or the *big early morning hard-on*.

It's not like I never have erections. My aging body hasn't completely betrayed me. But I don't wake up with them daily anymore. Erections are complicated events, the result of psychological and physiological factors including length of sleep as well as stimulation, which can be classified as "mechanical" or imagined. NPT is more complicated still. Nobody knows all the science behind NPT—which, in a solid night of sleep, occurs as many as three to five times, with erections lasting approximately thirty minutes apiece. Yes, half-hour long erections that grown men *sleep* through. Serious wasted energy.

What is known: Data exists that NPT can be influenced by the introduction of exogenous testosterone, or testosterone that's entered the body externally (the scientific findings report definite gains in rigidity, if not circumference). The testosterone, which is also called "male hormone," apparently gets inside your head.

"We do know that male hormone increases libido. Essentially, you're hungry for sex," says Dr. Richard Sherins, who specializes in male infertility and spent twenty years working as a researcher at the National Institutes of Health. "When you get hungry, you want to eat."

Practically everyone I speak to in the anti-aging community swears that an increased sex drive is an early indicator that supplemental testosterone has begun to work its magic. One of the first measures of increased sex drive, anti-aging folks say, is more frequent and pronounced morning erections.

Here I am with NPT, lying next to my beautiful wife.

She's asleep.

I look at her. She's facing me, her brown hair suggestively drifting across her face like a sheer curtain. Her lips look soft and moist. One of her nightgown's straps dangles off her shoulder. Man.

My next move should resemble a logical extension of those "after" shots posted on the anti-aging websites—the photos where the men all look buff, confident, and ready to pounce like tigers. The sheets rustle. I graze her arm with my arm, and her leg with my leg. I move closer to Juliana, and slowly wake her with soft strokes of her hair. Smile suggestively when her eyes open. Move closer still.

But the erection appears in Andrew Tilin's world, which doesn't exist on some silver—or computer—screen. Juliana's and my sex rituals don't include waking each other up in the middle of the night to have intimacy. That part of our relationship, for better or worse, has been built on sensitivity, as well as fear and restraint, rather than surprise and indulgence. Sex—really, even the idea of sex—almost always defers to everything else in our lives, whether it's sleep, work, my cycling, Juliana's morning yoga classes, or taking the kids out for Sunday morning bagels. Asking my first testosterone-fueled hard-on to change our ways is asking a lot.

Really, it's asking too much. I don't move toward Juliana. It's Friday, a day that already has its rituals. There's Therapy Tuesday, and then there's Yoga Friday. Juliana always wants plenty of rest before her Friday morning yoga class. Waking her up right now for sex wouldn't feel right. It isn't us.

TO THINK FOR A SECOND that more testosterone and erections would automatically mean more great sex was foolish of me. But it's a lot easier to ponder such a fantasy than it is to face the complex truths of one's own sexuality. Why, while lying in bed next to my sleeping wife, I decide to contemplate the latter—I'm not super sure. I thought I'd just peek at my sexuality. In the process, however, I end up trying to reconcile the typical male glamorization of sex with the modest and self-critical sexual being who I believe I mostly am.

Climbing Mt. Everest would've required less energy.

When my body begins to produce more testosterone, as it does in boys ages nine to fourteen, I am—like most boys—plenty disoriented. Puberty will deepen my voice, thicken my muscles, and sprout hair

on formerly smooth parts of my body. By seventh grade, I live in fear
of a schoolteacher asking me to stand up and write something on the
chalkboard. What am I supposed to do with all this, this *life force*? I'm
too embarrassed to ask anyone.

I become only more confused. It's the summer of 1981, I'm sixteen
years old, and Michael and I sneak into the R-rated movie *Body Heat*.
We already think we've seen it all—*Three's Company* (starring my
anti-aging buddy Suzanne, no less). *Charlie's Angels. Animal House.*
But watching William Hurt and Kathleen Turner perform their sexual
tangos leaves Mike and me crossing our legs and nearly unable to swallow our popcorn. Can't get much steamier.

Now I know how it's done!

Indeed, thanks in part to all of those Hollywood images, Michael
and I are just two young men in a nation of young men that take the
romanticized bait. We are convinced that intimacy in America should
always involve incredible looking women in tight-fitting clothes, the
occasional breaking down of doors to reach those women, and partners who always climax together. Of course, we're sure that our now
soaring, post-pubescent supplies of testosterone (men's T levels peak
in their late twenties) will help us in our quests, and in the groin I'm
confident that I'm every bit the man that William Hurt is. But the girls
I make out with and feel up from my high school dress in preppy rather
than clingy clothes. Plus they're not even breathing hard when I ejacu-
late in my underwear.

Michael doesn't help my growing feelings of sexual inadequacy.
"We ordered pizza and then did it by candlelight," he boasts one
Sunday morning, when we compare notes from Saturday-night dates
over the phone.

My date was nothing like that.

Whether or not my pal is lying, we're both striving to grow into the sex gods that we're sure we'll become.

The natural order of things. Right?

I think that even my mom wants me to hone my game. At least that's what I believe as a hyper self-conscious teenager when, one fall day in 1981, she takes me shopping for a new bed.

"How about a waterbed? That'd be cool," she says.

She thinks I'm totally uncool.

I'm aware of the fact that her comment makes no reference to sleep. Of course my mom doesn't mean anything negative. Mom, as usual, is all about indulgence—indugling herself, indulging me. Walking around the waterbed showroom, she has a lit Marlboro cigarette in her right hand, yellowing her teeth and fingers and stinking up her designer clothes, and she's been unapologetically hooked on tobacco ever since she was a little older than I am now. For the thirteen years that my parents were married, my dad begged her to quit. But he couldn't force her to change, just like he couldn't keep her from buying things at the city's finest stores with money we didn't have, arriving late (but perfectly coiffed) for every engagement, and ignoring the red paint on the curbs and parking wherever she pleased. But it was difficult for anyone to rein in my small, squeezable, chirpy Mom.

"Neat. You can put your clock radio there," she says, pointing to one of three compartments in the polished wood frame. Her voice has the positive energy of a puppy's bark.

I sit on the bed, and my weight doesn't move much of the water. I'm small for my age, blessed with big brown eyes, thick and wavy brown hair, and a nice face with some freckles. I have hair under my arms, but I'm still chosen last when schoolyard pickup teams form.

"I don't know," I say, pushing down hard on the mattress with my left hand. A wave rolls to the other side of the bed and comes back, and my body goes up and down as it passes, sending a tremor through my responsive, testosterone-happy groin.

The waterbed has Naugahyde covered frame pads and dark-stained wood trim. It's sensual. It's silly and cheesy.

"Kind of weird, Mom."

"Oh, live a little, Tilin!" she replies, crossing her arms, the smoke now drifting upward from the left side of her body.

Several months later, my girlfriend's huge, bare breasts move with the waves of the waterbed mattress. Not a lot—she is sixteen, and her body is ripe but hardly soft. I watch the two domes, and she watches me watch them, slightly list. Slowly her perfect flesh shifts, rhythmically. I have my girlfriend, as a matter of speaking, right where I want her: Atop my giant piece of moving, one-hundred-gallon, fuck-your-date furniture.

I am the man!

Soon after we start rubbing and smacking, the bed pitches us one way and then the other, like an ornery horse. My testosterone ebbs in what I think is a funny moment, on a funny bed.

I pull my lips away from hers and awkwardly giggle like a boy.

My girlfriend's mouth waits for mine again. It's open, soft, and desirous. Her eyes are half-mast.

I roll off her and shove my hips into the mattress, full force, to create an even bigger wave, which sends one of the bed pillows flying to the floor. I like to laugh. I like irony. Apparently, sometimes goofiness prevails over horniness.

She is not amused, and frowns. She pulls the comforter over her chest and turns over. I'm not taking the moment, or the passion, seriously enough. I am a joker. But am I wrong for being nothing in the sack like the William Hurt of *Body Heat*? I'm *living a little* on this here waterbed, and so what if it's not in some candlelit moment of intimacy. There's more than one way for two people to connect and enjoy each other. There has to be.

The girlfriend does not turn back over for a while. Sexual mythologies run very, very deep.

I am not the man.

Dad's San Francisco apartment torpedoes plenty more of my young and fragile machismo. His two-bedroom, two-bath place is a gay man's pad, fastidiously maintained with carpeting that's always vacuumed crosshatch-style, healthy indoor ferns and a ficus, and perfectly polished wood furniture, including a baby grand piano. His living room boasts nearly floor-to-ceiling glass that looks out onto San Francisco's Marina neighborhood and busy Richardson Avenue. Not the city view he'd always wanted for himself and for entertaining company, but this apartment is what my father can afford. The bathrooms have colognes arranged just so on the bathroom sinks. There isn't a swimsuit issue to be found in the place.

Dad dates, but seldom do I meet his lovers. He doesn't want to weird me out—his heterosexual teenage son, who thinks a lot about girls and sports—with men that I might perceive as odd or effeminate. I know that he's not keen on some unfiltered story about life inside San Francisco's bathhouses and gay bars dropping unexpectedly, like pigeon poop from the sky, into some conversation between one of his lovers and his teenage boy. Because, while I profess to be tolerant of his unorthodox world, in retrospect I think my father knew me better than I knew myself. As a kid, I don't think that I could completely handle his sexual life. But at the same time I have no anchoring model for my sexuality.

BEFORE ENTERING A RELATIONSHIP with Juliana in the summer of 1990, I have a number of sex partners. Some are modest, others zingy. But in intimacy I often feel like the chameleon, taking on my partners' personalities, and not asserting my own. Not knowing exactly how to act. Shortly after Juliana and I get together, however, I decide that there's no need to dwell on past uncertainties, whether it's my sexual misfires, mixed images of masculinity, or a murky sense of self as a sexual being. One of the thrills of a new romance, after all, is the opportunity to reinvent oneself. Or at least that's my false hope, one cool fall day in 1990, when I'm hanging out over at Juliana's place and she returns from a run. Within minutes I hear her turn on the shower. I take a fateful risk.

We're at her house in Boulder, Colorado. The one-story home is spacious, with two separate living areas and two roommates, and yet the house itself gives off an odd feeling. It's inviting and also cold, with the heat always turned down and the cupboards lacking much dishware. The garden, however, is voluptuous—fertile with vegetables, flowers, and rich, moist soil. Different dwellers contribute different vibes.

I pinch open the door to Juliana's small bathroom. Juliana is wrapped in a towel, leaning over, working the shower knobs. I catch lots of leg. She doesn't know that I'm sneaking a peak. Steam pours over the fogged glass of the shower door. I don't know where Juliana's roommates are, and I tell myself not to care. The fact that a roommate's bedroom shares a wall with the bathroom means that, if I make the right moves, the roommate could hear Juliana and I in a vocal moment of passion. *Oh well!*

I open the door wide enough to slip into the bathroom and then reach to unbuckle my belt, with the full intention of getting into the shower with my new girlfriend. Juliana doesn't hear me because the water is pounding, hot and in thick streams, against the back wall. The mirror over the sink to our right fogs. She starts to peel away the towel when she sees my reflection in a corner of the mirror, the last small space without fog.

She turns and looks straight at me. Juliana's smile is fast and sweet. But her left hand, anchoring the towel to her body, doesn't move, and Juliana laughs an uneasy laugh. "You're not getting in," she says, maintaining a half-smile. "No."

I'm in a house, a full foundation underneath me. But I feel like I'm walking a tightrope, balancing lust and decorum. This moment isn't so much about Juliana: Her reaction is hers, and it's my turn. Maybe I push on, standing my ground a little longer, insisting that this is where we both want me to be. Soon those long legs of hers could be moving in twitchy ways, in the shower, and I would happily glimpse at the hot water streaming down them. The moisture would bring smoothness and a shine to every inch of us. We'll have the kind of sex American men envision having. The type of loud sex that sends uneasy room-mates out of the house. The sex we men are *supposed* to have.

Instead I button up my pants and leave. I shut the door on the other side of Juliana and the steam. I'm in a cold hallway, feeling vulnerable, defeated, and exposed, even though I'm the one still wearing clothes.

One failed attempt at intimacy does not necessarily define two people's sexual relationship. But really, the shower episode was just another attempt in my life to define who I was as a sexual being, and another moment ending in confusion. The resulting story that I will frequently tell myself, for the next seventeen years: *When it comes to sex, wait on Juliana's cues. Taking big risks could hurt, a lot.* So I don't often try.

JULIANA IS STILL ASLEEP when Sophie enters our bedroom. I hear the signature slapping sounds of her groggy feet as they make their way over our hardwood floor. I know that she wants to be under the sheets with me and her stirring mother. Unfortunately that means Sophie could be getting close to my NPT-silhouetted body, too. Yes, my erection, my morning accomplice, endured all of my sobering recollections, apparently maintaining its strength courtesy of images of a young Kathleen Turner, Andrew's Waterbed Girls, and Juliana in the shower. And of course, courtesy of the testosterone.

Sophie feels her way in the dim light, climbing onto the bed and probing for where the down comforter stops and the pillows and an edge of the sheet begin. She slides under the covers and between me and Juliana, and snuggles against her mom. I have my back to her—duh. But then Sophie's hand pulls gently on my left shoulder. She wants me to move closer to her, to make a "Sophie sandwich" between her two parents. I shimmy over to her while keeping my maleness pointed in the other direction.

The anti-aging doctors don't tell you about this glorious moment. *You'll have to hide your hard-on from your kids.* That isn't bullet-pointed in the Wiley Protocol for Men paperwork.

Then I hear the slap of Benjamin's heavy feet. I know that he wants to get in bed with us, too.

Where do I hide?

He climbs onto the foot of the bed.

"Benjamin, I get this spot!" says Sophie in a combative whisper. I can feel the mattress compress as Benjamin, who's at my legs, wants to wedge himself between me and his sister.

"Sophie, move over!" Benjamin demands.

"There's no room," Sophie insists in a whisper that's really not a whisper. My face is close enough to hers that I can feel and smell her muggy, sour morning breath. Did she brush her teeth last night? I always tell the children that their perfect pink gums and white teeth won't last without brushing. Youth doesn't last forever! Your mouth isn't made of plastic and metal!

"Get on Daddy's other side," hisses Sophie. She extends her arms and legs, pressing her limbs against my back and presumably against some part of Juliana's body like a starfish so that Benjamin can't lie down next to her.

My lithe and lightweight, forty-five-pound son makes a snap decision to crawl onto the other side of me. I can feel the pressure changes on the mattress as he rears up from all fours onto his knees and moves to straddle me. I hear the tapping of the beaded necklace swinging around his neck. Juliana bought it for him, I don't know, somewhere, the summer before. Benjamin is a style king, impressively dressed and accessorized at eight years old, and makes me realize my apathy toward my own appearance. On many days, it's enough for me to get dressed, occasionally shave, and go to the office. Meanwhile my kid takes rock-star aesthetics with him to bed.

Sensing that my son's foot or knee is about to come down somewhere along my front side, I scrunch up into a tight fetal position. I'm virtually wrapped around my boner. Please, I think to myself. *Don't touch me there!*

"Dad, straighten out," says Benjamin. His voice is high pitched and free of the influence of male sex hormone.

"Uh . . . well . . ." I say.

"I won't take much room, Daddy," he whispers. "Will you scratch my back?"

He leans hard against my body, shifting his weight with the expectation that he'll soon slide into the narrow space left between me and the edge of the bed.

But I can't unroll. Not with the morning wood.

Instead I lift abruptly from the waist up, taking Benjamin with me as I move into a sitting position. He's on my side, and grabs my neck to keep from flopping over.

"Dad, what are you doing?" he says, surprised by my sudden movement.

"I have to . . . I have to get ready for work," I say, prying him off me. I've pulled the covers off of both Juliana and Sophie.

"Go ahead, lie down, Benjamin," I say, rotating my hips until they're square with my side of the bed. "Plenty of room for you now."

I adjust my boxers. It's still lurking in there!

In the dull morning light, I stand up and walk away from the bed.

I go into the kitchen, hoping to bring my middle limb to earth. I think mundane thoughts. Like lunch—kids' lunches. I hate making the kids' lunches for school. That should do the trick.

I reach for Benjamin's lunchbox, which sits on the counter. It's a purple and yellow, metal container decorated with a 1970s-style likeness of Elvis Presley that looks better than Elvis ever did in the 1970s. Lunchbox enhancement. Hormone enhancement. I look down. The spike in my shorts is somewhat smaller.

I find Sophie's lunchbox perched on a low-lying kitchen shelf, right next to some cookbooks and on top of a bunch of half-consumed bottles of vitamins that don't hold Juliana's and my attention. We always purchase such supplements with optimism—we get the fancy, government-favored, "Current Good Manufacturing Practices" vitamins, thinking that we'll take them and add to our health, longevity, and vitamin C stores. Then the clouded, plastic bottles inevitably sit idle and gather dust until, when Juliana and I enter some rare but manic purge mode, we grab the cylinders and see that the vitamins are past their expiration date. Then we throw them away and impulsively buy more.

I lift Sophie's lunch bag off the dusty bottles and open it. Inside are soggy slices of red bell pepper. I look down at my boxers. That worked. The erection is finally gone.

As I make the kids' lunches, I think more about the persistent hard-on. If I wake up every single day for the next year with this T-overloaded appendage, I'll be in the fetal position a lot. There's sweetness to the four of us spooning, and I know the children will soon outgrow their snuggling phase. I'll miss it forever. The doping could end such a phase prematurely.

Or maybe the time has come for Juliana and I to use the lock on our door. The kids are getting older, and I'm not getting younger. The additional chemicals inside of me have only just taken effect, and I still hold out plenty of hope that the new levels of hormone in my body will elevate my relationship with my wife, making intimacy not just as easy as it was before, but easier and more direct than it's *ever been*. Plenty of people think I should be grateful for the opportunity at hand: Across cultures and throughout history, men have searched desperately for ways to stave off the loss of youth and manliness. In an age of Viagra and testosterone supplements, we take the possibility of a lifetime's worth of erections for granted. But the history of science in pursuit of virility is a tragic compendium of ghastly cures.

Many remedies, for instance, have focused on genital consumption. Writers of very old Sanskrit texts recommended ingesting sperm-generating tissue to address impotence. Oil-soaked donkey dick, claimed one ancient Roman philosopher, had magical sexual powers.

In the early days of modern medicine, doctors, researchers, and various members of the general public were just as interested in harnessing the power apparently emanating from male parts.

For example, in 1889, a seventy-two-year-old French physiologist named Charles-Édouard Brown-Séquard told a stunned audience of Parisians that he felt much younger after injecting himself with a concoction derived from the balls of a dog and a guinea pig.

"The injections had increased his physical strength and even lengthened the arc of his urine," author John Hoberman writes of Brown-Séquard's thinking in his comprehensive and detail-filled book, *Testosterone Dreams*. Hoberman adds, "Extravagant claims of crude testicular extracts circled the globe, creating a therapeutic market that ran far ahead of the efforts of experimental physiologists to confirm their efforts."

Brown-Séquard's self-assessment, Hoberman also notes, was highly inflated. But the race was on to pinpoint the catalyst in testicles believed to provide sexual, life-affirming energy. Around the early 1900s, Austrian doctor Eugen Steinach performed vasectomies on senile men that reportedly improved their sexual prowess. French-Russian surgeon Serge Voronoff transplanted slivers of monkey testicles into the scrotums of well-off, aging men who believed that their flagging sex drives would surge. Steinach's and Voronoff's frightful and ultimately vain attempts to soup up men's sex drives, however, couldn't compare with the experiments on male virility going on in Northern California's San Quentin prison.

San Quentin, California's oldest prison and a towering, beige and red structure in Marin County that I've driven past hundreds of times, was a virtual ball-transplant factory. Spearheading the effort was the prison's longtime chief surgeon, an Oregon-born, prematurely gray-haired physician named Leo L. Stanley.

Stanley, who held his post at San Quentin from 1913 to 1951, was obsessed with male potency, which he believed was under siege in an era of growing women's rights and factory automation. The doctor thought that he was performing important and pioneering medical work when he turned his attention to the young field of hormone and gland science known as endocrinology, and in particular focused on testicles. Beginning in 1918, Stanley began to sew the testicles of recently executed convicts into the scrotums of living prisoners whom he felt lacked spunk.

"What is the ego," the good doctor once wrote, "but the combined functioning of the glands!"

In August 1918, he implanted two testicles inside a twenty-five-year-old man with "mental and physical languor" and "diminished sexual activity." Never mind exactly how the doctor determined the latter.

"Three months after the operation the patient had shown considerable improvement physically, mentally, and sexually," the doctor wrote in a medical journal in 1920.

Stanley went on to report that another recipient of his procedure enjoyed daytime erections like never before. Another had an erection only five days after surgery. Yet another, Stanley wrote, "had frequent erections, and declared that he felt one hundred percent more passionate, besides feeling better in every way."

When he ran low on a supply of human testicles, Dr. Stanley performed similar experiments with prisoners while using the ground-up glands of deer, goats, boar, and ram. In 1931, he performed 520 such procedures. By 1940, more than 10,000 various implantations had been notched at San Quentin. No catastrophic effects were ever reported.

But neither did the scientific proof ever side with the work of men like Brown-Séquard, Voronoff, or Stanley (who, for all his medieval experimentation on inmates, was rewarded with a second career as a cruise-ship doctor). The science of glandular extraction, however, did prime the pump for the hormone therapy that was to come. Right around the same time that San Quentin prisoners were gingerly walking the confined grounds with their newly enhanced packages of manhood, scientists from the Dutch pharmaceutical company Organon completed a paper titled "On Crystalline Male Hormone from Testicles." For the first time in history, researchers had isolated the hormone/anabolic steroid that they would name *testosterone*.

IT'S DINNERTIME ON a Wednesday night in the busy Tilin kitchen, a couple weeks after the NPT first materializes in our bed. The kids do their homework at the breakfast table. Juliana cooks. I'm fresh out of the shower, bare-chested, and rushing to get out the door. I have somewhere to be, across the Bay Bridge, in San Francisco.

I also have another erection. Apparently my penis, independent of the rest of my body, has become a time traveler, taking me back again to those awkward moments at the chalkboard in seventh grade. Over these last two weeks, growing sexual urges have run in parallel with my numerous hard-ons, too. I've been attracted to certain baristas, piano teachers, and moms of my children's friends, although I confess that far more unusual things have also aroused me. Warm, shiny, noisy, vibrating things, like fire engines that rush through traffic. Whistling teapots. Then there's Juliana. I can't overlook my attractive wife, who nowadays looks fetching whether she's soaping herself in the shower or folding clothes and dressed in sweatpants. Juliana has noticed me watching her—she's picked up on me staring at her, and seen the bulges in my underwear. She's become as intrigued by testosterone as any pioneering hormone scientist ever was.

"Did you apply it this morning?" she asks me with a twinkle as I button up my shirt, standing next to the stove. The cotton sticks to my wet back. I haven't been out of the shower five minutes.

"How are you feeling?" she adds in a suggestive sotto voce. "What are you thinking about right now?" She glances down at the fly of my pants and looks back up at me with a sly smile.

I believe my wife is getting randy.

Yes!

Alas, our timing is off yet again. I'm all for Juliana's enthusiasm, but for weeks now the growing sexual energy between us has been stuck in the air. The daily grind has prevented us from taking advantage of the enhanced Andrew. Juliana falls asleep while reading to Benjamin, or needs to edit photos. I wake up early to go to the gym, or stay up late to work.

"I'm thinking all sorts of interesting thoughts, which is why we should continue this conversation later," I say to Juliana, smirking, and then nodding to Sophie, whose blue eyes meet mine. My daughter walks over to us and stops at her mother's hip to show off a blue felt finger puppet that she made earlier in the day at school. Eight years into parenthood, Juliana and I know how to talk above the kids. But we can't exactly give them crayons and coloring books while going at it atop the kitchen counter.

The kitchen counter. Listen to me!

"I really need to leave," I add.

Sophie stretches her arms toward the ceiling in the universal child expression for "hold me." Juliana picks her up and supports Sophie in her left arm. She removes the lid on a steaming pot of broccoli with her right.

I look at my two girls together—Sophie is Juliana in miniature, with her rounded chin, calm demeanor, and rascally, arching eyebrows.

"Stay home, Daddy," says Sophie, bobbing the finger puppet in front of me like it's doing the talking.

"Yes. Why don't you stay home?" asks Juliana, replacing the lid on the pot. This time my wife's tone of voice is heartfelt, with a trademark, slight elevation of tone that I know connotes genuine love. It's the same pitch that I'd heard back in 1993 when Juliana responded to my marriage proposal while we stood at the edge of the Pacific Ocean, on San Francisco's Baker Beach. When, with her fine brown hair blowing easily in a December gust and her long arms wrapped gently around my neck, she pushed her straight, soft nose up against mine. "Really?" she'd said in that same tone.

With Sophie still in her left arm, Juliana opens the oven door.

"We'll have a nice dinner," she continues. "Put the kids to bed early."

Damn. I wanted to say yes. Badly. It was an offer I had to resist.

"I have this thing in San Francisco tonight," I say, tucking in my shirt. "Susie Wiley will be on a speakerphone," I add. "A bunch of women in a living room, all talking to Wiley about their lives on hormones."

Sophie looks at me blankly. I'm confident that neither she nor Benjamin thinks anything in particular when I use words like "hormones" and "testosterone." I try not to speak the word "doper" out loud. Benjamin knows that word from the sports pages.

Juliana lowers Sophie to the floor, and our little girl wanders back across the kitchen toward her brother. It's a nice kitchen, decent sized, handsome in granite and honey-color wood, kind of rectangular. But like much of the rest of Juliana's and my two-story, four-bedroom house, and similar to our own lives, the kitchen could use a boost. It seems somewhat worn, with loose cabinet hinges and dented appliances that sputter. Throughout the place, the wood floors are uneven. The chimney leans, and the paint on the electric garage door is peeling. Undoubtedly, hot water still runs through the pipes, and smoke from our fireplace reaches the sky. But Juliana and I both believe that our home will soon need a boost to avoid feeling old. Its walls' cracks will deepen like wrinkles, and the bubbles in its paint will grow to resemble warts.

"Listening to old ladies go on about estrogen or staying here and having fun," Juliana says to me, a naughty grin creeping back onto her face. "What's more important?"

I should enjoy my wife's flirting, and my kids' chilling in the kitchen. Instead I'm growing stressed out and irritable. There could be a traffic backup on the Bay Bridge.

"Don't do this. I'm going to be late," I respond coolly.

I struggle to pull a sock onto my left foot while balancing on my right standing leg. Sophie and Benjamin both look up from the break-fast table and laugh as I nearly fall to the floor while hopping around to keep my balance.

I frown. Nearly cracking my skull is not funny, at least to me. Nobody can enjoy comedy that comes at the expense of my clumsiness, or perhaps my eroding physical skills.

I look back over at a winking Juliana. She's a really bad winker. She waits for me to laugh, and to change my mind about going to the city.

She's pissing me off.

"So now I just have to say no to you. Well, NO," I say in a raised voice. "I have to go."

Her smile dissipates. Juliana turns her back on me to put dinner on three plates.

I can hear the couples therapist now: Think of a nice way to tell Juliana that you're really committed to tonight's engagement, and that you'd love to take a rain check.

A wife who propositions you. The humor of a wet dad hopping on one leg around a kitchen. Those are the fun moments in life! I should be laughing too.

But the testosterone has me feeling horny *and* edgy. I'd done some homework—experts dismiss the notion that supplemental testosterone radically alters behavior. They cite studies to back up their statements.

I don't know, maybe I'm experiencing the placebo effect. The belief that if this drug helps a sixty-year-old Sly Stallone play an angry Rambo, and turns bike racers left for dead into Tour de France front-runners, that even the myth that testosterone makes its users amped and assertive is having an effect on me. Scientists also say that testosterone's power of suggestion can't be underestimated.

Whatever the reason, I'm wound up, like I've been downing one cup of coffee after another.

Or maybe I'm edgy because, a month and a half after commencing my hormone-replacement protocol, I'm not having the experience I envisioned. I'm one unsatisfied doper. Of course I realize that I'm still stuck in a pedestrian life. Magazine editors press me for stories, kids need chauffeuring to piano lessons, and piles of laundry require folding. My race training hasn't exactly turned me into Greg LeMond. But beyond those challenges are other frustrations. My sex life ignites just as I must walk out the door.

I fish around in my pockets for the car keys while standing over Juliana and the kids as they dig into their dinners. Benjamin ignores his chicken. Sophie avoids her broccoli.

"We do have date night on Saturday," says Juliana, extending the olive branch that I'm too worked up to offer.

"You remembered, right?"

I nod, which is a silent lie. I'd talked to Michael earlier today about racing on Sunday, over four hours away and in California's Central Valley. Date nights preceding bike-racing days don't go together.

"Let's talk when I get home," I say.

"Actually, I'm pretty tired," says Juliana, putting down her fork. "I'll probably be asleep when you get back."

A WINTER RAIN PUTS a gloss on the Bay Bridge, and soon I reach San Francisco streets that take me back decades. The city's quiet and tree-lined Richmond district was home to many of my childhood friends, as well as the synagogue where I went to Sunday school and was bar mitzvahed. I frequently ran on trails among huge eucalyptus trees in the nearby Presidio, the onetime military base where the city's inhabitants could roam through generous stretches of undeveloped land, some of which butts up against the bay and ocean.

It's appropriate to be tripping down memory lanes, considering my imminent rendezvous with Susie Wiley. She wrote the book on a different kind of nostalgia. For half a decade, Wiley has pushed her brand of hormone-replacement therapy with the promise of turning mature women of almost any age, at least in terms of some of their key hormones, into girls in their twenties. I hadn't yet spent an appreciable amount of time with any woman on the Wiley Protocol. But Wiley herself had informed me of her female clients' sexual friskiness.

"To run with these dogs," Wiley had bragged to me in a phone conversation, "you got to get off the porch."

I park in front of a row of Richmond district homes that definitely don't look like sex dens, even though, admittedly, I don't know what a sex den looks like. These homes are made of materials like sturdy brick and handsome shingles, and indeed are representative of what is largely an upper-middle-class neighborhood. These are residences where people undoubtedly gather to converse about investment strategies, kids' soccer tournaments, and, apparently, estrogen, progesterone, testosterone, human growth hormone, and the like. The truth is, physician managed, hormone-replacement-therapy programs are largely for the wealthy and privileged. The hired help costs you: My visits to Dr. Patil cost $250 each (cash only). My monthly supplies of testosterone and DHEA run me about $75, and my lab work is about $200 every three months. I know that other people pay as much as $2,000 per month for their hormone treatments and medical oversight, and I'd been told that celebrities can pay almost four times as much for "concierge medicine." Meanwhile, I read that do-it-yourself dopers can buy a month's supply of injectable steroids on the street for around fifty bucks. The catch is that DIY steroid users have to play physician, pharmacist, and customer all at once. If something goes wrong, the bargain-hunters' options include Internet chat sites and emergency rooms.

I ring the doorbell of a two-story home. I wouldn't hesitate for a second to send Benjamin and Sophie to this big, wood front door on Halloween night.

It swings open. "Well you must be Andrew," says a woman whom I presume is Adrian Cordet.

I'd learned of tonight's meeting from one of Wiley's people, and Adrian had graciously invited me to the gathering via email. She is tall, big-boned, and blue-eyed, and her nearly seam-free face and head of monochrome brown hair hide the fact that she's undoubtedly in her menopausal years (otherwise she wouldn't be on the Wiley Protocol). Dressed in a long, ribbed white sweater and a luxurious looking, green scarf, Adrian appears very respectable.

"Please come in. Join us," she adds, proper as proper can be.

I walk into the living room and meet five other women who create similar impressions. They're all dignified and attractive, and I'd guess mostly between the ages of fifty and sixty-five. Among them are a biotech industry consultant, a nurse, and the owner of a landscaping business. Really, they're a well-appointed group: I notice diamonds on fingers, pressed slacks, and plenty of polished leather boots. Adrian's house is inviting—oriental rugs, a healthy fire in the fireplace, and a big triptych painting on the wall.

We all briefly chat about traffic and the wet weather while filling small plates with gourmet olives and warm quiche. Then we sit in a loose circle of chairs and furniture around a glass-topped cocktail table. On one side of the circle is a speakerphone.

"I believe everyone's situated," says Adrian, playing the perfect hostess, picking a small piece of quiche crust off the floor. She sets down her glass of mulled cider next to the speakerphone. "Let's call Susie."

Looking into my glass of Italian sparkling water, I figure that if anyone can liven up this gathering, it's Susie Wiley. When Wiley unveiled her protocol in 2003, few listened. But now she has those thousands of clients, and one way that the spunky Wiley keeps up with her chemically tuned constituency is via small groups of Wiley Protocol users who occasionally organize a conference call so that she can dispense her feedback (a physician joins the call to provide medical oversight). Tonight, a half-dozen women and I make up one of those groups, and we each wait patiently for Wiley to come to life over the ringing phone line.

APPROPRIATELY, THERESA SUE WILEY was born in 1952, in another era of confusion over supplemental hormones. Synthetic testosterone had been successfully developed in a lab in the 1930s, and Premarin, which is a form of estrogen, or the female sex hormone generally produced by the ovaries, was first marketed in the United States in 1942. But for years to come, society and the medical community were too conservative and concerned to show unified support for hormone supplements that promised to make people feel younger and more sexual. *The Journal of the American Medical Association* wrote of supplemental hormone use as potentially "promiscuous, ill advised, and unwise," and condemned "fantastic advertising claims for sex hormones." In contrast, William H. Masters, the gynecologist who would become part of the famous Masters and Johnson human sexuality research team, at one point dejectedly concluded that the prim society all around him was foolishly overlooking the power of hormones, and might as well classify a "third sex" of "former males and females": sixty-year-old adults, who had uniformly lost all interest in physical intimacy. Talk about being put out to pasture.

A young Susie Wiley, meanwhile, wandered around in more fertile fields. She grew up an only child, a farm girl in northern Illinois and a medical curiosity herself. Wiley's mother became pregnant with two children at the (then) relatively ripe age of thirty-six, and Wiley's twin sister died at birth. For Wiley, however, the world was full of possibility. On the family's corn and soybean farm, a young Susie lost herself in science, staring at the stars through a telescope, and arranging links of metal chain so that it looked like strands of DNA. Wiley buried herself in books, and studied hard enough to get off the land and into college. In 1970 she left home, outdoor toilet and all, and majored in anthropology at Webster University in St. Louis.

She never graduated, walking through the ceremony with a blank diploma after falling a couple of classes short. However, after wandering down several career paths, returned to her scientific studies. She returned, that is, in her own way. Married to her college sweetheart, they bounced from New York City to St. Louis to the California coastal town of Santa Barbara, having babies throughout their journey. Wiley had the big family she'd never experienced growing up, giving birth to five children between the years of 1978 and 1991.

Men, whose hormones often soldier along quietly and without drama, can't fathom what Wiley experienced in those years—the often powerful and generative feelings of pregnancy, the body as scientific marvel, and the symphony of receding and onrushing hormones. Follicle-stimulating hormone sparks an ovary! Human chorionic gonadotropin triggers the ovary to produce more progesterone and estrogen! Progesterone maintains the health of the uterine lining! And estrogen, the queen of all female hormones, fuels the growth of the uterus, aids blood circulation, and helps enlarge the breasts! All the fireworks of a Fourth of July picnic.

But in the mid-1990s, Wiley's trustworthy body began to misfire. A lump developed in her breast, a grapefruit-sized fibroid tumor in her uterus, and a cyst in an ovary. The doctors ordered mammograms and whispered the C-word—there's always the specter of cancer—which terrified her. At the same time, Wiley's periods grew shorter, and she knew that her reproductive years, as well as her sex drive, might soon be behind her. Her physiological inventories of estrogen and progesterone weren't what they once were.

That's when Wiley wondered if there was a connection between her failing health and her receding hormones.

The thought wasn't random. Wiley wasn't the only one in her house feeling lousy. When Wiley took one of her children, who was suffering from a migraine headache, to visit a local female endocrinologist, the two women hit it off, and Wiley reached into her science-minded past and began boning up on endocrinology. Wiley and the doctor attempted to write a diet book together, and although it never materialized, Wiley continued to read scientific journals and attend lectures. She befriended and shadowed a scientist named Bent Formby—a Danish biochemist, biophysicist, and molecular biologist. In 2000, Formby and Wiley co-authored a provocative book called *Lights Out*. (Wiley's formal/pen name is T. S. Wiley, which she says has "gravitas, like T. S. Eliot—I didn't want to be pigeonholed as just some woman writing about rest, weight loss, and menopause.") The book argues, in depth, exactly why Americans need more sleep. *Lights Out* explains that failing to synchronize your sleeping patterns with the daily cycle of natural light will compromise your hormonal systems and ultimately your health. Basically, Wiley writes, the light bulb is about the worst thing that ever happened to mankind.

But her magnum opus was still to come. Wiley and Formby hooked up again, along with Julie Taguchi, a local Santa Barbara oncologist, and published *Sex, Lies, and Menopause* in 2003. Complete with eighty-three pages of footnotes, the book repeatedly argues that middle-aged women suffering from menopausal symptoms and even poor health can thrive by applying creams filled with "natural" (often referred to as bioidentical) hormones. These hormones, say the authors, should be applied on a "rhythmic" dosing schedule, which is patterned after the varied amounts of hormone that a young woman's body typically generates over the course of each (approximately) month-long menstrual cycle. Wiley ties the cycles of seasons and light—particularly the moon's cycles—into her argument for this specific hormone replacement therapy, which ultimately came to be known as the Wiley Protocol. She also says that because women are the pictures of health and at their sexual peaks when young, the Wiley Protocol prescribes notably high levels of estrogen and progesterone. (Wiley's recommended doses can be as much as four hundred percent greater than her peers' doses.) In fact, the dosing schedule aspires to restore women's hormone levels to what they were in their twenties.

Sex, Lies, and Menopause arrived at just the right time. Only a year earlier, the huge, federally funded, and widely publicized Women's Health Initiative trial testing the safety of traditional hormone replacement therapy ended prematurely because researchers found that the hormone-using subjects, taking a combination of estrogen and pro-gesterone-like progestin, were at increased risk for stroke, blood clots, and breast cancer. The aborted study, as one might predict, hit supple-mental hormone sales like a body blow. In particular, sales of Prempro and good old Premarin, the two patented hormone products used in the WHI test, quickly sank.

But many menopausal women who gave up hormones cold turkey after the WHI fiasco ultimately went back to their doctors (like my doc, Dr. Patil), begging for the relief hormones previously gave them. Some patients didn't want anything to do with Premarin or Prempro. They didn't like that the drugs are made from the urine of pregnant mares. Nor did they want those drugs' largely "static" protocols.

They wanted the Wiley Protocol. There are stories of women car-rying *Sex, Lies, and Menopause* right into their doctor's offices. They opened the book to page 219 and pointed to Appendix I, which is titled "Recommendations for Access to Natural Hormone Replacement Therapy." The women simply said, *put me on this*. Plenty of doctors balked at the mega-dosing protocol, and called Wiley crazy and irresponsible. Others read their patients' copies of Wiley's book and ultimately followed its instructions.

One of Wiley's earliest and most important believers was Suzanne Somers. When Somers came out championing bioidentical hormone replacement therapy and the Wiley Protocol in her 2006 book *Ageless*, Wiley's name was suddenly in lights.

"I have been cycling rhythmically for almost two years as of this writing," Somers wrote in *Ageless*. "I have to say I feel great."

THE SPEAKERPHONE COMES to life, and suddenly I get nervous.

I have to analyze my balls in front of these people.

"Hello?" says a hoarse and husky voice. Susie Wiley sounds a little tired, and unnervingly unfeminine.

I throw down the rest of my sparkling water like it's a tequila shot. I quietly crack my knuckles.

That low voice—maybe she's on the Wiley Protocol and then some. Then again, it's already dark outside. Is it past her bedtime?

"Hello?" she says again, and then clears her throat.

Adrian, the night's hostess, hovers over the speakerphone.

"Hi Susie, it's Adrian Cordet in San Francisco, here with several other Wiley Protocol users. We're ready to talk shop. We've all got questions."

"Hello everyone," says Wiley, her voice rising an octave. "Thank you all for your courage, and your support."

I bite down hard on one of the ice cubes in my empty glass.

Courage? This woman should reassure me. She's the hormone guru.

One of Wiley's MDs calls in immediately after Wiley does—standard procedure for these client consultations. Wiley is careful to have a doctor available in case the conversation requires advice best provided by someone with a medical license.

"Let's get started," Wiley continues.

Inside of Adrian's living room, the six women and I look at each other. I don't want to go first, and I'm not sure I want to hear what everyone else has to say. Women discuss their hormones like people talk about battling a cold. Women are used to addressing hormone-related issues. Men, on the other hand, are not. I don't discuss, say, the quality of my erections with any friend. Not even Michael.

Please, God: Don't let the discussion turn to vaginal dryness.

"Hi Susie, my name is Denise Reynolds," announces a tall, thin woman with straight gray hair that falls, rather girlishly, down to her shoulders. Reynolds speaks loudly, and I'm not sure if she's concerned that Wiley can't pick up her voice or she is just hard of hearing.

"Thanks to you I'm finally interested in sex again. I used to find it a colossal waste of time," Denise says, sitting back into her chair with a smile. Then she confesses that she's seventy-two years old.

I try to gauge crowd reaction without swiveling my head. Personally I'm thinking Reynolds is too old for all this. Wiley differs.

"Wow, I'm impressed with myself," says Wiley.

The others clap.

"Can we talk about progesterone and estrogen?" Denise asks. I understand enough about women's hormones to know that, simply speaking, supplemental estrogen will generally provide a woman with more libido, fewer hot flashes, and improved sleep. Progesterone, meanwhile, prevents the supplemental estrogen from promoting unhealthy amounts of cell growth in the lining of a woman's uterus. Cell growth that can lead to cancer.

"Do I stop the estrogen or the progesterone on day twenty-six?" asks Denise.

"Progesterone," says Wiley. The doctor concurs.

Next to speak is Monica Buchanan, who's a nurse.

"Hi Susie. Remember we last spoke about treating my dry eyes? You suggested putting more estrogen on my carotid artery midday," Monica explains.

"Did it make a difference?" says Wiley.

"Not really," says Monica.

The two of them and the doctor discuss thyroid issues for a while.

A petite woman named Joanie Ailey talks about breast soreness and her nipples getting huge on day twenty-six of her cycle.

How huge is huge? Thick like the knob on a combination lock? Tall like a stack of dimes?

I say nothing.

Paula Stern, who runs her own landscaping business, asks Wiley about the wisdom of having mammograms. Inez Mayer, a consultant in the biotech industry, wants to purchase her hormone creams from a different pharmacist. Adrian inquires about blood-sugar levels. Then everyone looks at me.

"Susie, we're very excited about having a new member of our user group, and he would like to speak with you about his protocol," says Adrian. She gives me a nod.

I feel like a cross between Neil Armstrong and a *Playgirl* model. The Wiley Protocol for men was introduced only weeks before I started it. Wiley thought men could also benefit from taking varied doses of hormones—hormones specific to them—over the course of each month. Plus she wanted a men's protocol so that aging guys could keep up with her invigorated female clients.

"Hey Susie," I say. "Long time no see."

"Sure, we met at the anti-aging conference," she replies. "How's it going?"

I tell her that I'm dutifully applying the testosterone between my scrotum and inner thighs. I'm trying to rub it in right over the femoral artery. I explain that I don't yet feel a huge boost of energy when I'm on my bicycle. Wiley has no idea that I think of myself as a doper. Not her world.

"What about erections?" she asks.

I knew this was coming.

"Are you waking up yet with morning erections? What about nocturnal erections?" she asks. "Do you have strong erections in the middle of the night?"

Suddenly my mouth is dry. I lick my lips.

You like Wiley because *she is a woman. Women know hormones up and down, inside out. This woman knows how to make you more male. Speak!*

"That would be yes, yes, and yes," I say, staring straight at the speakerphone to avoid eye contact with the women in Adrian's house. This is embarrassing.

"And how old are you? Like, forty?" continues Wiley.

"Forty-two," I say.

"That's young," she says. "Good chance that you could look at a woman from across the room and get a big hard-on," she says.

I hear some chuckles, but continue to stare at the phone.

"How about night sweats?" Wiley adds.

"I'm sweating now," I reply.

Everybody laughs out loud. Wiley and the doctor tell me that I'm doing fine. The erections will likely get better—harder, and more numerous. The night sweats should subside as my body becomes more acclimated to the exogenous testosterone. If the sweating persists, she says, send up a flare.

I thank her for her time. A few minutes later she signs off.

I stand up to pour myself more sparkling water. Inez, the biotech consultant, approaches me.

"I know Susie doesn't officially recommend it. But I'd suggest that you shave your balls and apply cream right to them," says Inez without hesitation. "My husband does it. He's got something standing up in his pajamas every single morning."

Monica, the nurse, overhears our conversation and walks over to us. She chimes in. "Mine too! I always wake up and think, he's hard again this morning? Well, damn!"

I glance at Monica and Inez, who start sharing detailed recollections about morning sex. It dawns on me that I need to relax my shoulders and loosen my sphincter muscle. The hormone science behind stoking a mature woman's sex drive can include upping her estrogen as well as T levels (women naturally produce some testosterone, but far less than men), and courtesy of the Wiley Protocol, Monica and

Inez are clearly good to go as far as the former chemical. The ladies are also freaking me out. They look like they belong at a Goldman Sachs Christmas party. But they have total potty mouth.

Come on, you've heard all the exploits, from your buddies any-way. More times than you can remember.

I give pause, and then decide that the decorum I should maintain inside of Adrian's cozy, manicured living room is the decorum that I maintain in a men's locker room. Her house may not have a sauna or shaving cream. But I'm hearing vaguely familiar tales of conquest, and likely some fish stories, too. Hey, we're all just having a good time get-ting raunchy.

"You know, I'm not sure my wife is ready to shave my nuts smooth," I say to Inez. "I don't know if that would get her all wet."

"Just have the hair *lasered* off," says Monica.

You can do that?

"Then your wife will want them in her mouth more," says the landscape gardener, Paula. "I know I would."

We all look at her.

"You can't take me anywhere!" she laughs.

I PULL INTO THE DRIVEWAY of a dark house. Once inside, I mini-mize the floor creaks by treading lightly down the hallway. I brush my teeth in the kids' bathroom so as not to wake Juliana, and carefully, patiently rub the testosterone in my groin area until every speck of cream disappears. Just for good measure, I rub my scrotum with my left palm—the same palm I used to rub on the T—before washing my hands. Worth a try.

I gently slide under the sheets of our bed and close my eyes. I can feel sensation in my loins, although not, to my mind, courtesy of the testosterone that I just worked into my skin. What I feel is the result of accumulation: The six weeks' worth of testosterone that I'd already applied.

I hear Juliana's breath, and then I breathe deeply. Tomorrow is Yoga Friday. Maybe, I think to myself, tomorrow night will be the night. *Our* night. The testosterone's night to fuel some intimacy.

I turn onto my side, stretch my legs, flex my big toes, and finally nod off.

When I awaken hours later, the room is still dark. There are no kids in the bed. It's just me, Juliana, and my new, persistent pal. My penis is up before I am.

I lie there for a minute, and debate the merits of masturbating. Or perhaps I should just lie face down, on top of my hard-on, and try to suffocate the erection.

Not this time. No. I don't feel like being disciplined. Like maintaining control.

I move across our huge mattress until I'm close to Juliana, close enough that I can stroke her hair and body with my hands. Her back is to me. In the dark I softly work my fingers through her hair, caressing her scalp, lightly rubbing the silky skin in the indentation in her neck at the hairline. I rub her shoulders and work my way down, into the small of her back, onto her sacrum, her ass. I slowly run my right foot up and down the long, perfect arc of her right calf.

This feels good. I feel great. Super-great.

She slowly moves her head and right arm, and she's still thick with sleep and probably unaware of what's waking her. That these are *advances*. Uh-huh. None of the funky memories of my sexual past, not the waterbed, Victoria Principal's picture, an aborted shower with Juliana from a zillion years ago, or glamorization or myths or blah blah blah, slows me.

For once you're letting the damn erection do the thinking.

I am in love with the touch of this moment, and I feel assertive and gloriously hungry and *male*, and ready to envelop my wife. As she comes to, I continue to caress her and believe that yes, this is the right thing to do, screw Yoga Friday, who cares if the kids walk in, to hell with the morning workout.

And then, in the dark, Juliana shifts away from me, my arm having to extend further to reach her hair. But there is no time to feel disappointed or that I've risked my sexuality, my masculinity, and again lost. Because before I can think much of anything, Juliana rolls over her left side. And she doesn't stop until her chest meets mine.

inner dope-o-meter

The next day, I take an unpleasant bike ride. The weather is fine. The route is familiar—a relatively modest thirty-mile ride from my home through the East Bay hills running past the Oakland Zoo that local riders know as the Zoo Loop. The problem is the company. My riding partner is none other than my cycling coach, Roman Holmes. Holmes lives in the Pacific Northwest, and drove down to Northern California the day before our ride to visit family who live in the area. From his perspective, the trip affords Holmes the rare opportunity to pedal alongside one of his long-distance clients, to give out the back pats and on-the-road guidance that email, no matter how personalized, can't deliver. But from where I'm sitting—atop my stiff, dark gray bicycle saddle—the face-to-face, two-hour meeting with my coach is torture. Spinning my pedals alongside him forces me to think about what I imagine every doper grapples with: the truth.

"Oh yeah, I've been here before. I remember this. There's a sweet downhill coming up," says Holmes, as the two-lane, quiet strip of pavement we've been climbing side by side has flattened out. He's right: Soon our route tilts downward. There's a curvy descent of tree-lined Redwood Road.

Without looking and in one fluid motion, Holmes grabs the water bottle held in a cage on his bicycle frame and takes a quick drink while his long, powerful legs push his pedals faster. Wrapped in stretchy, gray and orange nylon "kit," or racing-team-style cycling clothing, Holmes is as trim as the blade of a propeller. His tapered and efficient body is shaped by a disciplined lifestyle, and where regular folks might see a beanpole I see youth and speed. Holmes is cut to move really fast atop an equally stripped-down, sixteen-pound, two-wheel machine. I wear the red, blue, and black kit of a local amateur team that Michael and I both ride for—essentially we're members of a club. Otherwise I'm just a slightly thicker, three-quarters version of the tall Holmes.

My coach quickly surges ahead of me and with a head nod indicates that he wants me to move right behind him.

Holmes had called me days ago and insisted that we ride together when he travels through the East Bay. I reluctantly agreed to meet him.

"Get on my wheel," he yells, twisting his head over his right shoulder to be heard. He takes his right hand off the handlebars long enough to point at the area directly behind his rear tire where I'd enjoy the aerodynamic benefits of riding in his slipstream. I catch the grin on his face as he pulls a little farther away from me on the flat stretch leading up to the descent. Holmes is paid to do this, to ride his bike on Saturdays and show his clients how it's done.

Just wait 'til the testosterone kicks in and we go for a ride together. I'll motion for Holmes to tuck in behind me. That'll be an interesting moment.

I stand on my pedals, lifting my butt off my bicycle saddle in order to accelerate and close the gap between us.

Look on the bright side. He'd be pleased with my progress!

I sit back down and try to build more speed by maintaining tension on the pedals as they go round and round. I'd learned that trick years ago, really it's part of road-riding 101: As best you can, don't just mash on the pedals as they go down. Push and pull on them as they go around.

Bright side?! Holmes might wonder what I'm doing to get so strong. As if I could tell him. Yeah, right. He'd fucking hate me.

I start down the grade perhaps ten feet behind Holmes, attempting to mimic his every motion. Like a ski racer navigating gates, Holmes takes the straightest path through the crooked road, steering his bike close to a curve's apex and then smoothly drifting as far as the lane's opposite edge to keep from scrubbing off speed by moving or braking unnecessarily.

To your average bike-path rider, the nuances of Holmes's descent are lost. His weight invisibly shifts over the pedals and sides of his handlebar in subtle ways that maximize the traction of his tires. His eyes focus on exactly where he wants his bike to go, the way a baseball player locks in on a fastball and has confidence that his bat will, almost magically, meet it. His body remains relaxed. Tiny steering adjustments help Holmes avoid small pavement seams and the stray pebble that might easily send him into a tumbling, thirty-five-mile-per-hour fall.

I fall further behind my coach with every curve, but I briefly forget all about him, as well as the drugs. I am also at one with the descent, energized by the pull of both lateral and vertical forces on bike and body, my skinny tires miraculously pushing me toward the inside of every turn. I am not Andrew Tilin—doper, father, husband, deadline-obsessed writer. I am Paolo Salvodelli—*Il Falco*, the other pro cyclists called him, because the Italian flew like a falcon. I am the long, lean, and fearless Englishman Sean Yates, a racer who distinctively pressed one thigh and then the other against his bike frame through high-speed turns. I am Samuel Sánchez, a crazy man on a descent who finished in the top five at the 2010 Tour de France.

I return to earth. The road flattens again, and Holmes, who isn't too far ahead of me, slows. I think unhappily of coming up alongside him. It's easy to slather on a bunch of testosterone every day in the pursuit of great sex, some swagger, and the expectation that I'll become stronger on some casual bike rides. None of those things are lawless or unethical. But that same cream feels dirty when it's undermining truth and trust, and the trust between an athlete and his coach is like the trust between teacher and student. In the presence of Holmes, the supplemental T circulating through my body makes me feel as corrupt as a kid who smuggles a cheat-sheet into a final exam. In the eyes of my coach, amateur racers, and race organizers, I am officially a doper, a bike-racing criminal.

Holmes stops and waits for me on the shoulder of the road, and I coast up to him. He's still perched atop his saddle, with his left foot unclipped from his pedal and extended to the ground. His mouth moves, and his head nods emphatically. I'm sure he's giving me advice and encouragement. But I don't hear him. I'm preoccupied. I feel toxic.

"I took drugs and cheated myself of my honor," the Irishman and former Tour de France rider Paul Kimmage confessed in his book, *Rough Ride*. Kimmage recalled how, the night after the first day that he'd injected himself with performance-enhancing drugs, he had laid awake in bed, wrapped in sheets and guilt. "I'm a million miles from sleep," he wrote.

"Let's get moving, easy effort and high cadence through this next section. No need to stress yourself," I finally hear Holmes say. "Especially if you're racing tomorrow. Okay?"

I still don't know if I'll compete in the morning—Juliana remains under the impression that tonight is date night. But I don't get into it with Holmes. Holmes is immediately likable, right down to the way he talks. He has a deep, relaxed, mellifluous voice. He sounds more like a late-night jazz-station DJ than a drill sergeant. Already I notice how he sometimes dwells luxuriously on his long a's. His "okay" sometimes comes out "okaaay." "No way" is "no waaay."

"Plenty of time to build your strength," Holmes adds, pushing his pedals slowly as we resume riding. "We've got the whole season to plaaay."

Two months earlier I'd hired Holmes because he seemed both mellow and tireless. ("Hey, miss a workout and it's no problem. I make an adjustment for the next day or two.") He'd sent me a photo of himself, sans helmet: Holmes has thick waves of boyish brown hair and the perfect teeth of someone who never indulges in sweets or soft drinks.

From our first phone conversation, it was also obvious that Holmes lives to ride. He's competed in all types of cycling events, and has survived a yearlong, grueling tour of duty in Europe, where the road racing is historically toughest. He's a self-confirmed technology nut capable of interpreting all of the data that can spill from a sophisticated power meter (like mine), and boasts of this coaching certification and that. I talked to some other potential coaches, too, but they all sounded young and too hyped about racing. I liked that Holmes was a mature thirty-eight years old, and had a previous career in the tech industry. Even without kids, he seemed to understand the demands of my commitment-filled days.

I am, after all, Holmes's prototypical customer: the middle-age man willing to spend $300 per month for a coach that will help keep me from growing old. Guys like me are the face of amateur bike racing. According to 2009 data from USA Cycling, the sport's leading governing body, its licensed members are predominantly male (eighty-seven percent), between the ages of thirty-five and fifty-four (fifty-six percent), and overwhelmingly hail from sunny, affluent, and body-obsessed California (nineteen percent). Like so many of my peers, part of my inspiration comes from Lance Armstrong and his seven Tour de France victories, as well as from Armstrong's coach, Chris Carmichael. Back in 2000, a year after Armstrong won his first Tour, Carmichael advertised the promise that his training magic could work for amateur athletes, too. Propagating technologies like email and the Internet, as well as the growing use of electronic training tools like heart rate monitors and power meters, made it possible for Carmichael and his staff to coach athletes across the nation, and over the years his business has expanded, and his client numbers have entered the many thousands. Overall, USA Cycling went from licensing about 200 coaches in 2000 to more than 1,400 in 2008. Aging athletes in other sports also have ample mentoring options. USA Triathlon, for example, has certified nearly 2,000 multisport coaches. There's a lot of training advice out there.

Michael has a coach, as does my friend Innis. My buddy Luke recently fired his coach and is considering someone new. The coaches design workouts that ebb and flow in terms of duration and intensity, and they give structure to their athletes' training. In a perfect world, the coaches help bring riders like Mike, Luke, Innis, and me to levels of "peak" fitness for races that we'd circle on our schedules as priorities. Similar to the way that the best road-racing pros point to July every year, which is when they meet at the Tour de France.

But the coaches and sophisticated training also turn me and my hardcore riding buddies into skinny, gray-bearded, clucking hens. We often discuss our coaches' philosophies, and compare workouts and training approaches. Our long conversations often address topics like pedaling cadence, weightlifting, gearing, interval times, core strength, rest, race tactics, injuries, sports drinks, bowel movements, and "maximal lactate steady state," which is also known as "onset of blood lactate accumulation," "lactate threshold," "anaerobic threshold," and "functional threshold power." All of these arcane terms attempt to characterize the highest physical effort that a performing athlete can consistently deliver for a given stretch of time (generally sixty minutes), and improving that metric (which can be quantified in heart rate or, even more accurately, in watts on a power meter) is what we all obsess over the most. A rider's "threshold" figure, with other key factors like body weight and aerodynamics being accounted for, is the number he hangs his helmet on. Threshold is to the dedicated bike racer what horsepower is to a car nut. The number can never be too high.

"Easy here, we'll work up to your FTP," Holmes cautions from behind me as we approach the top of a short yet unforgiving hill that leads into the small community of Castro Valley. FTP is short for the aforementioned "functional threshold power." I'm working hard. My gloved hands lever off the rubber-sheathed handbrake casings attached to my handlebars. My legs and back strain, and I can feel the heaviness of the headband that I'm wearing underneath my helmet. It's soaked with sweat.

"Slow down!" insists Holmes. "You've got nothing to prove today, crazy-man. This isn't a race."

He's right—I shouldn't be going hard for extended stretches of a pre-race training ride. Another thing coaches are good for: Yanking on the reins of their many Type A clients. I look at the power meter anchored to my handlebar. The digital readout displaying the watts I'm generating bounces around—243, 235, 262, 245. I figure I'm averaging about 250 watts right now, which for me, and for this moment, is too much. Directly beneath the power meter, I glance at a small piece of paper that's taped onto my stem, or the tube that connects my handlebar to my bike frame. Many of my peers' bikes feature similar adornments. It's a printout—in nearly microscopic point size—of some key power-related figures. Really, it's as much a hood ornament as a reference guide, a true sign of my membership in the little world of road racing. It lists my FTP at approximately 260 watts, and in this stretch of today's ride I shouldn't be anywhere near that figure. If I were a top professional rider, however, the numbers I'm generating would be meager. At threshold, some top pro riders produce well over seventy percent more power than I can.

I ease up on the pedals, and we roll through a corner of the city of San Leandro on our way toward the zoo and some hills. The ride feels schizophrenic, as routes through Oakland and the East Bay often do. Twenty minutes ago we were cruising through regional parkland, and now we're on a gritty stretch of MacArthur Boulevard, looking straight ahead, minding our own skinny-ass business as a pair of brightly painted Buick LeSabres, complete with oversize chrome rims, thumping car stereo speakers, and silver and black Raiders flags flying from radio antennas rumble by us.

I remind myself to get out of my head and just enjoy the ride. This is fun. I'm enjoying having my coach along for the ride, him watching my every move and guiding me with an expert eye. Usually I upload my "power data" to Holmes each night, and he analyzes the resulting numbers and squiggly-line graphs the way that a doctor reads a patient's chart before often sending me a cheerful email. Not much real contact. Having him here is far better, and for a minute I indulge in the idea of using a local coach. The exercise-centric Bay Area is filled with coaches for hire, and while none of my fellow racers have reason to be suspicious of me using a faraway coach, they might consider my choice undesirable. All of my friends' coaches live and race locally. My buddies and their coaches often ride together, and they sometimes huddle at races to talk strategy. Local coaches provide shoulders to lean on.

Maybe someday, Tilin. Not now. Don't contaminate some local coach's business.

Holmes and I pass the zoo and start slowly up Golf Links Road, back toward the hills and my house.

"Okay, let loose a bit," says Holmes, reaching into the back pocket of his cycling jersey for a snack—an energy gel packet. "I want you doing three three-minute repeats, each at about 260 watts. Several minutes of rest in between. Good prep for tomorrow."

A small set of relatively short, high-intensity intervals essentially prime a rider's muscles and cardiovascular system for the next day's race. I begin the first repeat. Holmes says he'll catch up.

Climbing toward Skyline Boulevard, from where I'll soon have great views of downtown Oakland and the bay, I push my body. Quads contract, lungs expand, shoulders scrunch. But I can still think, and guilty thoughts at that.

Repeat after me: Don't ride with Holmes. Don't become chummy with Holmes. It's not fair to him.

The back of my USA Cycling racing license specifically states that nobody in the sport wants to be associated with someone like me:

"My use of this license," it reads, "confirms that I agree to know and abide by the applicable rules and regulations of USA Cycling and the UCI [another of the sport's governing bodies], including the anti-doping rules and procedures . . ."

I'm the reason they make these rules.

I look down at my power meter. Around 240 watts. I'm ninety seconds into the interval. Calves are tightening. Unhappy sensations come from my lower back. I push harder.

Am I messing with his career? Could I ruin his livelihood by letting him associate with me?

Another minute goes by. Actually feel decent. I make the left turn onto Skyline.

Don't be such a drama queen. Get over yourself, you're just one guy.

I ride another hundred yards.

Still. Probably best to see him as little as possible.

Then another fifty.

So you ride with him every couple months . . .

I finish the first interval, and after spinning easily for a bit I come to a stop on Skyline, which is a largely empty, two-lane road. I can see far west, including much of the South Bay. The hard work feels invigorating. I'm motivated, and I feel strong. I'm *training*.

Then again, I'm a scumbag doper.

But it's more complicated than that.

I look south. I see Holmes, motoring up the hill toward me. We catch each other's eyes from behind our sunglasses.

He smiles, and waves.

"WHY ARE YOU so wigged out?" Michael asks me over the phone the next morning as I tell him that all is not right.

I am home. Michael is at his place in the Silicon Valley. We both bailed on this morning's race. He didn't want to wake up in darkness and drive four hours to the start line. Too stressful. I didn't want to make the journey either, I tell him, especially after keeping my commitment to Juliana. Last night, she and I had a lingering Italian dinner at Pizzaiolo near downtown Oakland, and then went home to relieve the babysitter and, with the kids already asleep, watch *Hairspray* on DVD. John Travolta's uncanny estrogen act did nothing to stop me from getting a hard-on, and I made a pass at Juliana, who fended me off, albeit with a smile on her face.

"Maybe your balls are shrinking," he jokes. "I'll research solutions on the Internet."

"Don't bother," I say. "Thanks. My balls are fine."

I should be calmer, like Mike. Mike tries to keep stress out of his life, which is why he aspires to maintain a simple existence. He rents an inexpensive, humble apartment so that he doesn't have to live with a roommate. He doesn't have a nice car or fancy furniture that beg for polishing and care. No dog, cat, or even goldfish. And definitely no foreign, performance-enhancing substances in his body that might saddle him with concern over possible side effects, or guilt. One of the few burdens he's willing to add to his days is lending support to a best friend who's twisting in his own skin as he whines on the phone.

"I still don't understand," Michael says over the phone. "So you're wound up because you didn't have sex? Or missed the Pine Flat race? It's early in the season. That race is in the boonies. This situation calls for calm."

I'm not upset about Juliana rejecting me. Before testosterone, the misfire we'd had the night before probably would've cost us an entire Therapy Tuesday couples session. We would've used words like "validation," "risk," and "curiosity." But Juliana's smile had reassured me. It didn't say *rejection* so much as *not now*. Besides, we both knew that there were plenty more erections to come.

"It's neither of those things," I say. "It's that I hate lying to Holmes."

I stand up from where I'm sitting at our dining room table to see where the kids are. They don't need to hear my confession. I walk down the hall, cordless phone against my ear. Benjamin is in his room, wearing a too-small Batman costume bought for a Halloween of years ago. He's repeatedly driving a remote-control car into the baseboards. I guess that's fun. Sophie is on her bed, reading an *Ivy + Bean* book. They're entertaining themselves, and not by teasing each other. The stars have aligned. Juliana must be downstairs, in our home office.

"I mean, I'm a doper. I wonder if I should tell him," I say quietly into the phone, retreating to the dining room table. "Holmes knows that I'm a journalist. Maybe he'll go along."

"Go along with what? You're giving this doping project an awful lot of thought and energy," says Michael.

I can hear a loud noise through the speaker on my phone. Something is tearing.

"What are you doing?" I ask.

"Damn. Wrong ones," he says. "I bought a bunch of tubes online, and just opened the package. Not what I wanted," he says. "The valves have threads. Threaded valve stems. Not good. Problem."

Michael wasn't bred to contemplate such minutiae. He wasn't supposed to care that securing and removing the rubber-sleeved head of a tire pump is easier if you mount it to inner tube valve stems that are thread-less. Thread-less valve stems are smooth and therefore relatively friction-free. Really, Mike was never supposed to know what a thread-less valve stem was. Instead he was supposed to know how to maybe manage a hedge fund, or expertly work a judge and jury, and fret over small, intricate things like wine labels and anniversary jewelry.

After Mike went to Town School with me, we both attended San Francisco University High School, and then he went onto Stanford. Mike's parents were always great to me, but they could be tough on Mike. They had very high expectations. They believed that with Michael's grooming and highbrow education that he'd someday marry the gorgeous girl, have the perfect family, and become a lawyer or maybe a Fortune 500 CEO. He had a lot of the right stuff to fulfill such vast expectations: Mike was smart and a hard worker. Tall and slight but muscular, with dark skin and wavy brown hair, he attracted a lot of women. He was always a great athlete, too—sharpshooter with a basketball, and considered turning professional in tennis.

The problem was Michael's head. Partially in response to stress that I always believed was tied into the expectations surrounding him, Mike's thinking increasingly took left turns. As far back as grade school, he couldn't be convinced that authority was good, and that he should become part of some establishment. Sometimes he'd let his teachers and parents know how he felt, and he'd get into trouble.

Mike ended up saying no to the world that lay in front of him, and grew repulsed by it. No to WASPy girlfriends and high-society parties. Screw you to the business, legal, and financial worlds. Instead he became a passionate schoolteacher of history and western civilization, and even taught in Switzerland for a couple years on hiatus from his life in Northern California. He ultimately rejected most professional sports, too—the sports that he and his family always watched while we grew up. As kids inside the multi-floored Piesco house, Mike's handsome mom fed us sandwiches made with fresh deli turkey while we tuned into the Giants, Warriors, Wimbledon, the Masters, the 49ers. We screamed and cheered at their Sony TV.

But when Michael grew up, those sports—particularly professional football, baseball, and basketball—came to represent the status quo, and he thought that the big three were full of overpaid and lazy jocks. Mike identified more with professional cycling, an underdog sport where even the few superstars, the rare guys who make maybe six or seven figures, have to work themselves to the bone to be competitive. He found truth and something noble in the riders' suffering, especially for relatively no money. When Mike himself wasn't on his bike, or teaching, or looking for a woman with his kind of sensibilities, he liked nothing more than to sit in his extraordinarily messy apartment and watch European bike races on cable television. He loved the races' hinge points, when the roads turned comically steep and the competitors' stoic expressions would finally give way to sagging shoulders and tightened jaws. For Michael, these were moments of truth not just in racing but in *life*—confronting pain, suffering, and doubt absolutely head on. Nothing was more real to Michael than such visceral feelings, which were so far away from what one might experience while hosting an attorney-client lunch, or gathering at the dark-wooded bar of some exclusive club. So Mike would lose himself while viewing clashes like the Tour of Flanders or the Giro d'Italia, where the emotions were obvious and the expectations were blessedly free of nuance or social standing. Just pedal! Indeed, Mike's own passion and orneriness for life would be fueled as he faced his glowing TV, and was surrounded by vast collections of cycling clothes, bike wheels, energy bars, water bottles, and inner tubes. Preferably inner tubes with thread-less valve stems.

There's more racket coming from Michael's end of the phone line. "What are you doing now?" I ask Mike over the phone.

"Taping up the package. Returning these tubes. This shit is unacceptable. I'm going to get what I want. The tubes aren't cheap."

"Oh. Well, what should I do?" I say.

"About what?" he asks.

"The *coach*. My *doping!*"

"Don't tell him what you're doing," he says. "He doesn't need to know. What he sees is you putting in all that effort. You're working plenty hard. Tell him about the drugs and he'll probably refuse to work with you, and also have to do something responsible. Like report you to USA Cycling. And all because of what . . . ?" he asks.

"What do you mean, because of what?" I say, my ears pricking up. "I'm rubbing this crap on my body, every day. I'm *doping*."

"So far I haven't heard any news that your doping is doing much for you, outside of the sack, anyway. Which means it would serve me no purpose," he cracks, and we both laugh. Michael had sent me an email days earlier with a subject line that read, "single forever." The link in the mail took me to a story about how racers think cycling is more important than everything—work, relationships, family. We both knew it described him a little too well. In Michael's life, the right woman hasn't appeared yet, though not for his lack of trying. Still, the one constant is the bike, and the purity of riding long and hard.

"Ever think about using some other performance-enhancing drugs?" he continues. "You're just on testosterone. You already had testosterone in your body, and now you have more. If you want to really duplicate the doping experience, maybe you should be taking a lot of stuff. Aren't these guys on everything? Can you imagine, all those drugs and still all that incredible suffering they go through!"

"Wait a minute. *Just* testosterone?" I ask, defensively. I'm waving my right hand in the air. "This stuff is super-potent. Is what you put inside of a gun *just* a bullet?"

Michael isn't the only who thinks I could do more with my doping protocol. I'd brought my friends Innis and Luke in on my doping secret, too. They'd practically yawned when I first told them that I'd be doping with testosterone and DHEA.

"Bank a little blood," Luke wrote me in an email, referring to the practice of blood doping, where endurance athletes like cyclists inject concentrated forms of previously stored blood (usually their own) to increase the amount of oxygen that can be transported to their muscles. Luke, like Michael, thinks that I should go "whole hog" to really maximize my performance, and that I'm taking the path of least resistance to putting a citizen doper story in print. "While you're at it," he continued in the email, "make me out to be the alcoholic super-racer in your book. Even if I don't merit either title."

Easy for my buddies to seek the highest truths regarding doping in sport. Their bodies aren't at risk. Their consciences don't hang in the balance.

MY FRIENDS MAY JOKE but I know what I'm doing is serious stuff. American pro cyclist Floyd Landis, after all, lost his 2006 Tour de France crown for using testosterone. The winner, busted for T! That says something about how seriously I'm taking my project! But whether or not my friends fully realize it, the truth is that nobody knows if testosterone betters the physical performance of an endurance athlete—be it an elite competitor or a spindly, 145-pound, utterly mediocre, road-racing weenie. The latter would be me.

Supplemental testosterone unquestionably does something big to a body. In 1942, *The Journal of the American Medical Association* observed that, in understated fashion, "androgens exert a tonic and stimulating action." It was a prescient statement, considering that the editors at *JAMA* were unlikely to have a vision of the steroid abuses to come, nor were they terribly aware of the already longstanding enthusiasm overseas for testosterone's apparent power to make power. Austrian physiologist Oskar Zoth took a page out of the book of Charles-Édouard Brown-Séquard, the French physiologist who swore back in 1889 that he found the fountain of youth when shooting himself up with liquefied guinea pig testicles. Zoth injected himself with a juice derived from smashed-up bull nuts and claimed that he became stronger—at least in the one finger that he poked in the name of science. Zoth immediately saw potential in the world of sports.

"The training of athletes," Zoth wrote in 1896, "offers an opportunity for further research in this area."

Stories exist that Nazi scientists were actually the first to identify and synthesize testosterone, with the hopes that they could turn members of the Third Reich into super-soldiers. But author John Hoberman, who has written extensively on testosterone, wrote to me that such rumors "are all nonsense." Hoberman did say that Adolf Hitler was on the T shortly before his death. We'll never know the kind of boost der Fuhrer felt.

What's unquestioned, however, is that supplemental testosterone flowed into the Eastern bloc nations in the years after it was first synthesized. In the mid-1950s, an American physician named John Ziegler, who served as a doctor to the United States weightlifting team, learned that the extra-extra-large Russian competition was benefiting from injections of synthetic testosterone. Ziegler, who was also a bodybuilder and had a deep interest in chemistry, returned home and in 1958, via the company Ciba Pharmaceuticals, rolled out an anabolic-androgenic steroid (*anabolic* meaning increased protein production and therefore the building of muscle; *androgenic* referring to male sex hormone) that closely mimicked testosterone. It was called methandrostenolone and would be marketed as Dianabol. There were visions of Dianabol aiding the wasting bodies of the old and infirm. Then the bodybuilders got hold of it.

Like testosterone, Dianabol stimulates protein synthesis inside of cells, which accelerates the recovery of working muscles. The result, for the power hungry, is a beautiful, closed loop: The faster that muscles can recover, the more work they can take on, and the more strength and mass one can build. Because of its specific chemical makeup, Dianabol helps form muscle even faster than the T, which is why Dianabol became the bulk-builder's darling.

By the early 1960s, the American weightlifting crowd, as well as football players and track-and-field athletes, used Dianabol. The drug truly paved the way for the testosterone and closely related (and man-made) anabolic steroids that any gym enthusiast in search of pectorals shaped like Half Dome can buy illicitly to this day.

But when it comes to doping, the gym crowd lagged hopelessly behind the cycling world. Cycling has been synonymous with suffering and misery since the nineteenth century, when six-day bicycle races, held on tracks in front of big crowds at venues like New York City's Madison Square Garden, challenged sleep-deprived, often hallucinating competitors to ride more and rest little.

At the start of the twentieth century, the men in charge of the French newspaper *L'Auto* had a sadomasochistic epiphany: Organize and sponsor an ultra-endurance-type race called the Tour de France that would travel the country. The newspaper followed the action, telling the tales of men racing for up to seventeen hours a day and bringing the most obscure parts of humongous France, including its one-cafe villages and faraway mountaintops, to every reader of the paper. In a car- and plane-less era, such dispatches felt like they arrived from outer space.

Many of the early Tour competitors were humble men with little to lose. What started as a five-week-long race (it's now three weeks) sometimes covered thousands of miles (nowadays the Tour regularly runs around 2,000 miles), and was torture consisting of cramping, boredom, hunger, hypothermia, dehydration, fear, and exhaustion. The race was about surviving as well as winning, and nobody much begrudged the rag-tag riders for seeking creative ways to ease their own suffering. Relief and added power came from tobacco, alcohol, strychnine, ether, cocaine, amphetamines—and that was just in the Tour's first sixty years. Drugs pushed Tour competitors to win, convulse in the middle of the road, foam at the mouth, and drop dead during the race.

"In short," one rider said during the 1924 Tour, "we run on dynamite."

Today the Tour de France is a huge, internationally renowned race, with endless media coverage and heaps of corporate sponsorship. Its organizers regularly beat their chests about the event's tight anti-doping measures. But there are plenty of indications that the race's original, drug-laced ways are written into the Tour's—really, professional cycling's—DNA. Nowadays busts are commonplace among pro racers at the Tour and many, many other events. The competition inside of the competition, the sport's critics say, is keeping doping riders spinning their wheels under the anti-doping radar.

One drug-taking offender in particular sobered me on the sport. Joe Papp, the former pro who I profiled for *Outside* magazine, had doped recklessly, using virtually all the substances that he could find or were handed to him, including amphetamines, strong liver detoxifiers, and nitroglycerine, which is also employed to make explosives and treat heart failure. Papp loaded up on synthetic erythropoietin, too. EPO is a hormone that occurs naturally and in limited amounts inside the body, and it stimulates the production of red blood cells, which are responsible for transporting oxygen to an athlete's working muscles.

Synthetic EPO, which must be injected, does more of the same, and while it provides a huge kick for racing cyclists, EPO can also turn one's blood as dangerously thick as sludge. Papp showed me secret videos of his teammates apparently shooting up EPO or something, and gave me the impression that many pro riders dope like mad. Whether or not the perspective is fair, he made it hard for me to believe that any competitive pro cyclist is clean.

But Joe Papp himself was a no-name until testosterone made him famous when he was busted for it in 2006 at the obscure Tour of Turkey. A year later, in May 2007, he found himself at a Southern California arbitration hearing being held for one of his sport's titans: Floyd Landis. A drug test near the end of the 2006 Tour had indicated that Landis had cheated by using exogenous testosterone. During the nine-day hearing, Landis's attorneys argued that not only was their client's drug test mishandled, but that testosterone wouldn't have benefited him even if he had used it. Why, the lawyers argued, would Landis be so foolish as to use an illegal substance that had no beneficial effect? The prosecution, meanwhile, introduced Papp as one of its expert witnesses. He argued that testosterone and road cycling are made for each other.

In researching my magazine story about Papp, I scoured the transcripts of that hearing, which essentially put testosterone on trial. During nine days of testimony, the arbitration panel heard multiple opinions on the effectiveness of the steroid. Don Catlin, a (now former) professor and physician at UCLA who founded and oversaw what is currently the world's largest testing facility of performance-enhancing drugs (the UCLA Olympic Analytical Laboratory), testified that testosterone can unquestionably benefit a hard-charging cyclist, particularly in terms of recovering faster from hard bouts of exercise. Meanwhile John Amory, a former consultant for the United States Anti-Doping Agency and an internist (and testosterone expert) at Seattle's University of Washington Medical Center, cited scientific research arguing that testosterone doesn't aid endurance or recovery.

As for Papp, he stated that testosterone unquestionably helped him bounce back after days of hard racing. Defense attorneys attempted to dispute Papp's testimony as unscientific, and they were right—Papp's doping regimen involved the use of multiple drugs. His approach to taking them, by researchers' standards, was hopelessly messy. But long after the hearing ended, Papp remained steadfast in the belief that he knew his body, and that testosterone had performance-enhancing effects.

"That courtroom was bullshit," Papp told me months after the Landis arbitration hearing. "Of course there's no empirical study confirming testosterone's benefit for recovery during multi-day bike stage races. You can't ethically study that.

"They said Joe Papp isn't experienced, that he's talking about a placebo effect," Papp also said. "Uh, maybe. But if so, there are a lot of guys being fooled by the placebo effect."

Another cyclist who's a confirmed believer in testosterone, as it turns out, is Landis himself. Yes, later in 2007, the arbitration panel concluded that Landis violated cycling's anti-doping rules, and it stripped the rider of his Tour title. Then in spring 2010, Landis confessed that he had used performance-enhancing drugs, including testosterone, for much of his career (although he maintains that the T wasn't part of his doping arsenal during the 2006 Tour).

And yet, the jury is *still* out on testosterone. Despite the arbitration panel's decision against Landis, and his subsequent revelations, science has tried and failed to prove the steroid's benefits for endurance athletes. Some scientists actually wonder if less testosterone might improve cycling. *Less.*

What's an utterly confused, truth seeking, citizen doper to think?

At one point during the Landis arbitration panel proceedings, testosterone expert John Amory said he wouldn't be surprised if hard racing caused a cyclist's testosterone levels to drop. Amory wasn't in a position to articulate whether such an adaptation was good or bad for athletic performance, but science exists that argues for the former. In 2004, researchers from the United States, Spain, and Finland published a paper about differing levels of testosterone in athletes after submitting three distinct groups of subjects—including trained weightlifters and amateur road cyclists—to tests of endurance (on a stationary bicycle) and explosive power (using weight-bearing exercises). The scientists found that some of the best endurance-oriented performances on the stationary bike came from subjects with the least testosterone. Maybe, the researchers opined, the superior performances were a result of select subjects having less body mass, more blood in their veins, or additional stress, which independently or combined reduced the concentration of the hormone. But they weren't exactly sure of the correlations. All they knew was that less testosterone might equal better cycling.

"Individuals with lower serum anabolic hormones [like testosterone] may be able to reach the highest maximal and submaximal workloads," they wrote.

I decide not to divulge this scientific nugget to Michael, Innis, or Luke. They'll find it too funny for my liking.

IT'S A CHILLY Saturday morning, and Benjamin stands half-dressed and goose pimpled in his dimly lit room. He has a pair of white, nylon baseball pants in his hands.

"Try on the pants," I say, looking at the blue baseball socks that come far enough up his thighs that they almost reach his underwear. The socks aren't supposed to extend that high.

I lean over Benjamin's bed to open the window blinds, and as I do sunlight brightens Benjamin's car posters and Elvis Presley memorabilia that includes figurines and old record albums. My son the budding performer, learning the piano and plucking at guitar strings, is a huge fan of the King of Rock 'n' Roll. Elvis—that crooning, sideburned, tower of Tennessee testosterone.

"Let's see the pants," I say. Juliana stands next to me, ditto Sophie, and we all watch Benjamin, with his small, perfectly proportioned body, slip into his new baseball uniform pants. It's early March. He has Little League photos today.

Benjamin pulls them on, but they're so big around the waist that they nearly fall off him. The pant legs are way too long. They go down to his feet.

He puts on his green and gold jersey, which has ATHLETICS stitched across the chest. There's a big vertical crease in the top, and short sleeves that hang well beyond my kid's elbows. Suddenly I can feel irritation building inside of me with the ferocity of a fireball. Benjamin's masculinity—no, the masculinity of *both* Tilin men—has been swallowed by a goofy-big Little League uniform.

I turn to Juliana. She's beaming.

"He looks cute," she says, adjusting the top's collar, which is practically falling off our son's shoulder.

"Cute?" I say. I've told my wife before that boys and men don't necessarily see the upside in being called "cute."

"You look *good*, Benjamin," she responds with a nod and a smile. Benjamin looks relieved, and moves around a little in his uniform, trying it out.

"Huh?" I say sharply, crossing my arms and turning toward her. "How can you say that? Everything is huge. The pants, the socks, the top. The boy needs different everything. A uniform that fits!"

The air inside of Benjamin's room becomes very still. This house never feels still. Benjamin always jabbers at a loud volume, Sophie whistles, and Juliana fills the air by playing the piano or downloaded songs from artists that I don't know. Unlike my hip wife, I've given up on trying to keep up with new music.

Finally Benjamin breaks the silence. He cracks his knuckles, which he does when he's nervous. Sophie picks at the stickers pasted all over Benjamin's sliding closet doors. She makes annoying little scraping sounds.

Juliana swallows hard and takes a breath, her yoga practice keeping her centered in a way I can't seem to maintain. She looks straight at me.

"Do you have to talk to me like that?" she asks.

"It's the truth," I say.

"What is up with you? Those are the smallest sizes," she says. "And he looks fine. You're being nasty."

"It's nasty to say that I want him to look right? Like a ballplayer?" I say, hooking a finger onto Benjamin's pants' huge waistband. Benjamin takes a step away from me and faces the floor. He keeps pulling this way then that on the waist of his pants in an attempt to keep them from falling down too far. He won't look up. I'm shaming him. I hate myself. But I can't stop, either.

"That's not what you said," Juliana replies, grabbing the uniform's belt and adjusting it. "Maybe you need to rephrase your thoughts."

I look at the full-size Elvis cutout next to Benjamin's desk. The King's yellow-sequin outfit fits him perfectly. Clothes hanging off him would be all wrong. They would undermine his sex appeal and maleness. I really want to ask Juliana if she'd let Benjamin dress for a piano recital in slacks that drag across the stage. Piano and music lessons are her department. Little League details are mine.

Stop with the comments. Don't let a uniform become an issue. Move on.

I'm twitchy from forehead to feet.

"We *need* to see what else is available," I say, hands on my hips. "That's what we *need* to do."

Whoa. Am I having some hormonal meltdown?

Scientists repeatedly say that there's scant evidence that men with more testosterone are automatically more aggressive. They say linking levels of testosterone with high levels of aggression with "'roid rage," is largely a fallacy. As a matter of fact, there are experts who argue that supplemental T actually puts many men who were previously low on the hormone—some of them suffering what's been called "Irritable Male Syndrome"—in a better mood or mind space.

Yeah, and science also argues that endurance athletes don't benefit from taking testosterone. Landis didn't wait for the right double-blind test results to come along before arriving at some conclusions.

Now nobody in Benjamin's room looks at me.

I consciously relax my jaw.

This could be just a completely juvenile snit. Lord knows I've had them before. How does one know the difference between 'roid rage and a temper tantrum? I sure don't.

"Okay," I announce to Juliana and the kids, running my hands through my hair. "Let me back up. Perhaps we can double-check to see if Benjamin can't find a better-fitting uniform," I say. "If not, we'll make do. Benjamin will be fine."

Juliana stays calm but doesn't seem appeased. Not that I can blame her. She frowns but speaks quietly.

"Andrew, let's not make an issue over the fit. These are the right sizes," she says, and turns from me to our son.

"Benjamin, you look great. Daddy forgets that Little League uniforms are made to fit boys of all sizes," Juliana says, pulling at the jersey so that it sags a little less. She threads the uniform's belt through Benjamin's pant loops and buckles it tight. "There you go. Now you're set." She smiles at him, and then lifts him into her arms. He cracks a small, sweet grin.

Benjamin looks at me. His shoulders soften. He picks his nose. He's ready to move beyond the conflict. He's not obsessing over how someone is supposed to look in a baseball uniform, about how society and magazines and all those page-views at sfgiants.com and maybe the exogenous testosterone have shaped my beliefs about what is masculine and male hormone-y.

I feel tightness inside of me release. My shoulders soften too.

I turn to Juliana.

"I'm very sorry," I say softly, stuffing my hands into my front pants pockets.

Juliana gives me a sympathetic if not completely warm smile. The expression is kind, but I read into it. Maybe she's thinking, *Thank God I'm not you. Thank God I'm not poor, confused Andrew.*

In Juliana's childhood world, bluster and conflict seldom walked through the door of her grandparents' West Texas home, where she inherited many of her values and sensibilities: Don't create issues. Every thing will be fine. No sense in making a huge fuss. But there's obviously a big difference between a home with minimal dysfunction and one where involved family matters go under-addressed. As a kid, Juliana already knew that her family life was complicated and far from idyllic. For starters, there was the largely absent dad, and a grandfather who staggered home from work each night, not because he was tired. Nobody talked much about her grandfather's breath, which smelled like a distillery, and would help explain why, on most nights, he went straight to bed instead of the dinner table.

For years, Juliana watched her grandmother, as small as my mom and equally full of life, work to take up the slack. She was dedication and practicality as much as my mom was extravagance. She'd tuck in her husband at night, clean the house, water the jade plants, read the Bible, and soldier on in the kitchen, making roasts, potatoes, and black-eyed peas for everyone: her four children, and frequently spouses and grandchildren, too.

Juliana had plenty of respect for her grandmother. However, that didn't mean she wanted a future that remotely resembled her grandma's life. West Texas was austere and isolated, and she'd inherited her father's wanderlust. When her family encouraged her to stay close by for college, she instead chose to attend the University of Texas at Austin, hours away from home. When they hoped that she'd settle in

Texas, she moved to Colorado, where she met me. When they thought she might settle down and have children, Juliana instead convinced me to travel to Southeast Asia and the Indian subcontinent for many months, and turned us both into dedicated yoga practitioners. But where I eventually stopped doing downward dogs by the dozen, Juliana continued, and became a yoga instructor before becoming a photographer. She practiced as well as preached equanimity, and learned to make peace with much of her past, including her elusive father and sometimes repressed family.

Juliana also came to cherish certain aspects of her grandparents' house. Like the lack of drama. As matriarch and patriarch rolled into one, Juliana's grandmother headed an estrogen-dominant house of three daughters and only one son, and everyone there got by okay without an abundance of maleness or testosterone. Certainly nobody would've ever stomped their feet at the sight of a kid like Benjamin wearing a baseball uniform that's too large.

But now, for better or worse, my wife is living with ample testosterone, and apparently the commotion that comes with it. We're all living with some havoc. Hopefully my many stowed syringes full of exogenous male sex hormone won't blow our roof clean off.

While giving camera-ready Benjamin a hug and kiss, thoughts of a simple, testosterone-free existence tumble around in my mind like clothes in a dryer.

I'M PRETTY SURE there's another hormone at play in Benjamin's room on this Saturday morning. Testosterone shouldn't receive all the credit. I've had a complicated relationship with human growth hormone for much of my life. Because wherever there's HGH, there's talk about size. Yes, the S-word. Size size size size size size size. Unfortunately, size matters in our society, and from where I stand skinny and small isn't nearly as well regarded as sizable and strong. Even without doping with HGH, I've had multiple brushes with the substance. In fact, the story behind it is a mini-epic, that requires being told in three acts:

1.

I first hear the term "human growth hormone" in 1971. I am six years old, and a true small fry in my first-grade class, when I walk into a San Francisco doctor's office with my then-married mom and dad. I don't know what we're doing here. I don't know that my parents want to make me taller. I only know that I'm missing school, which increasingly seems like more fun than where my parents have taken me.

A dark-haired man who wears a tie but not a white doctor's coat, and whom I've never met, greets us in an office doorway. He softly grips what little meat I have on my shoulder.

"You're Andrew," he says, offering me his hand to shake. He seems friendly.

We all sit down, and my mom begins. She speaks quickly, as if she's unburdening herself.

"We're not worried at all about Andrew, and his behavior or personality. Or his . . . proportions," she says to the doctor, smiling bravely. I see lipstick on her teeth.

The doctor doesn't wear a stethoscope, either. What kind of doctor is he? His office has no glass jar with the wooden sticks that press down on your tongue. Instead there are a lot of bookshelves and books, and a desk.

"We want him to be normal. Like everyone else," my mom adds uneasily. I sit next to her, holding her hand. She looks down at me. Her breath smells faintly of tobacco. She often pops breath mints to neutralize the cigarettes' stench. "We want him to be happy," she adds.

"Can you tell us about what you do?" my father says. Like the doctor, my dad wears a tie, as he did almost every day to the insurance brokerage office that he shared with my grandfather on the sixth floor in the old Jack Tar Hotel on San Francisco's Van Ness Avenue. As a kid, if I stood on my tippy toes, I could look out one of the office windows, which were cool to the touch from that fog-filled air, and see the cars and buses rolling down the street below.

The doctor nods, slowly. He talks for a while, and mostly to my parents, because the conversation is beyond me. I hear words like "growth charts," "wrist and hand x-rays," and "Bayley-Pinneau tables."

Earlier, while driving across town to this man's office, my mother told me what kind of doctor he is. It's a mouthful: *pediatric endocrinologist.* She told me something else, too, that involved another big word I didn't quite understand. Our visit is *informational.* She didn't say, "You're too short." She only thought that.

"We were told that one potential option was human . . . hormone," says my dad.

"Human growth hormone," the doctor says.

My father nods. Then he asks the doctor about the syringes. My father understands that growth hormone must be injected.

"How big are the needles?" my father asks, uncrossing his legs before crossing them again.

Needles make my dad uncomfortable. He doesn't like blood, either. I remember my dad once gagging a lot on some blood running down his throat after getting his wisdom teeth pulled. His eyes grew wide and his face turned white, and he started making a lot of awful sounds, like he was choking to death. I got scared and covered my eyes.

The doctor holds out his two hands and his index fingers, maybe a few inches apart.

"How often would we have to give the injections?" my father asks.

"You'd administer two or three per week," the doctor says. "Maybe more."

At six years old, needles make me uncomfortable, too. I squeeze my mother's hand. She squeezes back, firmly. *I'm right next to you,* her squeeze says. Her fingernails are painted a pretty red, as usual.

"Why are we here, Daddy?" I interrupt. "I don't feel sick."

I don't. My stomach doesn't ache. Tracy hadn't punched me. I want to go to school.

We are here because, when it comes to height, I may not be ill, but I'm not exactly flourishing. I barely come up to the chests of some of my classmates. On the growth charts I'm perhaps in the fifth percentile, which means on a height-for-age table I'm shorter than ninety-five percent of the six-year-old boys in the reference population. My pediatrician had said I might only grow to be five-foot-five—or less. My mother is five-foot-one, my dad is over six feet. They had told the pediatrician that they would like me to grow beyond five-foot-five. In her mind's eye, my mother said, a man should be taller than that. Taller than the women he dates, and tall enough to move back the car seat a bunch when he drives. That's just how men are supposed to be, she had explained. The pediatrician suggested that my parents make an appointment with a pediatric endocrinologist. Maybe, he said, an endocrinologist can help.

In 1971, medicine had the means to make kids taller. Nearly sixty years earlier, a famous neurosurgeon named Harvey Cushing determined that the pituitary gland, which is about the shape and size of a pea and situated near the bottom of the brain, secretes what ultimately became known as human growth hormone. Cushing believed that children lacking in the hormone, which contributes to a kid's growth in multiple ways, might not grow as tall as others. But for decades his theory was impossible to prove. The pituitary gland secretes multiple hormones, and not unlike in the early days of isolating and identifying testosterone, both the medical and pharmaceutical communities raced to better understand the pituitary and its secretions. Then in 1958, two years after it had first been isolated, human growth hormone was used to dramatically jump-start the growth of a seventeen-year-old, four-foot-two-inch boy. The result struck a nerve in a society that, as far back as the early 1900s and into the present, has repeatedly indicated to behavioral scientists that men ought to be tall, and certainly taller than women. To this day, studies show that there's a correlation between height and income—taller people enjoy higher average earnings. Manipulating one kid's height introduced the hope that no boy would ever, like me or Benjamin, be too small, or swim inside a sports uniform.

One 1958 newspaper article, recalled authors Susan Cohen and Christine Cosgrove in their excellent and meticulous book about height manipulation, *Normal at Any Cost*, declared, "Hopes have arisen anew for a world in which few children would be destined to be midgets, dwarfs, or even 'shorties.'"

My parents listen to the pediatric endocrinologist's shorty-fighting strategies. In the thirteen years since HGH has been used to help one small boy grow, he explains, thousands of children have been successfully treated. But, he warns, issues remain: Some HGH is impure and might not work as advertised. Determining whether or not young Andrew is hypopituitary—suffering from pituitary failure—may require significant testing. Finally, the doctor explained, the hormone is hard to come by: HGH is extracted from the pituitary glands of human cadavers.

Mom and dad listen politely, and then we leave. My dad's reaction is almost immediate.

"I don't want to do this," he says to my mother in the medical building's elevator.

"Marsh, let's think about it," says my mom. "About what will benefit Andrew for his whole life."

"I feel good, Mommy," I say, watching the lights flash as the elevator descends past one floor and then another. "Do we have to come here again?"

"No," says my dad before my mother can speak another word. He's looking down and straight into her eyes. "Never ever. Cadavers? That sounds wrong, Angela. I don't like to think what chemicals from a corpse might do to a little boy."

My father looks down at me.

"You're fine, and you'll always be just right," he says.

We don't return to that doctor's office. I'm never "treated" for shortness.

Looking back, I swear that my dad's stand against HGH had little to do with fear. His resistance wasn't about hypodermics that made him squeamish. If he truly believed that I wasn't going to grow, and that I'd end up so small as to be squished underneath someone else's shoe, he would've pushed past his own hang-ups and given me the shots. No, on that day in 1971, I think my father stood up to society: some cutting-edge science of the day, as well as people's weighty expectations of how men are *supposed* to be.

2.

Thirty years later, I'm the father taking the gut check: One day in 2001, I'm confronted with a very upset wife, an undersize child, and the suggestion that I can shape a life with a very different form of HGH.

"She diagnosed Benjamin with 'failure to thrive,'" Juliana says to me on a wintry New Mexico afternoon in January after returning home from our boy's one-year checkup. Tears brim in her eyes. Benjamin is in her arms, chomping on one of Dee Dee's paws. Dee Dee is his kitty-cat doll. Benjamin is in a yellow onesie. He looks very satisfied with how Dee Dee tastes.

"She says that maybe Benjamin isn't eating enough. That his body might not be producing enough growth hormone," says Juliana. "She's worried about his height and weight. He's in the fifth percentile for length."

At least the Tilin boys are consistent.

After a workday spent in a downtown Santa Fe office, I set down my shoulder bag against a waist-high bookshelf in our house that's packed with exercise and yoga tomes. I'd just walked in the door.

"What's 'failure to thrive'?" I ask, wrapping an arm around my wife to pull her into a hug.

"I don't know exactly but Dr. Rosalo wants us to take him to a pediatric endocrinologist," Juliana says, stroking Benjamin's brown hair. "I made an appointment. We'll see her in a few weeks."

The three of us are supposed to celebrate Benjamin's first birthday tonight with Chinese takeout. I want to introduce Benjamin to pot stickers, and not just because I love them. I want Benjamin to thicken up, and some greasy Chinese dumplings might give him some heft. The poor boy was colicky out of the womb, and over the past year he's consistently worried me and especially Juliana with his fussiness and small appetite. We've spooned bits of every infant cereal and baby food on the store shelf into Benjamin's mouth. Given him breast milk, as well as baby bottles containing rich formula. Put butter on everything. When we take him out and about and see infants with round thighs and double chins everywhere, Juliana and I get chubby-baby envy.

We decide to spend Benjamin's birthday eating Chinese takeout while basking in the glow of a computer monitor. Since one possible cause of "failure to thrive," which is really a catchall diagnosis for a child who's considerably undersized, is a deficiency in growth hormone, Juliana and I wonder if we might make a bigger Ben through science. While we eat pot stickers and sautéed chicken with green beans, we perform Internet searches to find out more about HGH. Benjamin is with us, although not in body. He fell asleep before we began eating and searching, and now he's in his crib in the next room. We listen to him sleep via one of those low-fidelity baby-monitoring speaker systems. The sound coming from the setup is simultaneously ominous and sweet. Imagine a cooing Darth Vader.

"GEEEEEEE," Benjamin inhales, "HAAAAAAA," Benjamin exhales.

Juliana flips around between science and news websites.

"HGH," I say, seeing the words "human growth hormone" on one Web page after another. "I hardly knew ye." I polish off my second pot sticker.

Actually, I know nothing about modern-day supplemental HGH, which has been on a roller coaster ride since I last almost crossed paths with it in 1971. In 1985, the Food and Drug Administration halted the distribution of pituitary HGH because of its link to a degenerative and fatal brain disorder called Creutzfeldt–Jakob disease, or CJD. That same year, a Bay Area-based biotechnology company, Genentech, introduced a synthetic growth hormone called Protropin, and an industry was launched—other proprietary manmade HGH offerings that came to market included Humatrope and Genotropin. Thousands of children received prescriptions, and many of those kids unquestionably benefited from the drugs. In the most extreme examples, synthetic growth hormone helped kids who would've otherwise become dwarves. But the manmade growth hormone, like its cadaver-based predecessor, wasn't without controversy. The fact is, experts estimate that only a small fraction of the child population suffers from true growth-hormone deficiency. The drugs were sometimes marketed to— and sought after by—parents who just wanted to add height to healthy but short children. And some pediatric endocrinologists were obliging and then some. A few who were quick to prescribe HGH were reportedly benefiting from the companies making synthetic growth hormone in terms of receiving funding for studies or even nice vacations.

"So doctors might prescribe HGH for kids that have no obvious need for the hormone," Juliana says, grabbing at a green bean with her chopsticks. "You have to ask yourself what kind of advice we'll get."

"GEEEEEE . . . HAAAAAAA."

We found more. *The New York Times* debated the supplemental hormones' effectiveness to add real height to its users. Human growth hormone might only accelerate the growth that a child would ultimately experience anyway. Over the course of, say, a decade's worth of treatment, a child could endure thousands of shots, at a cost of almost $100,000, and maybe grow a couple of inches as a result. Maybe more. Or perhaps not grow at all.

"What a crazy gamble," I say, sitting back in my chair and putting my hands behind my head. "What if it doesn't pay off, and you've burned through an insane amount of money?"

Suddenly I had a lot of compassion for the debate that ran through my parents' minds decades earlier. A pediatric endocrinologist may find that Benjamin isn't growth-hormone deficient, but could voice concerns that he might always be very small. Our boy isn't yet walking, and we're already envisioning him running away from bullies in a schoolyard. I wonder, if Benjamin ever gets called "Shorty," if he'll laugh, be scarred for eternity, or get stuffed into lockers only to come out swinging. The idea of playing God with your kid's physical dimensions is intimidating. The worst possible news—that Benjamin has hypopituitarism—might be the easiest to address. Then, somehow and some way, we'd likely spend the money to put him on HGH and hope that it works.

"I'm almost five-eight," I say to Juliana, turning away from the screen. "No brain disease from a cadaver. Lifetime issues with size, but employable. And happily married. I turned out okay."

"You turned out more than okay," she says, leaning over to kiss me softly.

"GEEEEEEE . . . HAAAAAAA."

We read that if Benjamin is a candidate for HGH, treatments wouldn't start for at least another year.

"Could we ever get the insurance company to pay for the treatments?" I say.

"I know what my dad would've told us," I add. "He'd say, let Benjamin be who he's supposed to be."

Juliana and I both remain quiet for a few seconds. We listen.

"GEEEEEEE . . . HAAAAAAA. GEEEEEEE . . . HAAAAAAA."

3.

"Once you're all set with testosterone and DHEA," Susie Wiley tells me over the phone one day in March 2008, "if you want growth hormone, you should consider taking growth hormone, too."

The suggestion comes without drama, just a digression in the middle of a different, follow-up conversation we're having about night sweats. I'm experiencing *sleep hyperhidrosis*, as my body continues to transition from manufacturing all of its own testosterone to mostly absorbing the exogenous testosterone that I'm applying almost daily. Wiley says that my hormone system will soon adjust, and that my PJs and sheets will no longer require daily trips to the clothes dryer.

Then in a truly incidental, do-you-want-a-cherry-with-your-whipped-cream kind of mention, Wiley drops the bomb. She serves up the suggestion of growth hormone.

"Why would I want growth hormone?" I ask.

"Improves muscle mass," she says matter-of-factly. "Sleep, too. I can't prescribe it, of course," she says. "But I can suggest a dosing schedule."

Her offer takes me back in time, to when I'd been spared HGH treatments as a kid, and to when I psychologically prepared myself to potentially inject growth hormone into Benjamin. Fortunately his pediatric endocrinologist ruled out such a treatment. ("Look at this boy, he's full of energy," she said back in February 2001. Juliana and I were in an Albuquerque hospital, watching Benjamin squirm around on an examination-room table, jerking Dee Dee this way and that.)

But now the situation is different. Wiley and I discuss the notion of me, as an adult, reworking my own body. In her industry, the suggestion is hardly unprecedented, which is one reason why she's casual about the idea of adding a new ingredient to my doping diet. For many anti-agers and pro athletes, dosing on human growth hormone is de rigueur, as essential to a health regimen as protein shakes and steel-cut oats.

The supplemental HGH craze began sometime after 1990, which is when *The New England Journal of Medicine* published a study—a teensy, tiny study—reporting that synthetic HGH was essentially sit-ups and bench presses packed into a tiny bottle. Of the study's twenty-one subjects (all men in their sixties and older), twelve received injections of HGH. After six months on the drugs, the subjects appeared to have won a physiological lottery: Bone density rose! Adipose tissue—body fat—evaporated by double-digit percentages! Muscle mass increased dramatically!

The market for synthetic HGH soon jumped, from 1988 worldwide sales of approximately $100 million to an estimated $1 billion by 2004. In 1997, Ron Klatz, one of the American Academy of Anti-Aging Medicine's co-founders, wrote a growth hormone how-to manual, *Grow Young with HGH*. The book said growth hormone users enjoyed everything from improved sex to better memory function. Celebrities from Nick Nolte to singer/rapper Mary J. Blige have either admitted to taking or been rumored to use the drug. Sylvester Stallone doesn't attempt to hide his use of growth hormone, which in 2007 caused him considerable trouble. He was busted for importing a banned substance into Australia, when forty-eight vials of HGH were found in his luggage at a Sydney airport. Stallone explained that the drugs were for personal use, apologized, and paid a fine.

In the sports world, HGH has also been everywhere. Mark McGwire and Jose Canseco, baseball's gi-normous "Bash Brothers" of the 1980s, used to crowd into bathroom stalls, syringes at the ready, presumably full of growth hormone. Dubious journalists and sports doctors nicknamed the 1996 Atlanta Summer Olympics the "Growth Hormone Games." When I asked Joe Papp, the excommunicated pro cyclist, about HGH in cycling's pro ranks, he misunderstood the question. I wanted to know *if* cyclists used it. He was already on to *how* HGH is used.

"Best not to take that with corticosteroids [a specific form of steroids]," he replied. "The rule as I learned it: Don't use one while you're using the other."

Duly noted.

One morning soon after Wiley suggests that I consider using HGH, I join Juliana for a bit of at-home yoga. I enter into a downward dog pose, which unfortunately gives me the opportunity to stare at the wrinkles above my knees. *Those*, I think to myself, my head upside-down and between my splayed arms, *are not my legs. Those are my grandfather's legs.* And my mind drifts (like it's not supposed to in yoga) to Wiley's offer, and the HGH that will supposedly chisel my body.

I take a shower and stop in front of the bathroom mirror before dressing for work. My shoulders have some shape, thanks to the bent-over, row-type weightlifting I've been doing at the gym to keep my back from hurting during long rides. My legs, wrinkles aside, look very solid, courtesy of ten to fourteen hours of cycling a week. But under the flecks of gray in my chest hair, testosterone or no, my chest has about as much contour as Drywall. My arms still look a lot like spokes on a bicycle wheel. Plenty of elite cyclists actually aspire to this silhouette. It's the ideal shape for a gravity-fighting, hill-climbing athlete who doesn't want upper-body bulk dragging him down.

Call me vain. Even if I become slower on my bike, I don't want to be all lower limbs—a human frog. Maybe, I think while buttoning up my shirt, I should take HGH. I contemplate the idea while driving to work.

As with testosterone, the body's own production of human growth hormone diminishes as we age. In a developing child, HGH fuels the lengthening of bones, bulking up of muscles, and the growth of many internal organs. An adult shooting up with HGH (forget the pills, absorption only comes via injection) can expect his or her body to undergo a "repartitioning effect" that diminishes subcutaneous fat and leaves you more, well, cut.

Its performance-enhancing effects—the ability to help athletes sprint faster and recover more quickly, and the capacity to increase strength—are debated in the research community. Some scientists argue that supplemental HGH could work against athletes: Researchers think that growth hormone could accelerate the accumulation of lactic acid in muscles during exercise. Lactic acid buildup is commonly thought to cause the "burning" sensation that ultimately forces an athlete to slow down.

Despite anecdotal claims, HGH isn't proven to enhance vision or erase age spots. Healthy adults who take HGH may also experience joint pain, tissue swelling, the increased likelihood of diabetes, and enlargement of the organs.

I arrive at my office and poke around on the Web. I find the watershed, small study of HGH from the July 5, 1990 issue of *The New England Journal of Medicine*. I also read an editorial on growth hormone from the same issue of the magazine. It's as cautious as the study is optimistic.

"If it [growth hormone] is given, how long should it be given?" wrote Mary Lee Vance, a professor of medicine in the division of endocrinology at the University of Virginia in Charlottesville. "Since it is unlikely that the beneficial effects of growth hormone on body composition are lasting, lifelong use would probably be required."

Lifelong use. Even if human growth hormone works as the anti-aging and athletic worlds believe it works, anyone who wants to feel those effects is tied to it forever, wielding a needle as often as six or seven days a week. While it's only a small needle nowadays, it's still *a needle*. Drug addicts use needles. As an adult on HGH, perhaps I'll look in the mirror and see past my new physique. I may see a fitness junkie, in more ways than one.

I pick up the phone in search of another opinion. I call Dr. Patil. I figure that if Wiley endorses growth hormone, than Patil will too, and maybe she'll convince me that HGH is worth trying. Being thorough, Patil will probably ask me to have some blood work done, although I'm not sure how much. Determining true adult growth hormone deficiency requires comprehensive and multiple tests that include provoking the pituitary gland to secrete measurable amounts of HGH. The incidence of adult-onset growth-hormone deficiency (GHD), as defined by the Endocrine Society (and via the discovery of pituitary gland tumors), is approximately ten cases per million individuals. The incidence of adult GHD as defined by some anti-aging doctors, however, is much higher. Patil might determine that I'm HGH deficient simply via the volume of my complaints about waning energy, reduced strength, and occasional depression. Then, I imagine, she could write me a prescription for HGH deficiency, which is the only way for me to acquire the drug without wading into the eerie black market.

Nobody answers Patil's office phone. I leave a message. Later she calls back.

"It's Dr. Patil. What's going on?" she says, not wasting time or oxygen on a fuzzy greeting. We haven't talked for weeks. I forget how businesslike she is.

"Susie suggested that I consider taking human growth hormone," I say, and then prepare to tell the doctor all the reasons why I think we should approach an HGH protocol cautiously. "I know that the anti-aging industry overwhelmingly thinks . . ."

"I won't prescribe that," she interrupts.

"Pardon me?" I say.

"I don't prescribe growth hormone," she replies.

I'm caught off guard. "Don't prescribe" wasn't in my script. I'm supposed to have a healthy debate with Dr. Patil—my doping doctor and gateway to growth hormone—whereby we review the pros and cons of adding another drug to my hormone-replacement protocol.

I give her some history. The HGH that nearly encroached on my childhood, and then Benjamin's. I tell her I'm willing to pay the exorbitant $400 per month costs for human growth hormone, at least long enough to experience the drug's effects. I say that I'm sensitive to the fact that many doctors have run into legal problems for prescribing HGH to patients who don't really need it. She should honestly assess my condition before pulling out her prescription pad. Patil, however, doesn't care what I say.

"Susie has some crazy ideas. I don't agree with all of them," she replies. "If you want to make GH, the better way is to get more sleep."

"And after I get more sleep?" I ask.

"The answer will very likely be no. Have you seen some of the anti-aging doctors who use that stuff? Their faces are misshapen. No way."

In the course of a brief phone call, Dr. Patil both rejects and reassures me. I lose a potential opportunity to try HGH, and instead gain the confidence that Patil is actually doing her job. She's looking out for my health. Supplemental human growth hormone is full of promise, potential, temptation, and many unknowns. The misshapenness of growth hormone users that she's referring to is a condition that mimics acromegaly, a medical syndrome that's caused by the body's overproduction of growth hormone and results in abnormal enlargement of someone's hands, feet, and face. When Patil's and my conversation ends and I hang up the phone, I'm grateful and relieved. Maybe my last thirty-plus years of narrow misses with human growth hormone are a sign. It's possible that a syringe full of HGH is never supposed to pierce my skin.

IN EARLY APRIL, I line up at the tenth annual Wards Ferry Road Race in the Sierra Nevada foothills of Sonora, California. Days earlier,

Coach Holmes told me over the phone that I shouldn't have any expectations for this race. He says that I should treat Wards Ferry as just another workout. I'm still building fitness, he assures me, and results right now are unimportant.

"Go hard, get used to the pace," he said. "Doesn't matter where you end up."

If Holmes only knew the half of my tempered expectations. He's probably right—I'm still building my fitness, if my power meter is telling me the truth. I'm only generating about 265 watts in my occasional threshold-type, highly intense workouts. The 265 figure isn't much of a performance bump over where I was six weeks ago. I'm also feeling like one big doping wimp. I'm on testosterone, but not human growth hormone, amphetamines, EPO, steroids, corticosteroids, cocaine, strychnine, or nitroglycerine. I'll probably finish last at Wards Ferry.

Bike races are curious in that, despite the dozens of miles you cover during the event, your world is very small. Sitting for two hours or more atop a rigid, lightweight piece of metal or carbon fiber, you sense when the pavement worsens, improves, tilts up or down, curves, and narrows. You know where others riders are, which is to say they're frequently within inches of you—while moving at speeds of anywhere from five to fifty miles per hour—as almost everyone vies to tuck in behind their competition and therefore stay out of the wind. You're also aware of the sweat running off your forehead and the need to drink from your water bottle, or eat some food that's stored in your jersey's back pocket or wedged under the elastic of your shorts. Sometimes you hear the whirr of everyone's bike chains. The scenery, however, never matters. In a bike race, you're usually too busy to enjoy the sights.

I spend the first twelve-mile lap of the four-lap race riding right behind Innis, who's elbow to elbow with the half-dozen leading riders. Both Michael and Luke had decided to skip the two-hour journey to Wards Ferry, and often Michael races in a different and more difficult category (and thus heat) than the rest of us anyway. Innis, Luke, and I have only been road racers for a few years, and in the opening miles of Wards Ferry, my inexperience shows. The course has a lot of short but steep climbs and descents, and plenty of curves too. I brake in turns when I should coast. Veer too abruptly in a pack of a dozen riders. Nearly cause a collision behind me when I slow down by standing up on my pedals. I'm still learning my way, although I don't admit that to anyone else with much more than a soft spoken apology. I want the other riders to feel like I belong with them, and halfway through the four-lap race, I'm tired but still right behind Innis. He's in the top ten. I suspect that the other twenty or so competitors in the race are directly behind me.

Halfway through the third lap, I focus on Innis's shaven legs, with those subtle clefts in the calf muscles. I know every cranny in those muscles, as I've ridden in the shadow of Innis, and what I've always felt is his superior riding ability, for hundreds of training miles. Those legs are my carrots and I am the bike-riding donkey, and I crest another hill, respond to another acceleration, and stick close through another set of turns. As we roll along, I finally notice another rider next to Innis in light blue and black shorts. A third rider, in front of Innis, wears a red, white, and black kit. Another wears blue and red. Innis is in white shoes, and light blue and white cycling shorts.

At the end of the lap, the course kicks up, steeply. I change into my easiest gear and quickly wipe the snot off my face. Then, for the first time in about thirty-six miles or so of racing, the pace noticeably slows. I pull alongside Innis, and even momentarily look over my shoulder. There are only two guys behind me. Nobody else is in sight.

"What happened?" I say to Innis, running my tongue over my front teeth. They're lumpy with the scum of dried spit.

"What do you mean?" he says, looking straight ahead.

"Where is everyone?" I ask.

"Gone," he says, emotionless. "Just us now."

I am transformed. My legs feel light. My back loosens. We have *broken away*, dropped the rest of the group far behind. Seven of us, alone!

We circle the course once more, and I ride with confidence. At one point the racer in red, white, and black accelerates in an attempt to pull away before being caught by the small group. The rider in blue and red makes a similar move.

They're not going anywhere without me.

When there are just a couple of short, steep uphills left to the finish line, my will finally cracks. I let Innis and four of the others go. When I cross the line in sixth place, I believe that I've ridden my best race ever. After I high-five Innis and catch my breath, I'm thoroughly convinced of something else, too. My lousy, clichéd, mundane, run-of-the-mill, ordinary supplemental testosterone had something to do with my performance.

really good times

"**O**kay, Athletics. Bring it in," I yell from near third base at one end of an East Bay schoolyard baseball diamond. Benjamin plays in the Little League of a town that neighbors Oakland, and I'm an assistant coach on his team, the A's. Head coach Tom Hallstein kneels over second base, angling it just so, while eight-year-old boys swirl around him, throwing Wiffle balls and diving on the artificial turf. It's a chilly and clear mid-April afternoon—the time of year when baseball begins. Today we have a ninety-minute practice.

"Let's all do some stretching," I announce loudly. The boys drag their feet toward me. I'm standing in jeans, sneakers, and my dark blue, league-issue baseball hat. "Everyone in a circle."

A dozen kids finally gather, and an imperfect circle forms. Three kids—Riley, Aidan, and a tall, quiet boy named Nick—create a bulge in the arc, and they don't follow my lead when I stretch my arms to the sides and start rotating slowly at my hips. Instead, they do little-boy stretching: They see who can knock off the others' baseball hats with their flailing arms.

"Hey Nick, bring down your arms, slow the rotation," I say. "Pretend that you're a sprinkler watering a lawn," I add, slowly twisting my own chest from side to side. "Not a Weed Eater gone berserk."

The advice backfires. All the boys laugh and decide that they want to be rampaging weed whackers. The circle's shape deteriorates further, to the point that it looks more like the jagged perimeter of a circular saw blade. The boys all start whacking each other's hats.

"Come on now, focus," I say a little louder, and then I bend over at the hips, legs spread, to stretch my hamstrings. "Do as I do."

Still nobody listens, but I don't get mad. Strangely enough, I don't feel the impatience or intolerance that I'd experienced back when Juliana, Sophie, Benjamin, and I were in his room when he first tried on his baseball uniform. Or the agitation I felt when Juliana persisted in asking me to stay home three months earlier, before I left the house to meet with Susie Wiley's user group in San Francisco.

I've largely been in good spirits ever since Wards Ferry, but I can't imagine that I owe my disposition solely to how well I performed. And while I can't attribute my happiness—or my edginess—solely to testosterone, the T, ironically enough, could be providing me with a lift, a path out of the darkness that is the aforementioned "Irritable Male Syndrome." The syndrome, argue some behaviorists, apparently makes men in their midlives about as unpleasant as a woman in the middle of a menopause storm. That's right: Men can be cantankerous and edgy because they're low on testosterone, too. Without enough T, men can experience weight gain, muscle loss, and a reduction in sexual appetite that can unmoor them, bringing on stress, irritability, and lower self-worth. Research even exists that T makes a guy happy: A 1996 study published in the *Journal of Clinical Endocrinology* and Metabolism concluded that the spirits of hypogonadal men (men with low levels of testosterone) rose when they embarked on testosterone supplementation programs. Over a sixty-day test period, the scientists discovered that the subjects experienced decreases in anger, irritability, and sadness, and increases in friendliness and well-being ("full of pep," says the study). The scientists also wrote, "the improvement in positive mood summary scores . . . were correlated with sexual motivation scores." I drilled down further, and found that test subjects on the T enjoyed boosts in sexual daydreams, anticipation, desire, and flirting, and though the scientists didn't take the reporting another step, I would bet money that these subjects got laid more often. I know that I am. And I am also, apparently, a full-on flip-flopping product of my hormone-filled existence—aggro one minute, placidly enjoying the smells of baseball-mitt leather the next.

As Coach Tom sets up the field for a catch-and-throw exercise disguised as a relay race, I continue to stretch and do some quick calisthenics with the boys. The movement feels good. The T, I believe, is giving me an overall sense of vitality. I wake up most days feeling horny, strong, and *ready*. Without coffee I feel caffeinated and excited for the day.

Pretty dang great.

Plus, about a month since I looked hard into the mirror and was disappointed by the reflection, the testosterone has delivered aesthetic benefits, too. With minimal but consistent and focused weight work, my shoulders appear bigger, and my shirts and pants fit funny—they're tight. My biceps have legitimate contour. Never had that before. Abe

Morgentaler, an associate clinical professor of urology at Harvard Medical School and author of the T-championing book, *Testosterone for Life*, cites a study where men on a testosterone program gained about 2.5 pounds, which he argues was likely due to increases in lean body mass. Morgentaler also cites another study where men using supplemental T enjoyed seventeen percent strength gains in performing leg presses while on the T alone. When those same men exercised *and* took the T, strength gains increased by twenty-seven percent. The latter was only one study, and small at that (forty-seven men). Results may vary, the saying goes. But personally? I like what I see.

After twenty minutes of more practice/goofing off (and my patience remaining intact), the Athletics move on to the next drill: base running. Tom instructs a few boys to take positions in the field, and the rest are to line up behind him at home plate and run on the swing of his bat. When it's discovered that we're short a shortstop, I run onto the field with my mitt. The boys are still young enough to be impressed by a dad's athletic abilities, even a dad like me, who played some outfield and plenty of bench-warmer in high school.

"I've got shortstop!" I call out.

Sure you do, Derek Jeter.

Tom directs the first ball to Liam, a kid with a bad haircut who's playing third base. The ball gets by him and then by Nick, who's playing left field. Aidan, meanwhile, circles the bases for a home run. Coach Tom hits a second ball and a third one, and more errors give way to more homers. Players throw down their gloves in frustration.

"It's okay!" I tell them, the benevolent role model. "Keep the ball in front of you!"

"Let's see if we can have some closer plays," says Tom. "I'll give a few to Coach Andrew."

I do my best to look the part: up on the balls of my feet, knees bent, mitt at the ready. I'm prepared to pounce.

"Here it comes!" shouts Tom. He hits a slow roller in front of me that I run toward and field cleanly. I make an easy toss to Tom's son Jimmy at first. Benjamin is out at first base by twenty feet.

Tom hits another grounder to me and I make another clean grab, and this time throw it harder to Jimmy. Nick is out by twenty feet too.

"You're not throwing me out, Uncle Andrew," says Alec, who lines up behind Coach Tom and waits for the swing of the bat. Alec is Tracy's son. I'm thrilled that I have the chance to coach both my son and my nephew.

Tom hits the ball in front of me and to my right, and it's a difficult play. But I field the ball cleanly and am overcome by my own vigor. My movements feel fluid. I'm as agile as a Cirque du Soleil performer.

A doper's loose on the Little League diamond! That's gotta be a new one . . . or maybe it's not. Who knows!

Alec races down the first-base line, his untied Nikes grabbing at the fake turf.

I throw the ball to Jimmy. It's a beautiful throw, on a line, should reach the boy around waist height, Alec will be out by fifteen feet. But Jimmy, I forget in my blissed out, look-what-Coach-Andrew-can-do moment, is only eight years old. He misjudges the ball, which sails past his glove and burrows into his upper arm. Jimmy goes down in a sobbing heap. Alec is safe at first, and beaming.

Tom and I both run to first base.

"Nice toss. Kinda hard," says Tom, who gently pulls Jimmy's hand off the area on his left bicep where the ball hit him. Tom also pulls back Jimmy's shirt. The spot where the ball hit his son is red.

"You think pro scouts are here watching you?" he adds.

"Hey Jimmy, forgive me," I say, kneeling down so that his eyes can meet mine. "You've been catching everything I throw. You've been playing like a big leaguer."

Jimmy ignores me. He looks back at his dad, and the tears plop off his round cheeks.

I turn to Tom, who's looking at Jimmy's arm.

"Sorry Coach," I say to Tom. "I got carried away. Really heaved it."

I'm contrite but also doing everything I can to suppress a grin. I'm not proud of hurting Jimmy. I just feel like such a stallion.

Tom helps Jimmy up. Jimmy walks away from first base and toward the boys' gear bags for a breather.

"Sorry," I say again. "I guess I wasn't myself."

"Well whoever you are," says Tom, "can you take it down a notch?"

"BACK BEFORE SEVEN," I tell Juliana on a Wednesday afternoon in late April, while the buckle on my helmet strap fastens with a distinct "click." I reach down to wriggle my feet into my cycling shoes. "Feel free to start dinner without me."

Juliana, who's sitting in the living room at our upright piano and right next to Benjamin, calls out a quick "Bye!" but doesn't look up. Neither does Benjamin, who's struggling, despite Juliana's guidance, to get the song "Little Playmates" right. Sophie doesn't even notice me leaving. She lies on her back on our brown living room couch, with her long, light brown hair fanned across a cushion. She's completely preoccupied with the presence and rare friendliness of our seventeen-year-old, often aloof cat, Lola. Lola, a Russian Blue, defines anti-aging. She has moved with us six times to three different states, and she has outlived two other pets. Even Lola doesn't look at me. She usually only does when she sees the painted pattern on the bottom of her food bowl, which means it's time for a refill. And you know what? In the era of Andrew and the T, I'm fine with being ignored. Nowadays I feel a palpable change in my behavior. I'm often happy doing exactly what I want to do.

I swear, the drugs give me a thicker skin. I don't mind perceiving myself as sensitive, but I'd like to think that I'm not in need of constant acknowledgement or praise. Aging men—and women—in our society are supposed to have convictions as stout as I-beams. Right? All the glossy magazine ads for retirement planning, Mercedes-Benz sedans, and posh resort trips depict people that are graying, calm, and assured. They know what they're after. Even my father, nervous Marshall, had to up and declare his homosexuality to his immigrant parents one day in the late 1970s (after Tracy outed him). My grandparents had wanted to fit into San Francisco's web of upper-middle-class Jews. They belonged to a synagogue, hung my grandfather's sales awards on their hallway wall, and were members of the Concordia-Argonaut Club, with its prodigious buffets and a dining room full of white tablecloths. I imagine that my dad told my grandparents he was gay while inside their perfectly kept, two-bedroom condominium in Marin County's calm town of Tiburon, and I could see my grandmother, her thick and silvery, perfectly coiffed hair, weeping into her pressed handkerchief. Dad had to live with his parents' tears, anger, and, for a while, their backs turned to him.

He hated the family dynamic that his homosexuality created, and his parents' lack of understanding. But reluctant as he was about his identity, my father did realize what mattered in his life, and he was true to himself, in a schizophrenic San Francisco era when society outside of the thriving gay community remained conservative and intolerant.

Crazy as it sounds, before taking testosterone, I'm not sure I could get behind my own needs even the way my dad ultimately stuck up for his. Standing in our home's entryway, on an uneven wood floor made slippery by my plastic- and carbon-fiber-soled, white Italian cycling shoes, I think about how only months or even weeks ago I wouldn't leave the house for a bike ride before receiving affirmations. I waited to hear Juliana say, "Have fun," or "Good for you," or simply "See you soon." I hoped that Benjamin would wave. At some level, I sought their endorsement for my crazy addiction to fitness. I wanted to know that they're all right with me hopping on a contraption, for hours at a time, that most adults haven't touched for decades. That I am okay being myself.

All of that insecurity over a bike ride. You were one delicate mo-fo.

I guess that's it—I am an insecure adult, and obviously not the stuff of a retirement planning ad (I've never been diligent about the IRAs, and while I have a sweet old BMW, I am insecure, too, about the showy hood ornament). Am I so afflicted because I don't have parents? Tracy and I buried both Mom and Dad before either of us turned forty, and while I hate to trot out the tired, those-kids-were-orphaned-too-early lines, my sister and I did lose more than parents. We lost affirmations, the oft-repeated, sometimes unarticulated messages that we are safe, and that our parents love us, are proud of us, and will get behind our decisions both small and large. I'm jealous of my friends who still have both a mom and a dad, even as those folks age and become more child-like in their needs. Those lucky friends still receive parental pats on the back. At least in my mind they do.

I also know—I mean, come on!—that nobody's life is straight out of one of those godforsaken retirement-planning ads. Marketing mirages! And yet, armed with such knowledge and cynicism, I must repeat to myself that retirement-planning-ad models are just acting, and that the other parents of children at Benjamin's and Sophie's school don't live lives of serenity, no matter how crisply their pants are pressed. They walk around with heads full of chatter, too.

My doubts and second-guesses have, for years, compelled my therapist to ask the question, "What do *you* need?" Specifically, she poses the question to me when a patch of conversation makes it clear to her that I'm insecure about my marriage. I tell her that as Juliana and I grow older we do less together. Once upon a time my wife and I went out or traveled as a tandem, or not at all. Movies, music, vacations—we moved through life like synchronized swimmers. No more. Our relationship has matured, and while we both intellectually understand this evolution, the changes—and our increasing separateness—sometimes sting. The marriage reeks of a loss of innocence, as I once remember it being less encumbered by issues around intimacy, and the conditioned behavior whereby a single word or gesture can sour exchanges between us for too too long.

Which is a strong reminder, lab rat, to hail the T and its anesthetizing effects. The blithe life of a doper!

I can still step outside my experiment, however, and see that, as Juliana and I grow older, we lean heavily on Benjamin and Sophie to be our common denominators. I continuously work to become a better writer and cyclist. Juliana enjoys girls' nights out, trips to see her family in Austin, long photo shoots, and playing in a parent band—my forty-two-year-old wife is a rocker, talented at both flute and keyboard, and a singer, too. Sometimes watching her onstage feels fine. Other times I have the sensation of being a face in the crowd.

"What do *you* need?" the therapist repeats. Then, she's occasionally continued, "There's only one person who can really make you happy in this world. You."

On this particular spring day, I am totally happy. I know what's necessary to satisfy myself, and in part it's the father's little helper that I wiped onto my thighs and back just this morning. I mean, part of me just hates admitting that there's authenticity coming from the words and assurances of an overbuilt icon like Sylvester Stallone—that there's actually truth and merit behind his cheesy online championing of anti-aging medicine. I want to remain cynical, and not admit that this kind of medical assistance is the way forward. But now I believe that the T has infused me with some of that Sly swagger.

Researchers have my back. They think that testosterone somehow triggers chemical reactions in the nervous system or organs that make someone, ahem, more assertive in their interpersonal relationships, and that the T actually encourages "dominant behavior." The concept makes sense: Scientists have already proven that when men feel compelled to be assertive, like following a divorce (they're hunting for a new mate) and before competition (they want to prevail), their testosterone levels naturally rise. Nobody has connected all the behavioral dots, but one way to fill in the gaps is the great intangible, the placebo effect, the mere suggestion that boosted testosterone—*The legendary male sex hormone! Every man's chemical oomph!*—might be enough to make a guy on the T feel better about himself.

"So much of testosterone is mental," Allan Mazur, a sociologist at New York's Syracuse University who has written extensively on testosterone and behavior, explained later over the phone. "There are correlational studies that associate the elated state in victory with rises in testosterone. Which cause which, we don't know. We just don't know all the effects."

Whatever is happening inside of me, I feel like testosterone helps elevate my sense of self. And I'm all for it, whether I'm dealing with an angry editor on the telephone or preparing, in front of my family, to take a sizable bike ride.

So while the kids and Juliana camp out in the living room, I turn to the other thing that makes me happy. I put on my wraparound sunglasses and strut, in my clumsy cycling shoes, out of my entryway and into my garage, knowing exactly what I need. It's not a kid, a wife, or a wave, but a two-wheeled, titanium-framed, 39-53-chainringed, Continental-tire-equipped bicycle. Without a second thought, I roll the bike out onto my suburban driveway, close the noisy garage door, and don't look back.

WEDNESDAYS ARE OFTEN the most rigorous training days of the week, and for many weeks I had despised them. I'd occasionally grumble to the ever-pleasant Holmes via email or the phone. His responses were always filled with encouragement. One day he wrote me, "Pretty tough workout. I only reserve it for people who can handle it!" Another day his email said, "It's clear that you are strong enough to win."

But Wednesdays are different now. Credit the training, and the T.

My coach is right, I have grown stronger, to the point that I now enjoy Wednesdays. They're opportunities to improve fitness that is beginning to snowball for reasons obvious and . . . less than obvious, at least to a coach that knows nothing about one of his client's drug-using antics. Proof of my progress exists in the reams of data generated by my super-fancy power meter. My FTP, or threshold number, has climbed from 265 to 286 watts, an increase that Holmes pinpoints via some calculations made around carefully measured workouts. Holmes's diagnostic rides might include a nineteen-step fitness-assessment session that features, in precisely spaced reps, twenty-seven minutes and fifty-four seconds' worth of all-out, drool-inducing effort. Holmes also mines my workout data to look at my highest power output for stretches of time ranging from five seconds to sixty minutes, and goes on and on about the differences between "average" power and "normalized power." (You ready? The latter provides a metric as if my pedaling effort had been applied smoothly and consistently, and is derived via an algorithm that accounts for variables including headwinds, tailwinds, uphills, downhills, and probably the direction in which the birds overhead fly.)

Holmes relays some of the more esoteric information to me, and while I love technology and pride myself on being able to talk the tech talk, the particulars available are, even to my geeky side, data overload. I'm happy knowing my threshold and one other relatively easily digestible number: my power-to-weight ratio. I understand that if I can keep my weight stable, or even lose a few of my 145 or so pounds, and I can increase my power, that my cycling performance will improve. Power-to-weight makes sense: Shoehorn an ever-bigger engine into a lighter car, and the car will go faster. My power-to-weight ratio stands at about 4.3 watts per kilogram (the bike-racing community universally calculates power to weight in kilograms). The number is high enough to characterize me as a well-trained amateur racer, though I am nothing more than a respectable recreational athlete. Tour de France competitors achieve power-to-weight ratios somewhere above 6 watts per kilogram. They are both ridiculously lean and insanely strong. Flush their drugs down the toilet and they're still the most freakish of physiological freaks.

I slowly ride away from my house and up the incline of our curvy street. I reach around with my right hand to the back pockets of my cycling jersey and probe for the printout of today's workout. I feel my way, tracing the edges of my cell phone and an energy bar in one pocket, house keys and arm warmers in another, and a spare inner tube in the third. Finally I feel the folded paper printout—it's still crisp—just to the outside of my inner tube. I grab it by pinching my fingers.

In his shorthand, here's what Holmes cooked up for me for today:

Bike 2:30: LT, Sub LT, bursts

- *20 minutes warm-up, then do 4 x 10 minutes at threshold— 275-285-ish watts, with 5 minutes recovery after each*

- *Then do 20 minutes easy and then do 20 minutes at sub-LT 250-265 watts, with 10 bursts to 310 watts for 10 seconds and back down to previous effort.*

- *Cruise for 30 minutes and cool down.*

The two-and-a-half hour workout could be worse. The "bursts," which push my body to seek out more oxygen when it's already working near its limit, could be woven into the more intense "LT" efforts

("LT," or "lactate threshold," is synonymous with "FTP") instead of the somewhat easier "sub-LT" efforts. By themselves, those ten bursts of power aren't so demanding. What's difficult is recovering from each burst while maintaining a high "baseline" effort. Essentially, Holmes wants my body to learn to "rest" or "recover" while I'm still riding pretty darned hard.

I ride easily through the Oakland hills to the treed and quiet intersection of Pinehurst and Redwood roads, which is close to my house and a good launch pad into a series of hills where I can ride each ten-minute interval. One of the ironies of being a bike racer is that you frequently cover little terrain during your rides. Instead you stake out choice stretches of pavement (minimal traffic, few potholes, relatively consistent grades, and no stoplights), and ride them over and over again.

The first interval sucks. My legs feel slow, and my breathing is labored. Neck is stiff. My chosen stretch of Redwood Road isn't a perfectly uniform grade, so my wattage numbers wander as my effort unavoidably changes: 269, 274, 112, 305, 209, 330. Wattage figures almost always bounce around.

But I don't stress. I'm confident that my body is in a closed T-loop: More stimulus means more strength, and more testosterone means more ability to recover, which means I can take on more training stimulus and become stronger still.

Bring on the work!

The second interval starts better, and my wattage numbers smooth out. I ascend past the fire station and densely treed Redwood Regional Park on my right, and parking lots and trails accessing Anthony Chabot Regional Park on my left. The occasional motorcycle speeds by, its whine disappearing as quickly as it comes on. Despite the intense pace, my legs burn only to a point. I fall into a meditative rhythm. The third interval goes better than the second. I climb out of the shade of Redwood Road and close in on Skyline Boulevard, getting whiffs of the hay that's stacked at the equestrian centers near where the roads intersect. When I turn right onto Skyline I'm cooled by breezes coming from the west, off the southern portion of the San Francisco Bay.

I am in the zone, one with my titanium steed!

During my high-effort glee, I remind myself to look up instead of down at the tiny screen mounted to my handlebar. A woman who used to cut my hair (even pre-T, I couldn't bring myself to call her a hair-dresser) once told me that her husband had a terrible cycling accident when he became preoccupied by watching the data on his computer. Sounds funny, unless it happens to you.

After completing my four ten-minute intervals at threshold, I double back down Redwood Road, make a left on Pinehurst, climb up one side of a hill, descend the other, and finish the hard part of the work-out, complete with the ten short bursts each above 300 watts, while ascending a steep and twisty stretch of Pinehurst. The route is popular with cyclists, and I pass a bunch without one rider coming around me. Time and time again, I stand up on the pedals and surge.

On your left! On your right! Doper coming through!

Even when you're riding hard, pass enough people and you feel little pain.

At the top of Pinehurst Road I'm close to home, and I decide to turn the coach's recommended, thirty-minute "cruise" into a ten-min-ute spin back to the house. I feel very strong, and I'm excited to see what the data on my computer says. I roll up the driveway, open the garage door, lean my bike up against a ladder in our garage, slide off my shoes and helmet, unplug my power meter, and gingerly remove it from its mounting bracket.

Inside, Juliana is cooking. I haven't missed dinner.

"Hi Daddy," says Sophie, who intercepts me at the top of the stairs. She's barefoot, with her toenails painted blue. "Did you have fun?"

"I did. Would you like to see what my bike ride looked like?"

"What do you mean?" she asks.

I lift her up.

"You're sweaty and stinky," she says, but Sophie still throws her arms around my neck.

I sit down in our office, with my daughter on my lap, and attach the bike computer to a laptop. Soon a window pops up, and a bar slowly fills as thousands of data points download from my bike computer. After a few more clicks, Sophie and I are looking at a graph filled with four jagged lines, colored red, blue, yellow, and green. Yellow is the most important—it's a measure of watts generated over time.

"What does it mean?" she asks, dragging her right pointer finger across the screen and making a big smudge.

I can easily isolate and analyze the intervals that I just rode.

"It means," I say with more mouse clicks, "Daddy's getting faster."

Over the first three LT intervals, my power—my normalized power, mind you—kept climbing. My first repeat: 278 watts. Second: 283 watts. Third: 291 watts. I tired in my fourth repeat, only maintaining 273 watts. But I finished strong, keeping the throttle around 265 watts while squirting in all of Holmes's prescribed bursts.

I try to explain, in the simplest terms, the numbers to Sophie. She keeps her back to me, and seems more interested in the pretty designs than the data. The other information on the graph includes my speed, heart rate, and RPMS, or how fast I pedal in revolutions per minute. Sophie traces all of the lines, and leaves fingerprints all over the screen.

"I don't understand, Daddy," she says.

Daddy doesn't understand it completely, either.

Where does the training benefit end and the doping benefit begin? Vice-versa? Scientists admit that there's a dearth of evidence arguing for or against testosterone's performance effect on the well-trained endurance athlete's body. The researchers can't ethically, and perhaps safely, load up a bunch of great riders' bodies on testosterone and let 'em rip for weeks or months on end. For the same reasons, science has little knowledge of how the T fully affects an athlete psychologically.

Meanwhile you feel like a warrior, from head to toe. For what that's worth.

I upload the workout file to a remote data server that Holmes will access. I think he'll be pleased with my progress.

"Dinner!" Juliana yells from the top of the stairs.

"I feel graaaate," I write to my coach in a quick email, reaching around Sophie to get at the keyboard. I erase the last word, spell it properly, and hit "Send."

ONE DAY AT THE END of April, Juliana distracts me. It's the rare weekday morning where we're both home while the kids are at school. We're downstairs in the office, and I have to reach over her desk to grab a box of paper CD sleeves. I stand on my tippy toes, clinch the box on the cabinet shelf with my fingers, and glance downward so as not to hit Juliana, who's editing images on-screen, as I push away from the cabinet and come down. There is the top of her head. There is the collar of her maroon V-neck shirt, which goes around her long neck and dips down her chest. There are the edges of her breasts. There is the tensioning of my cotton underwear, as if suddenly it's shrunk a size.

I say nothing. Instead I slowly put down the box of CD sleeves on a desktop beside Juliana and begin to lightly run my fingers through her hair. She says nothing, and at first doesn't acknowledge me or my hands. Then I begin to softly kiss her neck and use my hands to trace the lines of her triceps, which have been built up from years of yoga. Finally I lift her fingers off the keyboard and massage her hands.

I wait for her to pull away, for her to tell me she has to work.

Keep going. What's the worst thing that can happen?

Slowly but surely, my hands creep back up her arms and onto her shoulders. I reach my left hand down her chest, and underneath her shirt and bra.

Juliana is excited too.

I swivel her office chair so that my wife faces me, and I lower to my knees. I begin to un-tuck her shirt.

"Let's move to the couch," Juliana says quietly, even though there's no need to be quiet. It's just us in the house, and Lola the cat. My wife smiles softly, her left cheek dimpling. Her eyebrows form a straight, serene line across the base of her forehead. Juliana takes my left hand with her right and we move into the den and onto the faded yellow sectional couch where Juliana and I never sit, let alone lie, with her atop me. We make love in front of the physio ball, my indoor bike trainer, and the multi-DVD set of *Little House on the Prairie*, which we won months earlier at a white elephant party. It's possibly the least romantic room in the house. Which makes the spontaneity of the sex feel all the more exciting.

I am on the den couch, my wife naked on top of me, on a Thursday morning, while waiting for a sewer-line repairman to show up.

This is awesome.

There is more *awesome.* A couple weeks earlier on a Sunday, we're in bed and Juliana reaches over me to put the phone back in its cradle after speaking with a friend. The friend said that she was about five minutes away from our house and driving up the hill to drop off Sophie and Benjamin, who were coming home from a sleepover. I grab Juliana's smooth thigh. "A quickie," she suggests with a grin.

There is awesome one night when I reach for Juliana's butt while she tries to squeeze past me in our tiny bathroom right after I'd applied the T and was pulling up the boxers that I sleep in.

There's awesome every Saturday morning that's free of kid activities and the occasional, five-hour training rides that I take with a group of local cyclists. We tell the children to go wild and watch all the Saturday morning cartoons they want, and then I try not to hit Sophie's back as I close and lock our bedroom door on her way out.

"Did I tell you what my therapist said?" says Juliana one Saturday morning in early May while we lie in bed after being intimate. The kids are watching *SpongeBob SquarePants* downstairs.

"She said that we're both sexually interested. But we both want a predatory mate," she says, grabbing another pillow and propping herself up in order to sit up without exerting much effort. Juliana seems relaxed, satisfied, and happily lazy—I can tell by the way she's unrushed in her movements. She pulls the covers up to just beneath her shoulders.

"She thinks that we both want someone that will come after us," says my wife. "I think she's right. I think that's been the case for a long time."

I lie chest down on the mattress and fold my arms under my head. I face Juliana, my head in line with her hips. I project my voice upward so that she can hear me.

"I've got my animal instincts now," I say. "I'm always thinking about jumping you."

"The funny thing is, you're not the only one who's been more in the mood," says Juliana, crossing her arms. "I've wanted more sex too. Maybe your horniness is contagious. I feel less inhibited. And I feel closer to you."

"Maybe therapists should start prescribing steroids," I say with an abbreviated laugh. "I should've checked in with your gal about growth hormone. Does she hand out tester vials of EPO?"

Cut the joking. Don't ruin the moment. Don't screw with the momentum.

As long as Juliana and I have been together, she's sought out depth both in her life and in our relationship. Her yoga practice is spiritual as well as physical, and she's attended many meditation-style workshops and retreats and picked up all manner of relationship books. I've almost always sought out more linear answers, namely from the therapist that I've been in contact with for over a decade. When Juliana's and my relationship encounters turbulence, we historically retreat. She accuses me of over-intellectualizing my feelings and our relationship. I roll my eyes and think irrational things, like marriages aren't built on mantras, and then speak my irritated mind to my wife. Juliana feels judged and dismissed. I feel like she can be needy and unable to roll with my biting attitude.

The teenage girls couldn't roll—literally—with your make-waves waterbed humor, either. Too bad the T can't flat out cure your edginess.

We've discussed our clashes ad nauseam with our couples therapist.

"I want you to do this work with a pad and paper," our therapist has said many times during our Therapy Tuesday sessions.

"Juliana, tell yourself, 'How I'd like to act and feel when I feel needy is . . .'"

"Andrew, tell yourself, 'When Juliana feels needy, I want to feel . . .'"

When I'm not digging my fingernails into my palms, and I really try and be in the moment, I seek a deeper connection with my wife. I believe that she is wiser than me.

I want to feel open! Accepting!

"Sometimes I don't know when to turn off the sarcasm, Juliana," I say while we're still lying in bed. I slide my hand under her thigh. It's not the sweetest sign of affection, my knuckles digging into her hamstring. But I'm feeling lethargic. I just got laid. Not every moment surrounding sex, even on testosterone, is poignant.

She doesn't move away.

Lying there in bed, I give some credit to Susie Wiley and her hormone protocol, too, although sometimes it's as hard to get my logic-oriented sensibilities around the messages of Susie Wiley as it is around the teachings of some Zen roshi. Wiley's book, *Sex, Lies, and Menopause*, isn't easy to follow—frequently it's an amalgam of pop-culture references, clichés, and compelling and complex scientific theory about women's hormones tying into rhythms, the modernization of society, and outer space.

"While we are young, the ups and downs of estrogen and pro-gesterone month after month strike the beat that keeps us rocking and rolling with the stresses of life that could negatively affect our health," Wiley writes in the book. "When the cycling rhythm of 'on and off' ceases, we can no longer handle germs, fatigue, and hot or cold weather; maintain our body temperature; or control our appetites under stress. We are beginning to die. Sometimes death can happen in as little as three years, or it can as long as an agonizing twenty or thirty. When our hormones stop humming the tune of the Sun [sic] and the moon and start keeping the beat of an artificial environment, our internal systems—which have evolved over millennia to adapt for survival—are being driven by artificial signals. When this happens, what was the dance of life becomes a malignant pas de deux."

Wiley argues, of course, that women can continue rocking and rolling if they dramatically up the stores of female hormones (like estrogen and progesterone) to match the levels they had in their youth and follow her schedule of fluctuating dosages.

When I first met Dr. Patil back in January, she told me that, ideally, Juliana and I would both be on the Wiley Protocol so that our hormonal cycles would be perfectly synchronized. Wiley hasn't published a book about men and hormones (she says she's working on it), but she argues that men have rhythms, too. "Oysters know to feed at high tide, and human males know it's fall when the freshman girls appear on campus," she writes in *Sex, Lies, and Menopause*. Specifically, Wiley argues, men's hormones ebb and flow courtesy of external forces like light, food supply, and women. When women are at their most fertile, both monthly (around the time of ovulation) and seasonally (in the fall, which Wiley calls "mating season"), men should also be at their sexual peaks.

But Juliana's women's health doctor is opposed to Juliana going on the Wiley Protocol, with its radically high hormone dosages. Wiley, however, is unfazed by the fact that Juliana is on a different hormone replacement therapy program than her own. My guru is confident that my protocol will still work its sexual magic with Juliana. "You'll build to a crescendo on days sixteen to twenty, which should be right over her female ovulation," Wiley had told me in a separate conversation.

Indeed, our sex around the middle of the month—when my dosage over a one-week span exceeds 1,170 milligrams of testosterone, or over three times the amount of testosterone that a urologist might prescribe—is frequently super spicy. After Juliana and I get up from bed on that Saturday morning in early May, I look at a calendar. My next spike of exogenous T, I notice, happens to coincide with Mother's Day.

SEVERAL DAYS LATER I'm in my testosterone-cream-rubbing morning routine, sitting on the toilet with my pants down, leg wedged against the door of the tiny bathroom off our bedroom, dutifully wiping this morning's dose of 50 milligrams of T with my left hand onto my inner thighs, putting the thin residue remaining on my hand onto my scrotum (it's now habit, like rubbing a good-luck charm), when I look at the white and gray syringe that I'd just left perched on the bathroom sink. I grab it.

I've been wiping what I'm pretty sure is testosterone on my body for the last three-plus months, and yet all I know is that the testosterone and DHEA I'm taking come from some pharmacy in the central California town of San Luis Obispo. There's no iconic corporate logo on the syringes, or an emergency 1-800 hotline listed on the packaging.

This cream could be laced with arsenic or tin or who knows. I could start coughing up blood, or one of my testicles might swell to the size of a coconut. Or shrink until it's half the size of a frozen pea.

Remaining seated, pants and underwear hanging around my ankles, I sigh.

Calm down, bud. You're fine. So far, anyway.

Still, as I look at the syringe and the white cream packed inside of it, a valid concern sprouts among the many weeds of paranoia regularly shooting up inside my head during this year of doping: Am I getting, you know, good shit?

The answer, I discover, is multi-headed and controversial. Among the anti-aging community, established medicine, and the pharmaceuticals industry, the question has been posed for decades, although it has likely been posed more eloquently, and not specifically aimed at Wiley's testosterone brew (remember that I'm cutting edge; Susie Wiley's men's hormone replacement protocol has only been on the market for several months). And after many years of debate, the bickering parties still haven't come to a consensus.

In the 1980s, before American Academy of Anti-Aging Medicine founders Ron Klatz and Bob Goldman embraced HGH, a couple doctors out West, with an assist from some pharmacists, tinkered with the hormone blueprints they prescribed for menopausal women. Jonathan Wright (near Seattle) and John Lee (Northern California) worked with pharmacists to create "natural" hormone replacements that were unlike, say, the estrogen content in the drug Premarin, which (as I mentioned earlier) came from the harvested urine of pregnant mares. Wright and Lee both argued that "natural" hormones could be made structurally identical to women's endogenous hormones, and would therefore better perform inside human bodies, meshing perfectly with the chemical receptors the way "a key is for a lock," as Lee wrote in 2003. Lee called these hormones—created using molecules identical to those found in soybean and wild yam—"bioidenticals," and the name stuck. Many practitioners in the anti-aging industry, which often characterizes its medicine and drugs as alternatives to what is being offered by big pharmaceutical companies, ultimately rallied around bioidentical hormones, insisting that these chemicals are superior to "conventional" or "synthetic" hormones (since we're rolling up our sleeves here, bioidenticals are also technically "synthesized"). In 2002, when the Women's Health Initiative delivered bad health news about menopausal subjects taking synthetic hormone replacement therapy drugs Premarin and Prempro, faith in those drugs' recipes nosedived right along with their sales. To the hormone-seeking world, bioidenticals were in step with organic strawberries or free-range eggs: a supposedly healthier and more desirable option.

Some of anti-aging's influential voices, as you might imagine, are all too happy to weigh in on the subject.

"We now know that natural (bioidentical) hormone replacement therapy, when clinically indicated, can improve a person's physical and mental status to that of a person ten to twenty years younger . . ." writes anti-aging doctor Ron Rothenberg in *Forever Ageless*.

"Bioidentical hormones are . . . completely different than synthetic hormones," Suzanne Somers writes in *Ageless*.

"Natural substances are herbs, vitamins, minerals, water, and hormones that are derived from plants. Almost every drug that has ever been proven useful . . . came from a natural substance that would have done the job as well or better than the synthetic, altered form," Susie Wiley writes in *Sex, Lies, and Menopause*.

The testosterone that Patil prescribed for me, of course, is bioidentical, too.

The traditional medical community's response to bioidenticals: Pshaw! "Bioidentical," many hormone doctors say, is more marketing than substance.

"There is nothing different about bioidenticals. They are chemically identical to the test-tube drugs offered by traditional drug companies," Adrian Dobs, an oncology professor specializing in hormone disorders at Johns Hopkins University School of Medicine in Baltimore would later explain over the phone. "The body's receptors treat the bioidenticals exactly the same as the versions made by the pharmaceutical companies."

Establishment MDs are also quick to insist that no substantial, high quality body of research exists favoring bioidenticals over synthetics.

At this point in any debate between bioidenticals versus synthetic hormones, some members of the anti-aging industry refer to a dogeared script: Synthetic hormones, they say, are proven to cause harm (bioidenticals backers can recite the damage path left by the WHI from memory). The pharmaceuticals industry uses vast sums of money and PR power to consistently curry favor with the Food and Drug Administration, as well as physicians and medical experts. And conventionally trained doctors are often too busy and/or meek in their thinking to consider untraditional forms of medicine.

The pharmaceuticals industry responds that it does indeed manufacture some bioidentical-style hormone products, too. Most testosterone supplements—including two of the industry's most popular, Testim and AndroGel—are bioidenticals. Meanwhile plenty of doctors throw up their hands over the issue and simply see their anti-aging counterparts as interested in marketing as much as good medicine. I could sense the resentment in an email sent to me by a doctor friend who knew of my doping project: "There is a red flag when medical entrepreneurs believe they are at the cutting edge of science," he wrote, "and all of the academics are stuck in the mud, a confederacy of dunces."

The anti-aging industry thinks that it's the establishment, however, that needs to come to its senses, and stop chasing the dollars. Wiley and others rant about how the corporate pharmaceutical machinery keeps the anti-aging industry down by refusing to conduct thorough clinical studies with bioidentical hormones, which cannot be patented because of their molecular similarities to naturally occurring hormones. Bioidenticals' defenders also say that the drug companies simply—and irresponsibly—add an atom or group of atoms here or there to a bioidentical and then call the hormone their own. "A patent is where the money is," Wiley writes in her HRT book.

All sides in the bioidentical-versus-synthetic debate have compelling arguments, and chapters and entire books have been written on the wider issues (three examples: Jonathan Wright's *Stay Young & Sexy with Bio-Identical Hormone Replacement*, Arlene Weintraub's *Selling the Fountain of Youth*, and Marcia Angell's *The Truth About the Drug Companies*). The one conclusion that we can derive from the debate: No hormone replacement product wears the title of "best."

Which brings me back to my incredibly self-centered concern: Am I getting good shit?

WILEY'S PEOPLE STEER ME to the pharmacy where my testosterone cream is made, down in San Luis Obispo. I contact the pharmacy's owner, Dana Nelson, whom I'd met months earlier at the Wiley

Protocol booth in Las Vegas. He welcomes my call and invites me to visit his facility.

I make the four-hour drive into the hilly, relatively small college town of San Luis Obispo and pull into an old-time shopping center where clusters of one-story buildings stand in the middle of a giant parking lot. Near "Foothill Cyclery" and "SLO Kickboxing" is a sign for Nelson's Healthplus Pharmacy. A poster in one of the pharmacy windows says, "We are a Wiley Registered Pharmacy." Above the poster is a giant board that says "Flu Shots Here." Lettering on another pharmacy window says, "For You & Your Family."

Off to a good start. This place seems about as earnest as a barber shop in Mayberry.

I enter what feels like a serious pharmacy. There's no motor oil, cheap toys, or cylinders of Pringles on the shelves. Instead there are glass jars full of sprain-supporting wrapping tape of every width, and tubes with all manner of emollients. The pharmacy sells orthopedic shoes, a dozen different types of knee braces, "swab sticks," and surgical lubricant (whatever that is). I spot boxed walkers off to one side. An old couple waits at a big prescription counter for an order to be filled.

"My spiel is kind of simple," says fifty-nine-year-old Caty Asper, Nelson's articulate and forthcoming wife (the two are now divorced). She's offered to give me a tour of the brightly lit pharmacy until her husband gets off a phone call. "Dana and I bought this place twenty-two years ago. As the profit margins have narrowed, we diversified in order to survive."

At Healthplus, she explains, you can visit an acupuncturist or arrange for the fitting of a breast prosthetic. Or you can purchase your hormones.

Asper leads me into a scrubbed down lab area with all manner of cabinets, tall bottles, large plastic containers, and blenders with digital readouts that look like very sophisticated versions of milkshake mixers. A woman wearing gloves, a mask, and a hair cover carefully uses what looks like a caulking gun to begin pumping a white estrogen cream into a green Wiley Protocol syringe. Just before I'd walked into the lab area, the worker had mixed a powder form of the hormone with a cream base. Then she'd stirred, beaten, and whipped the blend until the powder was pulverized and the cream was quite smooth.

Dana Nelson walks into the area, shakes my hand firmly, and says hello. We chat about some shared experiences on the Wiley Protocol for Men, and watch as the worker carefully fills the syringe, a job that she'll repeat over six hundred times each day to keep up with the Wiley orders. Nelson watches closely. His bald head, beard, and rimless glasses help make the sixty-year-old man look wise and trustworthy.

I try to remain suspicious. Less than two years earlier, in February 2007, state and federal agents raided the Signature Compounding Pharmacy in Orlando, Florida. Though Signature purported to specialize in anti-aging products, authorities believed it was actually a multimillion-dollar supplier in a steroid trafficking operation involving physicians who wrote thousands of fake prescriptions for pro athletes. Signature's owners were ultimately acquitted, but other pharmacies were raided for similar reasons. The busts helped to place a harsh light on "compounding" pharmacies, or pharmacies like Nelson's where prescription medications are made on-site and tailored precisely to the needs of patients who seek dosage strengths, flavors, and/or blends that aren't offered by the pharmaceutical companies. Many in the anti-aging industry believe that the drug lobby known as Big Pharma wants these unregulated pharmacies shut down, because compounding pharmacies represent competition that plays by a different set of rules: Compounders, who are regulated by state laws, can sell drugs that aren't FDA approved. They can issue their house-brand medications (which are made with FDA approved ingredients) with unregulated warning labels. And perhaps some of Big Pharma's criticisms are well founded—I'd read of compounders that mixed their ingredients wrong, and had unsanitary lab areas.

"I'll play devil's advocate," I say, as Nelson and I walk out of the lab and into his office, which is filled with a miniature library of old and worn books with earnest titles like *The International Compendium of Practical Knowledge*. "Why should anybody have faith in you? Why should I trust you?"

"It wasn't too many decades ago that most drugs were made by compounders," he says, sitting down at his cluttered, computer-less desk. "The drug company reps used to talk with us about their meds. Now they only want to talk to the doctors who write the prescriptions." Nelson adds that tightening state regulations have forced all coumpounding pharmacies to clean up their acts. He asks if I want to meet his business's two staff nurses. Then with two hands Nelson grabs a green-and-purple binder that's hundreds of pages thick.

"Would it make you feel better to know that even if compounding pharmacies don't have universal standards, that Susie definitely does?" he asks, opening the binder and flipping through a few pages. He explains that Wiley sends the manual he's opened to all of the pharmacies that compound her hormone replacement therapies, and that participating Wiley Protocol pharmacists receive eight hours of training.

I look at one page and it reads like a basic cookbook: "Compounding directions for estradiol, 400 grams . . ."

"Everybody working with Wiley uses the same wholesalers, the same sources of drugs, the same methods, and we all send our samples in to be tested once a quarter to make sure that what we're making is within the ranges of potency," says Nelson. "They're all checked. Major manufacturing can't come back at us and say, well you don't know. We do know."

Nelson continues, explaining how in April 2007 Wiley testified on behalf of compounding pharmacies during a U.S. Senate Committee on Aging hearing titled "Bioidentical Hormones: Sound Science or Bad Medicine?" Wiley left dozens and dozens of pages in the congressional record that explain her protocol and its systematized production, and how only compounding pharmacies can deliver the dosage forms and strengths that she believes her clients need.

"So I'm really using the amount of testosterone you claim I'm using?" I ask.

"Yes," says Nelson, interlocking his fingers, sitting straight in his chair, and looking very professorial.

"It's a brand," he says.

"Well, it's not a brand brand," I say.

"It's a brand," Nelson says. "The Wiley Protocol is exactly what it says it is."

Soon he stands up to walk me out of his pharmacy, and with the sun still high in the sky I begin the long drive north toward home on Highway 101. I have lots of time to think about the testosterone I'm using.

You could go back to the urologist and ask him to put you on AndroGel, but why do that? What you're on is working. It's a hoot! Seems legit. You're not growing a second nose.

Five hours later, road weary, I pull into our driveway well after dark, and before I lock the car I grab the empty Subway sandwich bag that had carried my unspectacular veggie-sandwich dinner.

Juliana and the kids are asleep, which is exactly what I want to be. I drag myself into the bathroom, brush my teeth, and then dutifully grab a Wiley Protocol syringe half-full of the T from the zipped-up toiletry bag stowed in the cabinet under the bathroom sink. I push down my pants and underwear, sit on the toilet, and turn the syringe over in my fingers. Right next to my feet on the bathroom floor is the crumpled Subway bag.

Okay, so the Wiley Protocol is not McHormones, or the Subway of testosterone therapies. Maybe it's better. Maybe Wiley's testosterone is gourmet fare from a local restaurant. It's the hormone replacement therapy that would be in a Michelin Guide, if the Michelin Guide rated hormone therapies instead of food.

I'm tired.

Keep rubbing.

I apply the testosterone and go to bed.

"BERKELEY HILLS IS on Mother's Day," I say to Luke over the phone on a Sunday afternoon. I'm at home and in the kitchen, Juliana is paging through an Annie Leibovitz photo book on our bed, and the kids are in the living room, hosting playdates. They're all busy shooting pictures of each other's elbows, eyebrows, and nostrils with my iPhone.

Luke is one of my cycling mates who, unlike Michael, lives near me in the San Francisco East Bay. The Berkeley Hills Road Race, which is in a week, is in both of our backyards. He's considering racing at Berkeley Hills, or even just spectating. I've had the event on my calendar for months, and have been eager for the day to come. Or should I say, I was looking forward to it.

"Yes, Andrew," says Luke in his deep, slightly honking voice. Just hearing that voice makes me smile. He sounds funny. "It's always on Mother's Day," he adds.

"Why on earth do these race organizers pick that day?" I say. "Do they not have mothers? Do the male racers not have wives?"

"Sure they have moms and wives," says Luke. "But these are bike racers. Workouts versus wives. Chain-lubing before children. Racing first, the world a distant second."

"Those priorities don't work in my house," I say. "Will you race it?" I ask.

"One way or another," says Luke, "I'll be there. Sounds like you're ready. Air in the tires? Kit clean? Shall I bring you some raisins?"

Good old funny Luke. I hate Luke. Well, I don't hate Luke. I like Luke a lot. How can you dismiss a guy who shows up for a wedding, straight-faced, in a black skirt? That's what tall, lanky, eccentric Luke did, several years ago—a society wedding no less, which is where I was first introduced to him and his idiosyncrasies. He wanted to become a bike racer, and we started riding together and with Innis, who manages several climbing gyms in the Bay Area. We've all spent dozens of hours together on or around our bikes, laughing, panting, fixing flat tires, complaining about leg cramps or sore backs, and planning our next rides. Both Luke and Innis are fine company, but whereas Innis is a salt-of-the-earth type, a fairly mellow Oklahoman who talks with an endearing twang, quirky Luke does everything his own, frequently amusing way. For instance, the guy could live on mac and cheese. He often wears these full-fingered, red gloves when we ride (they're really ugly). Luke is a stay-at-home-dad with a baby son (his very nice wife has the corporate job) yet he usually manages to get in his miles. Actually, he is dead serious about getting in those training miles. He's irritatingly impatient and stubborn as well, but he has such a deadpan delivery that you can't stay mad at him. Also, like seemingly every other bike racer I know who's married, he enjoys a ridiculously long leash to train and race. That last point, that perceived freedom, any-way—that's the part about Luke that grates. I never see him sweat the bike-vs.-everything-else-in-life conflicts that wear on me.

"So I'll see you at the race?" Luke says.

"I think so," I say with a sigh.

I walk down the hall to our bedroom. I need to bring up the Mother's Day/bike race conflict ASAP. Waiting won't help. Juliana enjoys surprises, including lilies or generous helpings of fresh cilantro in her tacos. But bike races?

I walk slowly.

"Will you just stay in bed with me and for once not nurture the damn bike?" Juliana had said to me a month earlier, in couple's ther-apy, with tears in her eyes.

Her request had come so sweetly, I couldn't offer much more than an apology and real compassion. Even though the T had me feeling jumpy, I think I stayed off the bike for three straight days. If Juliana had gone to the typical race widow's refrain—"Why don't you just sleep with the fucking thing?"—I could've dug in my heels and kept on riding. I wouldn't have missed any of Holmes's prescribed workouts.

Sometimes conflict comes in handy.

I am so mature.

I reach the bedroom door, turn the corner and look at Juliana, who's sitting, legs slightly crossed, on the bed. She shuts the photo book and leans back easily onto the pillows. There's not an ounce of tension in her body. I don't know how she does it. I always feel tension.

"I love the shot in here of Annie Leibovitz's mom," she says, running her hand over the hard cover. "She was able to have her mother be so in the moment."

And I'm here to seek a hall pass. On Mother's Day, no less. Plus I'll be completely preoccupied the night before, when I spend hours cleaning my bike and packing and repacking every last thing for the race.

Juliana is wearing her thick-framed, cat-eye prescription glasses. She didn't need corrective eyewear for the first thirteen years that we were together, and then age crept into her eye sockets. I'm still unused to seeing her in glasses, but I've liked them on her from the start. Michael and I both have had fantasies about the clichéd tiger-in-a-librarian's-skin types ever since we were boys. Right now Juliana looks like a hot librarian.

I sit down next to her and fold my hands in my lap.

"What?" she says, looking at me with a suspecting grin. "What's the matter?" The corners of her mouth rise only about a millimeter each.

"Nothing's the matter," I say.

"Something's up," she says. "Tell me."

Ask for what you want.

"I wondered if we could celebrate Mother's Day next Sunday in the afternoon instead of the morning," I say. "And if you could skip yoga on Sunday morning too."

Whoa. Mother's Day on your own terms! Shooting for the moon!

"Why?" she says, her voice even.

I've been at this crossroads in a conversation with Juliana so many times. Bike rides, bike races, ski trips, working on deadline. I've tried apologies. I've negotiated trades—the nice dinner out or promise to plan a weekend away. I've become defensive, the cyclist's old "could be worse" approach: "You're lucky you're not married to so-and-so, he lives on his bike."

Ask!

"I want to race the Berkeley Hills Road Race. It's so close, it's like my home course. But some bonehead scheduled it for Sunday morning," I say.

Stay calm. Hearing "no" won't cause you internal bleeding.

Juliana looks at me with a broader smile. She looks down at the book. She looks back at me.

"That's fine," she says. "This is important to you, isn't it? Go enjoy yourself. We'll celebrate Mother's Day when you come home. Just be *here* when you come back," she says. "Present."

I nod.

I don't know if the T gave me courage, or if I actually am mature. Okay. *Maturing.*

I HAVE A ROUSING GOAL for the Berkeley Hills Road Race: Disrupt the entire dang competition. At a key moment, bolt into the lead, and therefore into the helmeted heads of all my fellow racers. If I do it right, and my training and chemicals serve me the way I hope they will, I could actually win the race. I've never done that.

Let alone done it as a cheater.

"Nothing better than being active in the mix," Holmes tells me via email. "Animate the race. Try to make it your own." Holmes has also been sending me emails wondering why I don't stay in better touch with him, and he gave me grief because I didn't ride with him when he'd hosted a four-day training camp for some of his clients only a forty-five-minute drive from where I live, in the hills of Marin County.

Just keep cashing my checks, analyzing my power data, and sending the workouts, coachie. I don't want to be your pal.

Too few athletes in my non-elite, amateur category of competition follow Holmes's advice to be aggressive. The way road races for inexperienced, older farts work is often like this: Start the competition together, ride behind someone else (to stay out of the wind) but close to the front of a giant clump of riders, and hope that everyone around you tires quicker than you—or figure that some of them will crash and pull out of the race. (It's best to stay near the front of a big pack to better avoid the occasional metal- and bone-bending crashes that occur when thirty to seventy-five competitors, many of them skittish and sometimes out of breath or distracted while drinking from their bottles or choking down energy food or wiping the sweat out of their stinging eyes or futzing with their glasses, headbands, jerseys, gloves, shorts, or shoes, ride in ridiculously close quarters.)

But the attrition strategy is A) boring and B) not suited to my particular physiological gifts, or lack thereof. Even if I'm part of a small pack of competitors remaining near the front until the final stretches of a race, I am a lousy sprinter. My smallish muscles weren't designed for sprints, and I haven't performed the drills—who has the time?—that would help me generate high numbers of watts, even for short stretches. Racers with lots of power, who have a strong final kick, can leave me behind in the final hundreds of yards to a finish line. Such was my fate at Wards Ferry.

Less than two hours before the race begins, I review my lead-taking strategy in my mind while performing one of bike-racing's silliest looking pre-race rituals. Along with dozens of other racers, I heat my muscles and generate considerable sweat while riding nowhere in a shadowed and chilly parking lot, which is located in an unpopulated area between the East Bay's rolling foothills near San Pablo Reservoir, and is also close to the start line of the race. Warming up on a portable "trainer," a device with a small, turning drum that provides resistance and keeps your bike's rear wheel off the ground, is convenient because you can prepare your body for the hard effort to come (sometimes the minute the race begins) without having to navigate traffic or other riders. But as I spin on my pedals and look at all the other athletes doing the same— there's a guy in green and gold kit on my right, two women wearing blue and white directly in front of me, and an angry looking dude to my left whose bike is turned toward mine, and he's staring right through me— I can't help but think how selfish bike racing can be.

We should harness all the energy generated right now in this parking lot to light up some low-income neighborhood of Oakland for a month. Or harness it to, I don't know, cure cancer. Why am I not in bed right now, looking at my wife and kids instead of looking at Mr. Game Face on my left? It's Mother's Day!

Which reminds me: I haven't seen Innis or Luke, and both said they would be here today. Where are those guys? The thought that they're still in bed with their wives makes me feel worse still.

Luckily my thoughts soon drift to training and doping. And not the guilty thoughts. To my thinking, my workouts and testosterone have combined to turn me into an intensity-loving machine. My body now craves Holmes's heaviest workouts, because I can, with some ease, both handle them and recover from them. Whether my strength is coming from Tilin Theory or science no longer matters. My legs feel like they have tons of snap. Testosterone is my anti-tiring drug. The race, I believe, will be fun.

IT IS NOT. The slow-moving amoeba that is our group of fifty-five competitors stretches and contracts over a rural and open, nineteen-mile loop that features three significant hills, which are named after the Three Bears. The first hill, Mama Bear, can't be a mile long, and the road is straight. The second hill is Baby Bear, and it's actually a pair of short climbs. The third hill is Papa Bear, and is approximately as long as Mama Bear. The second of three times that my group of racers ascends the Bears, I feel so inexplicably weak and vulnerable near the top of Papa Bear that I fall to the tail of the peloton, and nearly give up. My quadriceps feel very heavy. I notice that my breathing is labored, and my headband is already so saturated with sweat that salty fluid is irritating my eyes. My legs don't want to push the pedals around with any semblance of speed. The few people standing on the side of the rural road don't cheer me on.

"If you threw a penny at him, he'd be out of the race," Dutch writer Tim Krabbé wrote of a suffering fellow bike racer in his bike-racing classic, *The Rider*.

The backside of Papa Bear, however, is a long descent, and I earn a reprieve, and for some inexplicable reason suddenly feel much better.

What switch was just thrown? I wish a little "juiced" light came with my syringes, and illuminated when the drugs kicked in.

When we climb a short hill that officially marks the beginning of the third lap, I am near the front and feel strong. Again nobody cheers for me, but I can imagine the clapping.

Come on T! Come on Tilin!

Early into the almost full and final lap, a racer in black kit blasts away from the somewhat smaller amoeba.

"Don't let him get away," mutters a bearded rider right in front of me. His white and gold jersey is stuck to his big shoulders with sweat. I don't know the guy. I don't know anyone in my race. Innis and Luke are apparently at home with their wives and children.

In the split second I have to decide whether or not to join the racer in black, to put a huge amount of energy into riding fast until I catch him and then hope that the two of us can hold off the trailing peloton for an entire lap, I let the rider go. He's gambling that nobody will respond or speed up until it's too late, and he'll be able to hold off a furious-finishing group of riders behind him all the way to the end.

I tried such a tactic only weeks earlier in a race in the hills of Livermore at the Wente Vineyards Classic Road Race, and I was caught well before the competition ended. I had no strength left as we neared the finish.

I watch the rider in black pull further away. We all do. Nobody says anything but the pace steadily quickens as we pass the eucalyptus trees on San Pablo Dam Road, bisect the hillside homes on Castro Ranch Road, and roll out along the grassy stretches of Alhambra Valley Road. When we reach the last of the relatively flat stretches of Bear Creek Road before Mama Bear, there must be at least thirty-five people left in our group. As we climb the first third of Mama Bear, I feel a wave of strength and urgency wash over me. I begin to accelerate past a rainbow of team jerseys and shiny bicycles. When I reach the front I keep going. Halfway up, I pass the rider in black who had taken off earlier. He's moving very slowly. His strategy backfired. I don't look over my shoulder. Pangs of guilt about doping come and quickly go. Right now I'm busy.

From hormone to muscle, you're made for this moment. You are the un-tired machine.

I continue to accelerate and feel no pain. The sweat in my eyes doesn't bother me. I look down and watch my legs, smoothly shaven and sticking out of my blue shorts, churn.

Those are engine parts! You're in the lead! You're following nobody's Lycra ass!

One hundred feet from the top of Mama Bear, I look over my right shoulder. Twenty guys in single file, strung out down the hill, trail me.

I'm making them suffer!

I ease up at the top of Mama Bear, only long enough for the first ten racers to catch me. Then, hoping to demoralize them, I immediately accelerate again.

I lose five of them on the first spike of Baby Bear.

I drop four on the second.

"We're clear! We're alone!" a voice yells behind me. I glance back and see one rider in red and yellow. Nobody else.

"Take that, you motherfuckers," I say in a low voice at the grade's crest. "There's more."

We descend the backside of Baby Bear, and what I thought would be an opportunity to recover before my last, glorious climb up Papa

Bear is no such luxury. The descent isn't steep. My legs are weak, I am coasting. Fellow racers, pedaling furiously, begin to pass me.

I see jerseys of orange, green, black, white, blue, yellow, gold. I try to make a run at the leaders up Papa Bear, but halfway up I am pooped and give in. My pedals barely move as I cross the line.

I finish in seventeenth place, and I'm still happy. I made the race my own. I imagined victory, if only for a few wonderful minutes. I raced agressively, like a pro. As I roll down to my car, I believe that my mistake was largely one of tactics. I forgive Luke and Innis for no-showing. I forgive myself for doping. At least for now.

"Seventeenth," I say to Michael over the phone from the driver's seat of my car, headed home and to celebrate Mother's Day with Juliana, Benjamin, Sophie, and some friends in San Francisco at a dim sum restaurant.

Michael had raced the week before and decided to skip Berkeley Hills.

"In the lead just before reaching Papa Bear," I say. "Big thrill."

"Not bad, LeMond!" he congratulates me. "I guess you can't say that you lost because everyone else is on drugs."

I chuckle. He's funny.

"I'll tell you this," I say to him. "Come race day, the T is one hell of a recreational drug. Today was this old-man athlete's acid trip."

"Hey. I have a theory about those guys who finished ahead of you," Mike says. "Maybe they're better dopers than you," he laughs.

NEARLY TWO GREAT weeks go by. Holmes and I review the data from Berkeley Hills and he's impressed. In a thirteen-minute stretch near the end of the race, I average a glorious 323 watts. In that same time period, I log two-and-a-half minutes at 344 watts. Thirty seconds at 488 watts and twenty-five seconds at 553 watts. I was un-tired, over and over and over.

Meanwhile, Sophie prepares to "graduate" from first grade, Benjamin from third. Juliana and I plan the summer—as a family we'll travel to Austin to see her relatives. I'll compete in a huge, three-day stage race with Michael in Bend, Oregon. Between these trips, Juliana and I will both squeeze in our work. We're also getting along great. Emotionally and sexually, we're in a rhythm.

The testosterone, meanwhile, has been all upside. The sex. The cycling. The disposition. I mean, who are the fools among us? Those with the syringes, or those without? I'm discovering that it's harder to find fault with the steroids and easier to forget that I'm being dishonest. I'm not losing any sleep over playing the equivalent of blackjack with my long-term health. I'm having fun.

My cell phone rings while I'm at my desk. It's Juliana—her picture, smiling and with a knit scarf around her neck, appears on the little screen. I push away my computer keyboard and answer her call.

"Hey sweetie, how are you?" I say.

"I'm not sure," she says in a subdued voice. "I'm pregnant."

one big doping family

My doping odyssey is officially our doping odyssey. Not yet sure how many the "our" represents.

"Juliana. Sounded like you said you're *pregnant*. Bad phone connection, right? Can you hear me now?"

She doesn't laugh.

That's because this isn't funny.

"Yes, you heard that right," Juliana replies, slowly and matter-of-factly.

". . ." I say.

She does the same. Nothing.

I am forty-two years old and my girl and I just made the care-less teenager mistake. I didn't even make that mistake as a careless teenager.

"How . . ." I finally mustered.

"I don't know. Maybe one of those quickies," she says.

"I thought we were always okay, that this couldn't happen. We only had unprotected sex when you were sure this couldn't happen," I say. I push a pile of notes about some triathlete that I'm profiling to the side of my desk, and rest my left elbow on the bare space, and then put my head in my hand. I don't often get headaches, but I feel one coming on.

"Obviously we got it wrong. I don't know. Maybe there was a hole in a condom," she says.

Condoms—and timing—have been our form of birth control for the majority of our relationship. Juliana never liked the idea of living with an intrauterine device, or IUD, inside of her. As for the "Pill," it's a sore subject. Juliana stopped taking the Pill early in our relationship. She cited two reasons. For one, she thought it was bad for her (Wiley agrees, and dedicates much of a chapter of *Sex, Lies, and Menopause* to what she's sure are the Pill's many potential threats to one's health, including breast cancer and blood clots). Juliana also gave up the Pill because, in her mind, we weren't having enough sex for her to bother with it. She didn't confess this latter reason to me for years, because she thought I'd be hurt. She was right. I was. Nothing like your partner giving up on one of modern society's most convenient forms of birth control (says, ahem, the man) to put an exclamation mark on your relationship's lack of sexual zest and potency.

Then we find the T, and look what happens.

"Did you call your gynecologist?" I say that evening, walking into our bedroom from the garage. I'd left work early. I thought that this was a night to be home early.

"I didn't. Why would I call her so quickly?" she says.

"To discuss ending the pregnancy," I say, trying to suppress my irritation. I walk out of the bedroom to hang my jacket in our weird hallway coat closet, the one that's waist-high and requires a gymnast's agility to hook a hanger on the pole.

I walk back into our bedroom toward Juliana, who is opening the lid of the hamper in our hallway.

"I'm not sure ending the pregnancy is what I want to do," she says.

WHERE MY HEAD IS at this moment: Demanding but poorly compensated writing career. Unwieldy mortgage. Eroding inheritance. Ripening marriage. Cycling. Wife with part-time work. Two fabulous kids, although Benjamin came packaged with that turbulent entrance into this world, what with colic and the erroneous failure-to-thrive label hung on his diminutive shoulders. Cycling. Middle age.

Put into this same baby-debating position, some guys would say that all other issues pale compared to a successful conception, and that this microscopic life is an unparalleled gift, the largesse of the galaxies, a fistful of winning lottery tickets rolled into human form. I can appreciate the perspective. The births of Benjamin and Sophie were unbelievable. I remember holding dark-haired, peaceful Sophie in my arms on a late spring morning in 2002, soon after Juliana delivered her, the New Mexican sun angling through the window of our room in St. Vincent Hospital in such a way that it grazed the right arm she held over her head. *We made you! Little perfect fleshy you!* Sophie still sometimes sleeps with that right arm held just so, a slight bend in the elbow, the connecting shoulder relaxed. Way cool.

But I don't want another baby.

Where Juliana's head is at this moment: family, life, and youth.

"Another child could be good for all of us," she says, picking up Benjamin's dirty socks, which are right next to the hamper instead of inside it.

"A baby might bring the family closer," she adds, deciding after putting Benjamin's socks in the hamper to take all the clothes out of the hamper. I swear, parents lose more ability to think linearly with every passing day. "Besides," says Juliana, "I feel good when I'm pregnant. I feel young. I feel, well, *life.*"

I look at my wife unloading clothes out of the wicker hamper as if she were bailing water out of a badly leaking boat. The chores never end. But she seems lifted at the thought of being pregnant, her cheeks dimpling and generous lower lip pulling happily taut. She is a sweet and special person. Even after all our years together, the juggling of two children, and our relationship struggles and many moves, Juliana still looks happy and fresh-faced. I've called her "My Fresh-Faced Girl" ever since we started dating in Boulder nearly twenty years ago.

You're about to make that fresh face very sad.

"Juliana . . . I'm not sure having another baby will be a change for the better," I say, making piles of laundry in our narrow hallway. Whites. Colors. Special-care exercise clothing. Our smelly and stained recent history, recorded on cotton, nylon, and elastic, stretches out in front of us.

"Can you consider having another child?" she says, a soft and patient plea. "Just for a minute?"

I take a deep breath.

"We already juggle so much," I continue. "I don't think . . ."

"It's my body," she interrupts, albeit in a soft-toned voice. "I get a say."

"Absolutely," I respond. "Shouldn't we both make the decision? We'll both be raising another child."

"I'm the one who will bring it to life. Maybe my body is giving us a sign," she says, and then straightens, as the hamper is finally empty. Juliana looks right at me. Her eyes are wide open and seem as fragile as crystal

"A sign of what?"

"Youth. I'm still young enough to have a baby," she says.

"Oh," I say, transferring a black sock that had landed in the exercise-clothing pile to where it belongs, with the other colors. "I never thought of it exactly like that."

Take a moment with this one, bud. This is a big deal, Mr. Without a Uterus.

"Youth comes in different forms, Andrew," she says. "You're kind of reliving your youth. Sometimes what you're experiencing is great for me, and sometimes it's not, and I'm okay with it. But now we're talking about my youth, and my life."

I want to push the pile of whites out of the way and come toward Juliana. I'm uninterested in making love—of the many sexual fantasies that have come to me while on the T, none have involved doing it atop stinky socks, spotted T-shirts, and dusty baseball pants. I only want to be close to my wife. This moment *is* about hormones, and the T definitely played a role in us being in this situation. But the debate over Juliana's pregnancy has nothing to do with hormone-replacement therapy. It is about the window of opportunity that a woman has in her life to do specifically what her body alone can do, and how that window, as the days shoot by and we increasingly can't think through which way to throw our dirty socks, feels fleeting. For

Juliana, pregnancy means she isn't old. Her body is still firing on a lot of cylinders.

I let go of my resistance, if even for just minutes. I kick Benjamin's boxers out of the way, ditto Sophie's lacy white socks. I put my arms around Juliana and listen to her cry.

TWO DAYS LATER, Randy Ice calls me. He's the physical therapist I'd contacted almost a year earlier, the one who had first exposed me to the anti-aging industry. Ice is yet another person who's about to make my doping experience about more people than just me, myself, and I.

"Did you ever follow up on your research about hormones and the anti-aging industry?" he asks.

"I'm on a testosterone-replacement-therapy program," I tell him. "It's a trip."

"How do you feel?" he asks, his deep voice and happy tone immediately familiar to me. "Rejuvenated?"

"Randy, it's potent," I say. "Sometimes I feel like a world-beater. Other days the sensations are, frankly, almost overwhelming. I'm not sure how healthy it is to think that I can practically walk through concrete walls. Or win every argument that I have with my wife."

Ice tells me that he's unfamiliar with Wiley's dose-fluctuating protocol, and that I might want to talk to my physician about how much testosterone I use.

"I'm calling because I finally have names for you," says Ice. "Patients of our clinic on hormone-replacement therapies who have consented to talk to you."

I sit up straight in my office chair. *Other dopers next door!*

"That is fantastic, Randy," I say, busily opening a new Word document on my screen. "I really appreciate you circling back around."

"Three have already consented, and I'm waiting to hear from a couple more," he says. "Two of them are cops."

Policemen! Holy crap!

"One of the officers was a walking disaster when he came in," adds Ice. "He'll be a great testimonial."

I'd read in a recent issue of *Sports Illustrated* about policemen and prison guards, as well as private security forces charged with keeping U.S. officials safe in Iraq, all being accused of taking steroids. Sure enough, several years later and late in 2010, Newark, New Jersey's *Star-Ledger* newspaper would uncover evidence of nearly 250 police and firefighters who were taking HGH and steroids. Drawing lines between emergency services workers and their ilk with performance-enhancing drugs isn't hard to imagine: Jobs involving force and intimidation might be filled with men who will go to some effort to further puff up their chests (and their biceps, and their deltoids, and their . . .). But the idea that these men carry guns and are employed to guard the public, or to keep the peace? I wouldn't have wanted someone handing me a BB gun when Juliana and I butted heads that early spring day over Benjamin's baseball uniform. I still don't know why I'd become so undone, and I highly doubt I would've pulled a trigger. But what if the T makes a lot of people edgy, and some of them are often physically threatened? And carry weapons? And have permission to drive vehicles through city streets at breakneck speeds?

Ice and I hang up, and I soon leave messages with the three most compelling people on the six-person list: the two cops and a fifty-nine-year-old real estate agent from Southern California. I wasn't so interested in the others—a much older gentleman, a weight lifter, and a woman.

I don't hear back from anyone before more good fortune comes my way. An email pops onto my screen from a doctor associated with professional cycling who had originally introduced me to Joe Papp.

"I may have an unusual source of information for you," she wrote. "I have a friend who is a former European pro rider and now a cop in Florida. He says he noticed that some of the local riders ride a lot faster these days."

Other dopers next door who race their bikes! Pregnancies, citizen dopers, cycling dopers. Fireworks wherever I turn.

I quickly email back the cycling doctor and she makes an electronic introduction. I write the officer and another few days pass. No responses. No fireworks.

"One week and no response from any of these guys—dopers, Deep Throats, cops, nobody," I say to Michael one late afternoon while I barely push the pedals as I ride my bike up Old Tunnel Road. It's a curvy, cambered street between Berkeley and Oakland with a gentle but fairly consistent grade, relatively few homes, and therefore not a ton of traffic. Old Tunnel is a favorite among cyclists, and I've spent the last several months riding past plenty of them. But on this Tuesday I'm taking it easy—coach's orders ("Ride like Grandma," Holmes likes to tell me). I'm in midseason form and could use the rest. Plus in five days I'll race up San Jose's Mt. Hamilton. I'm keeping my watts around 150, chitchatting on my mobile phone, and doing something competitive cyclists seldom do: take in the scenery.

"You know how beautiful the views are up here on Tunnel?" I say to Michael, who's in his apartment, prepping for his training ride.

"South Bay, East Bay, City. One of the best vantage points in the Bay Area."

"Nice not breathing hard for once, huh?" says Michael.

"Every time I ride it, Old Tunnel gets easier," I say.

"It's called *training*," says Mike.

"Training, resting, eating right, and aiming the syringes just so," I say. "I can't wait to talk to these other guys about their experiences."

Mike doesn't respond.

"Hello?" I say.

What's up with Mike?

"How many times are you going to bring up these mystery steroid users?" he finally says. "You think people are going to talk? There's shame, weirdness, sadness, and all these societal taboos around these drugs. You're not exactly blurting out to the world that you take these substances."

"I don't want to blow my cover," I say, nearly riding into a pothole. "Why are you upset?"

"Come on. You're not telling *anyone* for a reason," he says. "It's not like dads at Sophie and Benjamin's school will turn you over to the U.S. Anti-Doping Agency. It'll get even stranger if you get a cop on the line. Will you out yourself to him?"

"I'm not breaking laws. Cycling's rules, yes," I say reaching the top of Tunnel Road and a stretch of really tall eucalyptus trees. They give off a menthol-like smell that takes me back. Mike and I have run and ridden by such trees since we were boys.

"Keep your secret and you'll essentially be lying to a cop. That's not natural," says Michael. "You think that the doping is a weird experience for you. Tell you what. It's kind of a weird experience for me."

"How?"

"I don't exactly know," he says. "It's not the secret. That's easy to keep. Maybe something about how you and I relate to cycling anymore. You seem to see it differently now. Less the sport we participate in and more like a . . . a big experiment."

"I still love to ride," I say, almost dropping the phone as I sandwich it between my neck and cheek so that I can free my right hand to shift into an easier gear. "Now more than ever."

For all that love, you're riding like some sort of oblivious jerk. Get off the phone.

"I see that you're having fun," says Mike. "But it feels to me like you believe you're in some game. Not just in the activity. Look, I have to go. Time for my ride. But we'll talk more."

I'm happy to hang up, only in part because the road ahead is about to slope downward. My best friend has given me plenty to consider.

I understand Mike's points. Sometimes the cycling, with all of my newfound power, seems very much like an out of body experience. As the lab rat, I often like to observe what I'm doing on the bike, and reflect more along the lines of *isn't that interesting?* as opposed to *what a blast!* I'll wonder aloud to Juliana if the amount of T that I'm using directly impacts my cycling abilities (jury is out). I'll ask Mike what he thinks about the strange mental games and moral justification that a doping cyclist likely engages in when he wins a race. What's it like to stand atop the podium knowing that you're a fraud, and will I have a chance to find out? Yes, I talk about winning—the outlandish thought of winning!—like it's the logical next step in a science project instead of a fabulous moment in the life of a recreational athlete. All this doper-cogitating means that, sadly, I'm now usually in my head on the bike, too. For so long cycling had been one of the few elements in my life that I didn't overthink. No more.

I sense something else is up with Mike, too, related to his irritation with me eagerly seeking out other dopers. I've been on the testosterone long enough that the T supplementation is part of my everyday life, and I think that the fading boundaries between me and the drugs has alienated him. Michael is behind the writing project. But Mike is the kind of guy who still chafes at the news every time another top cyclist gets busted for doping. He's still, somehow, amazed at their nerve, at their disrespect for the sport. I, on the other hand, have gone from convinced that the entire pro peloton is juiced to thinking that whoever isn't doing it is, quite frankly, missing out on—if nothing else—a wild ride. The two increasingly diverging perspectives have inserted a gap between Mike and me. Without him telling me, I'll venture to guess what he's occasionally thinking: Is Andrew one of us? Or is he one of *them*?

Stuck in doping's no man's land.

The answer is that I'm not sure.

ON A WEDNESDAY MORNING in late May, I receive a surprise call from a Florida area code. It's the cop—thirty-year-old Jimmy Anderson, who's the friend of the cycling doc who had contacted me. Anderson, who's also a very talented road racer, is willing to be interviewed. The guy knows a ton about narcotics—he's worked a lot of drug busts. I'm a doper. As I stumble over my words, Anderson unknowingly helps me take steps to figuring out where I belong in the riding community.

"So you believe that, like, you ride with, um, regular folks. Who take drugs?" I say to Anderson. "They're taking them to be faster riders?"

You're not Charles Manson. Just talk.

"I occasionally ride with middle-aged guys who, maybe a year ago, rode mountain bikes, and beach cruisers not long before that," he says. "They've come into the sport after all the doping scandals have happened. They know a lot about the drugs and ride harder than some of the fastest guys I know. For stretches, I swear they ride as fast as the pros.

"At first you think, wow, so-and-so came a long way in the off-season," he adds, with a little sarcastic chuckle. "But then you start hearing the whispers. About performance-enhancing drugs and 'roid rage."

I wonder if anyone is whispering about me. Or if I've whispered, and too loudly!

Anderson once rode as a pro in Europe, but he was told to take drugs in order to win. He was disgusted.

"The riders I raced against used heroin and cocaine to get themselves revved up, so that they could feel their hearts pumping," he says. "That's not an urban myth."

Once Anderson gave up on his aspirations as a pro racer, he ultimately went in the other direction. He not only played by the rules, he enforced them. He's a seasoned cop and now rides at the highest levels of amateur racing.

Our conversation continues, and I try to tease more out of the policeman, explaining my project in very vague terms. I'm researching a book about citizen dopers, I say, and I'm interested in all aspects of their lives: racing, relationships, their bodies' reactions to the drugs, and so on.

Are they like me? Am I like them? Tell me tell me tell me.

But of course I feel like I better be cagey.

"So why don't you go after these . . . troublemakers?" I ask.
"Maybe you could bust some dealers."

Do these guys get their drugs from the doctors or off the street?

"I'm looking for the more abused stuff," he says. "My unit tracks people trafficking the pharma-type drugs. Pain killers, depressants, anti-depressants. We're not looking at the people taking these particular types of steroids or drugs. Besides, they know that I'm in law enforcement. They're careful to ask me questions instead of offer me statements."

Dopers next door are nothings. They're small potatoes.

"So you just let these dudes ride on drugs right underneath your nose?" I ask.

"Everything in their world is contingent on them winning group-ride sprints," he says. "Who cares about those rides? They aren't even races. They're chasing nothing."

Dopers next door are pathetic.

"Plus they're dangerous out there," adds Anderson. "They're fast, but they're riding well above their skill level. The other day during a sprint some of the riders were forced to swerve into oncoming traffic. There have been crashes."

Riders who cause crashes quickly earn notorious reputations. They're idiots. Dopers next door are losers.

"They're monsters," Anderson says.

Dopers next door are monsters.

I ask him for names of some of the riders. I tell him that I'm curious to find out if the dopers feel any particular happiness or remorse. If they believe that they're alienating others in the sport. But at this juncture in the conversation, Anderson loses interest. He's a cop all day, and he's not too enthusiastic about playing detective for me on his bike rides.

Soon I thank Anderson for his time, and wish him luck in avoiding ballistic, over-fueled cyclists. We hang up.

Am I such a public nuisance—the equivalent of a child with a lot of matches, a teenager with a powerful car and a learner's permit? The dopers sometimes buzzing around Anderson sound like overgrown boys of the worst possible kind: stronger than they know, older than they realize, and more aggressive than smart.

Is this the guy I see in the mirror? That Michael has begun to see in me?

Before I can become too self-loathing, or seriously consider doing something cathartic but rash (like outing myself to Holmes), my phone rings again. It's one of Randy Ice's clients: The older, doping, Southern California real estate agent by the name of Ford Lewis. At first, Lewis seems like a ray of anti-aging light on my doping-in-sport darkness, a hormone-therapy booster whose life and perspective is far from the heavy and sad world of cheating athletes. He's a regular guy who also happens to use exogenous testosterone, and he's wonderfully un-self-conscious about taking the T, too. Then I find out that there are more chemicals to Lewis's story—many more. And I wonder if I'm actually communicating with the Ghost of Doping Future.

"It was about two years ago, I was smoking, and I had the big pot belly, when I changed my whole trip," says Lewis. "I altered my diet and started to exercise, and found a doctor who introduced me to HGH and testosterone. I went for it."

Lewis subsequently became the clichéd, anti-aging "after" picture. He tells me that in about six months' time he lost twenty pounds of fat and gained nothing but muscle. His energy level changed. He landed the beautiful girl.

"I hooked up with this little lady. She'd been a fitness instructor for many years," he says. "Then I put her on the growth hormone. In three months she gained fifteen percent lean body mass. She's sixty-one and has a body of a thirty-year-old." Lewis and his wife, he tells me, are at the gym five days a week, at 4:30 AM.

Lewis felt so good on his new drug and life regimen that he asked himself: Why stop at T and HGH? He's injected Sustanon (a chemically altered, commercial form of testosterone designed to provide an amped boost to the muscles), "ozone" (alternative medicine argues that the three-oxygen-molecule gas, which is also found high in the atmosphere, somehow improves the circulation of oxygen inside the body), and erythropoietin, too. EPO, as I've said, is a key hormone in the regulation of red-blood cell production, and synthetic versions help some people battle anemia and others (like elite endurance athletes, eager to load up on oxygen-carrying red blood cells) to improve their athletic performance. Lewis didn't fit either demographic, but he tried EPO anyway.

"Made me feel tired and down," he says. "Terrible, really. But if you want the name and number of my contact, I'll give it to you," he adds. "He's in Mexico, pretty sharp. Transfer money to his bank account and he'll send it to you. Everything works out fine and dandy."

"Why don't you just stick with the T and growth hormone?" I ask. "They seem to be working."

"Oh, they are," says Lewis. "But my whole premise is aggressive maintenance therapy. Yes, I feel great. I want to keep feeling wonderful."

Until you spontaneously combust, anyway.

I mention the notion that Lewis's unproven protocols could make him feel vibrant and vital in the short run only to accelerate the timetable where he'll suffer from some drug-induced illness that could make him quite sick.

Lewis scoffs.

"You know, I won't just try drugs on a whim," he insists.

I decide to drop the subject. Lewis is like many anti-agers in that he doesn't obsess over the idea of living forever. Rather he's interested in a very high quality of life for as long as possible. Lewis finds the logic in this approach, and in taking experimental substances, to be unassailable. He suggests that I consider taking additional substances with my T ("N1-T" and "Tongkat Ali" for releasing my "free testosterone"; Anastrozole to keep a cap on my estrogen levels), applauds me for having taken such an active role in boosting my hormones at a relatively early age, and thanks me for talking to him and fighting the anti-aging fight.

"We need people like you to get the truth out," says Lewis. "Imagine preventative medical clinics on street corners where you could get your blood work analyzed cheaply. If we could do just a little bit we could keep ourselves real healthy. We have to try and stay healthy."

I don't have issue with Lewis. He's a very friendly man. I commend him for his conversion from softy to health nut. But via using a steady stream of HGH? Sampling Mexican EPO? I'm not in lockstep with his approach to vitality. I'm not interested in risking my health, even with the chance of feeling better, with drugs du jour. At least not yet.

A couple days go by, and the steroid-taking cops don't call me back. But I feel like I've already learned plenty about my fellow dopers. I won't cast stones. I won't trade in my old friends, either.

On the Friday after speaking to Lewis, I call Mike. I haven't heard from him for a while. I worry that perhaps he wants to keep his distance.

"I've been kind of busy. Coming up on finals. What's going on?"

I'm just happy to hear my friend's voice.

"Nothing," I say. "Just called to say hi."

THEY LOOK LIKE ASPIRIN. Three white, chalky-looking pills, and next to them a small, orange, plastic cup of water. Sitting atop a delicate, silvery medical tray on wheels, the assemblage could model for a painting—art of the pharmaceutical era, a framed work that wouldn't be out of place in the gynecologist's examination room where I stand near Juliana, who is propping herself up on an examination bench, her legs and feet resting between the stirrups used by patients during gynecological examinations. The painting could be called *Steroid Life*: The pills are mifepristone, a controversial, synthetic steroid that is designed to terminate early pregnancies.

"Oh, boy" sighs Juliana, making crinkling sounds as she shifts her weight on the exam table, courtesy of one of those standard-issue white paper robes that she was issued when we'd first walked into the room. "My poor body."

Juliana stares right through the gynecologist, who is a young, thin, sympathetic woman and mother of two small children. She is not Juliana's regular doctor, who isn't available today. But even as strangers, my wife and the physician share a sensibility in this moment that is alien to me. The doctor knows about the creation of a life. She's experienced the way that a woman's body unfolds and expands during pregnancy, not like a burden or a storm cloud—but a flower, or the universe. My wife and this doctor, the two of them can celebrate the power and mourn the tempering of a woman's body like I cannot, and I say nothing as they discuss loss. I feel like an extension of Juliana's paper robe—cold, indelicate, and even abrasive, when what she needs is warmth, security, and comfort.

Initially after discovering what had occurred, we attempted to discuss and debate the issue in healthy fashion. She'd had an abortion twenty-five years earlier, before we'd met, and it had been a miserable experience. All of that violation—the surgery on her body, ending of a life, and the turbulent entrance into the first stages of adulthood. I'd assured Juliana that if we were to end the pregnancy, this time the experience would be as different as possible. I would be next to her and a constant presence. I told her I loved her.

Still Juliana and I had difficulty reaching détente. I knew what I thought was the right thing to do, but Juliana wasn't so sure. She vacillated between keeping the baby and ending the pregnancy. For days, Juliana had regularly fallen into reveries—while cooking a pot of pasta, or making the bed, or laying on her back on our small stone patio and absorbing the friendly, tempered heat of the Northern California sun. Sometimes she barely noticed me, and her dreaminess made me feel powerless to help her, to help us.

Couples therapy didn't do much. Again we were told to pull out a pad and pen. "If I hang onto my resentment, then . . ." I wrote as our therapist slowly sounded out the words. "If I let go of my resentment then . . ."

If I let go of my resentment then I'll be shopping for diapers.

I am a jerk, yes. And yes, this is how I feel.

The pregnancy touches on one of our core constitutional differences: Juliana likes to consider what's possible. I like to consider what's probable. Juliana equals optimist. Andrew equals realist. Or maybe equals cynic. Somewhere between the two.

Early in our relationship, the contrasts fortified our bond. It was Juliana who proposed that we travel through Southeast Asia, before children, but after we'd both spent many of our younger years working in the publishing industry. At first I resisted—I was launching my career, we'd bought our first house, and Southeast Asia seemed almost clichéd. Kathmandu, the Himalayas, India, *trekking. Outside* magazine, where I had been an editor, had already featured stories on those types of trips and destinations for years. By now, weren't there paved roads to the top of Mt. Everest?

But in 1996, only days into our five-month journey through Asia, I boarded a bus with my young wife. It was the slowest, creakiest, most overfilled bus I'd ever seen, and it would supposedly take us from Kathmandu to the sparse foothills village of Jiri, where we'd start our trek into the Everest region. I'd carefully packed the overstuffed backpacks—I was responsible for many of the journey's prophylactic details, the first-aid kits, water purification equipment, and Gore-Tex jackets—which sat on our laps, as they would for the entire ten-hour drive because, despite our purchasing plenty of seat room, we were hemmed in by the pushy locals. There were Juliana and I, alongside creased- and greasy-faced old men, chickens and goats, huge wicker baskets, and musty, old wool blankets. We were squeezed together to the point of nearly being one. We smelled Third World rawness—the bus exhaust, animal feces, and body odor. But nothing about that moment felt clichéd. I remember looking at Juliana, her hair pulled into a ponytail, her skin smooth and not yet layered with Himalayan grime and dirt that we wouldn't thoroughly wash off ourselves for months. She looked ahead and wore a big grin. I was so grateful for her curiosity.

The gynecologist points to the three pills.

"Do you feel at all rushed into the decision?" she asks. "The biggest regret you might have is not having thought it through."

"I've thought it through," Juliana says. And she had. She'd taken the time she needed, and finally arrived at a choice. A third child would've been daunting, she'd finally told me one night. She felt as though she finally had her life back after raising Ben and Sophie, and how fortunate we already were to have two healthy and happy children. In some ways the family felt complete. It's rhythms were established. She was ready to make this decision. When she told me, we held each other. I tried to think clearly. *Did I push too hard for this choice? Will we regret this loss of a potential life?* I only know there is no right call, and that I was relieved to have a decision made, and so much more relieved that in the end we both chose the same thing.

The gynecologist stands next to Juliana in such a way that I can't see Juliana's face as she reclines on the examination table. She sits up.

"Andrew," she says, extending her arm, beckoning me to approach and hold her hand. I step around the doctor and grip Juliana's hand. I smile a humble smile. Juliana does the same.

Mifepristone is an "antiprogestin": It will stop cells from producing or using the hormone progesterone. Progesterone is essential to a successful pregnancy, properly preparing the lining of the uterus for an embryo, fortifying the body's pelvic walls, and maintaining placenta function among its duties. Mifepristone is FDA approved but has endured decades of controversy. Following its development by a French pharmaceutical manufacturer in 1980 (and designated

"RU-486"), Mifepristone was approved for use in France eight years later only to be stopped in its tracks by antiabortion groups. Two days after distribution ceased, however, the French government ordered the drug's maker to resume putting Mifepristone in the hands of women wanting it, arguing that the drug was, essentially, a relatively safe and non-intrusive way to terminate a pregnancy. But Mifepristone, which has been available in the United States since late 2000, has never been a simple, foolproof, or completely effective drug for terminating pregnancy. Bacterial infections that might have been linked to Mifepristone killed a small number of its users in the drug's first years on the market. And the second part of the treatment—Juliana will likely have to return in forty-eight hours to take an oral "prostaglandin" to facilitate expelling the contents of her uterus—can cause the kinds of abdominal pains, bleeding, and contractions that many women associate with a miscarriage. Outspoken pro-lifers accused the FDA of approving Mifepristone without thoroughly vetting the drug.

And my wife, after taking a couple of deep breaths, is about to swallow the stuff. Unhappy moment.

"Whoops," says Juliana, dropping one of the pills, which falls to the ground. I lean over to pick it up and then hand it back to her.

She barely looks at the pill.

Steroids giveth, and taketh too? No, the T didn't make me do it. Testosterone didn't impregnate Juliana. Andrew did. Yet I still can't believe that we would be here, in this sterile exam room, if those syringes never came into my life.

Juliana slides the pills into her mouth and chases them down with the water.

ON A LATE JUNE DAY, I drive to Dr. Patil's dark brown, hobbit-home of a medical office. I'm about halfway through my yearlong experiment, and feel like I'm familiar with the doping routine and a lot of its sensations. Slather on the T and DHEA in the morning, slather on the T again at night, feel edgier toward the middle of my monthly cycle when the daily dosages reach their peak, feel horny and strong a lot of the time. Ahead of my appointment with Patil, I visited a lab for some blood work, and I'm sure the checkup will address my results— my testosterone levels, what's going on with my prostate, and so on. But one of Patil's first questions surprises me.

"How's your family?" she asks.

Strange question. Dr. Patil has never drummed up frivolous conversation before. Dressed in black slacks and an expensive looking red blouse, she looks as I remember her: surprisingly corporate.

Fine. How's your family, Ice Queen?

"They're okay," I say. "It's summer. I'm traveling to a bike race in Oregon for a few days with a friend. Then Juliana and the kids head to Austin in late July to visit my in-laws, and I'll fly down to meet them for the tail end of their trip."

"How's their health?" says Dr. Patil. "What's going on with your wife?"

"Have I told you about the pregnancy?" I ask. Time around that episode, only a few weeks prior, was blurry.

Patil shakes her head, and I give her the quick synopsis, including Juliana taking the Mifepristone. Juliana and I were anxious for the two days following her taking the medication. She experienced modest cramping and some bleeding, and went through a stack of DVD movies at home while I kept the kids busy and sent them off for play dates.

Juliana was sad and angry: about us, the pregnancy, and putting her body through such a brutal procedure. Two days later, an ultrasound revealed that her uterus was still lined and could support a pregnancy. The gynecologist gave Juliana two more pills to induce contractions and basically flush out her uterus. We went home and waited for a gush that never came, and wondered if Juliana subsequently needed a traditional, surgical abortion to make sure she wasn't pregnant. The poor thing. We'd tried to avoid such a procedure in the first place by opting for a termination by way of Mifepristone. Ultimately Juliana did not require the surgery. The episode, however, weighed on our relationship.

"I'm very sorry," says Patil, crossing a leg. "Up to the pregnancy, was Juliana responding well to you being on the testosterone?"

"It's been a mixed bag," I say. "A lot of urgent passion, which is fun in kind of a reckless way. The sex between us frequently feels new and carnal, that is when Juliana is in the mood. But sometimes her hormones misfire, and she's completely uninterested. Often I'm okay with that. Sometimes her rejections create tension. Then there's that edge that seems to follow me around."

"Her fluctuations could be wreaking havoc on your ecosystem," says Patil. "When the women flat-line, the men start feeling crazy. Have you talked to her about going on the Wiley Protocol? Did she read Susie's book?"

I told her that I'd made my suggestions. Juliana wasn't interested. Patil nods.

"Let's review what's happening with you," she says, and looks at her clipboard. Patil scans the results of my recent blood work and moves close enough to me that I can see the results, too. There are a lot of numbers.

My "total testosterone," measured in nanograms per deciliter (ng/dL), was 414. It had been 290 back in January.

"Improved," says Patil.

But there was also a figure for "free testosterone," which was 79.3 picograms per milliliter (pg/mL), which Patil explains is "still on the lower end." She also comments on other numbers for bioavailable testosterone, albumin, PSA, SHBG, DHT, and LH too.

"Wiley thinks you might want to add a couple more lines per dose of testosterone in the summertime," says Patil. "Juliana might like that."

Unlike a half year ago, I largely keep up with Patil as she runs through the other figures. I've done some homework.

Total testosterone is the most widely used metric for measuring one's testosterone levels. It's not, however, the most telling figure, because the vast majority of testosterone circulating through a man's body is bound to "carrier proteins" (like sex-hormone binding globulin, or SHBG, and albumin), some of which cling so tightly that the testosterone they've paired with isn't available to trigger responses in other cells, like in muscles or the brain. Lower SHBG counts, for instance, mean more testosterone is "free" to couple with other cells. I'm happy to say, my SHBG levels had gone down in the last half-year, which contributed to the rise of my free testosterone, which endocrinologists and hormone-minded physicians consider the truest measure of a man's testosterone levels. (Wiley, for what's it's worth, would later explain, "How much testosterone is free depends on your emotional and perceptual response to your observable universe," which is her way of saying that stress and the related cortisol hormone greatly influence free T levels).

Unfortunately, free testosterone can and is measured in multiple and inconsistent ways. Doctors and scientists have been frustrated enough by the inaccuracies of quantifying a person's T that, in 2010, the esteemed, ninety-two-year-old Endocrine Society gathered representatives from science, industry, and government in order to commit all parties to the more accurate measuring of testosterone in the human body.

Until the methodologies are all sorted out, doctors often go by total testosterone.

"Wiley wants you shooting for approximately 600-plus total testosterone," adds Patil. We're in the same exam room where we'd met for my previous visit. Reaching that number, she says, would put me in the middle of my test's "reference range" for what's considered a normal level of testosterone in a grown man (among concerned scientists, this is another touchy subject—the ranges are somewhat arbitrary).

Dr. Patil and I run through some other figures.

My PSA, or prostate-specific antigen, is 1.4 nanograms per milliliter, which is fine. PSA is a chemical created by prostate tissue, but also prostate cancer. My measure is sufficiently low.

My DHT score (dihydrotestosterone) is high—155 ng/dL, or twice as high as the upper limit in the reference range suggested by the lab that calculated my blood work. DHT causes male pattern baldness—yo, I can't act on *every* physiological shortcoming—and, some believe, stimulates prostate growth.

I'm too young to have a swollen gland make me pee every hour. Let alone prostate cancer.

"I'll get back to you on that one," says Patil.

My LH, or lutenizing hormone, which is a product of the brain's pituitary gland and stimulates the production of testosterone in the testicles, is way down.

"All this supplemental testosterone? Your testicles have gone on vacation," says Patil with a rare smile.

"I'm wondering if my balls are shrinking," I say, running my hands through what little hair I have left on my head.

Testicular shrinkage can happen to dopers who regularly dose up on the T, although Wiley insists that she's addressed the issue. Two days of the month I apply no testosterone whatsoever.

"Are you really noticing shrinkage?" asks Patil. "Let's stay stable with your dose. Let's not raise it if there's a threat of atrophy."

"I guess I haven't noticed them getting smaller. I definitely haven't . . . measured any reduction. Maybe all these side effects are in my head. Like the anger—I'm also wondering if the testosterone is making me angry," I add.

"I've had other patients in the early stages of hormone-replacement therapies who are also very sensitive," Patil says, standing up and straightening the wrinkles in her pant legs. Apparently the checkup is over. "They notice every little fluctuation or perceived change." We agree that, for the time being, I'll carry on.

I stand up and stretch, reflexively pulling my mobile phone out of my left front pants pocket, looking to see if I missed any calls, and then putting it into my right pants pocket.

Patil notices.

"Don't carry that near your testicles. Electricity and radiation," she says, with a dismissive shake of her head. "Think about those things."

So friendly, this one.

Patil gets back to business. "In regards to the hormones, is every-thing okay with your kids?"

More unexpected family questions.

"How do you mean?" I ask. "They don't know I'm taking testos-terone. I didn't think I could get them to understand my using it."

"I told you the first time we met. Be really cautious about getting the testosterone cream on others," she says, turning her loafer-covered right foot ninety degrees.

Apparently this is a lecture.

"Put on the T two hours before intimacy. Sponge off the areas where you applied the cream before having any intimacy," she says. "Make sure not to get it on the children. I've had female patients get high levels of testosterone because their husbands were on it."

"I'm trying my best," I say, zipping my phone into a pocket on my backpack. "But I confess, our house is hectic. It's not easy to follow every rule of hormone therapy as perfectly as I'd like. Sometimes my son grabs my shower towel, no matter how hard I try to keep it separate. Or I get tired and fall asleep in his bed, and I'm only wearing my boxers. I don't think I'm exposing him, but I'm not absolutely sure."

"You have to be disciplined," says Patil, standing straight. "This is about your family's well-being, too. Think about those things."

I nod.

Yeah, yeah. Think about those things.

A HUGE ROAD TRIP with Michael, long ago scheduled to commence only days after my visit with Dr. Patil, was just the escape I craved from my hormone-soaked reality. At least I thought it would be as we headed to Oregon, to Bend's Cascade Cycling Classic stage race.

"Which bike will it be for today's race?" I say to Michael as he turns off the ignition on his Honda minivan in a paved parking lot filled with bike racers unloading gear from their cars. It's a beautiful July morning in central Oregon, and Mike and I just spent the short drive heading west from our Bend motel looking out the bug encrusted windshield at the terrain ahead of us—green and treed, with a snow-capped mountain in the distance. "Which helmet will you wear?" I ask, turning around, looking at the small bike shop's worth of equipment filling the back of his car. Mike owns a minivan for the "little dears" in his life—namely his bikes, golf clubs, and other pieces of precious sporting equipment.

"Which outfit?" I add.

I brought plenty of stuff from home, but Michael went nuts. Beyond his two bikes, there were—among other things—his three helmets, seven pairs of cycling shorts, eight wheels, six jerseys, four pair of sunglasses, nine pairs of socks, and three grocery bags full of sports nutrition foodstuffs.

"You worry about your gear, LeMond. I'll tend to mine," says Michael, arms crossed. Then he unfolds his long, lean body out from behind the steering wheel. Michael is still dressed in regular clothes—a white T-shirt and red shorts—that show off the standard bike-racer body coloring: Farmer-tanned, deep brown arms and neck from where cycling jerseys' sleeves and collars stop, and very dark legs that turn ice white at mid-thigh. The drastic color change happens where cycling shorts usually end.

Michael and I begin unpacking and sorting our clothes and equipment, just as we have many times before. Trips dedicated to riding and racing our bikes have always served as the stickiest elements in the gobs of glue that creates our bond. We've scaled mountain passes in California, Wyoming, Colorado, Nevada, and New Mexico. Climbed perfectly paved roads in Switzerland. Raced up the French L'Alpe d'Huez, a cruelly steep mountain that's regularly included in the ever-changing routes of the Tour de France. Every beautiful place we've gone, Mike and I have enjoyed the sheer, ongoing pleasure of parting the air around us on such simple and quiet machines. To me, the T wouldn't be nearly the rush that it is if it weren't combined with the high I still get not just from riding, but from riding racer-fast.

Michael and I had signed up for the thrills that would no doubt be part of Bend's Cascade Classic months earlier. In one way, it was just another adventure involving heaping amounts of cycling gear, plenty of logistics, and teasing between friends. We've always bickered—Michael's slow pace and occasional obliviousness drive me nuts; I can be way too anal-retentive and combative for him. Only two days earlier, on the drive north toward Bend and nearing the California-Oregon border, Michael had driven past gas station after gas station only to notice, when we were on the emptiest stretch of highway, that the needle on the fuel gauge was below "E." I was irritated. I had insisted that we turn around. Michael said he knew his car a lot better than I did and that we'd be fine. My shoulders tensed. He looked straight ahead, cradling the steering wheel. Neither of us said anything when we motored into a gas station near the tiny Northern California town of Dorris.

But this trip *is* different than the others. During the nine-hour drive from the Bay Area, Michael and I both wondered aloud how many more expeditions like this are in us. The bike racing is a wonderful passion that we share. It not only keeps us extremely fit. We learn more about ourselves, and about our abilities to overcome challenges (long hills, flat times, stiff headwinds, the list goes on), with each logged mile. The competitions give us goals and hopes, people to ride with and, when the suffering is over, good fodder for stories.

But as the two of us grow older, we've also become increasingly aware that the racing life is all consuming, and sometimes excessive. The vain athletes, the obsessions over gear and threshold numbers, the money invested in coaches and equipment, the endless hours spent training and then racing the same people, repeatedly, on roads that lead nowhere. What, we sometimes wonder, is the point of it all? Benjamin and Sophie want more of my time, and Juliana won't complain if I'm more present. As for Michael, he wants an intimate relationship with something more feeling than bike tires and handlebar tape. And the two of us both know: Once we can look at our cycling obsessions with any sort of objectivity, we already have one cleated foot out the sport's door.

As for the Cascade Classic, we agree that it can unquestionably serve as one of the great memories of our racing careers. It's a huge event, attracting top amateurs from the west and some of the best pro riders and cycling teams in the country. Plus it isn't just one competition, but rather a "stage race," like the Tour de France but in miniature. Over the course of three days, Mike and I will compete in four different events (the pros compete in six races over five days): On the first day we race a short, fourteen-mile "time trial," where each racer starts individually and races against a ticking clock, and then a "criterium," or short course, riding laps for less than an hour around a six-corner "loop" set up on Bend's city streets. The second day's challenge is a seventy-one-mile road race ending at 6,300-foot Mt. Bachelor Ski Resort. Finally, on the last day, we race a sixty-seven-mile, hilly, four-lap "circuit" race. Before the event, Michael and I had assured each other that we are, like always, just in it to have fun.

Right, just for fun. Until the T kicks in. Then we'll see what fun looks like.

"Stay near the front until we top out on that first hill," says Michael, throwing a leg over his futuristically shaped, blue, black, and gray carbon-fiber bicycle. "We don't want to get left behind before the action starts."

In the paved parking lot where we'd disembarked from Mike's minivan an hour earlier, we're now talking final strategy and readying for the day's seventy-one-mile road race. Our numbers are carefully pinned to our jerseys. Wheels are perfectly centered between brake pads. Back pockets are stuffed with food. We've both already ridden up and down an adjoining road in order to work up a sweat so, if needed, we can start the race at a breakneck speed. We don't talk about the fact that, entering today's stage with two races already under our belts, I'm in eleventh place in my category out of nearly fifty riders. A top-ten overall finish would be insanely impressive. Michael, riding in a different category with stronger racers, is in fifty-second place out of sixty-six riders. His place in the pecking order is where, relatively speaking, I would often find myself, too. Today and tomorrow, his category and mine will race together.

"Don't spend energy trying to get away from everyone else early in the race. It's a long ride," he says, as we navigate out of the parking lot and toward a group of riders amassing at the start line. There will be 114 riders starting together. For me, that is a huge field.

"What if a group tries to get away from everyone else? Should we go with them?" I ask.

"All the significant hills are toward the end," says Mike, grabbing one of his water bottles and taking a long enough drink to swish around the fluid in his mouth. He swallows.

"That's when the race will be decided," he adds.

The race, at first, feels like a stampede—more than a hundred sets of legs sometimes moving pedals at seventy, eighty, or ninety revolutions per minute while gears grind, snot flies, and sudden movements cause scary ripple effects and barks from riders who admonish or implore people to ride for the good of the pack. At any moment, so many of us could spill over like high-speed, muscle-bound dominoes.

I ride close to Michael because I know he's a very experienced racer. I trust his knowledge of when to surge, and when it's okay to drift slightly backwards inside of the giant peloton. I steal glances at towering pines and firs. We round big and blue Crane Prairie Reservoir. We arrow through the dry but hot air.

With maybe thirty miles left to go, I ride up alongside Michael. There must still be eighty or so athletes clustered together, a Technicolor cloud moving almost silently down central Oregon's forested roads.

"I'm still okay. How about you?" says Michael, looking straight ahead while talking. I glance over at him. The black straps on his helmet are stained white with salt from his sweat.

"Not sure," I say. "This is stressful."

"It'll break up soon. You're strong," he says speaking through clenched teeth. "Come on!"

Mike is right. Around mile fifty the road ascends, riders just ahead of us begin to surge, and the group thins.

With fifteen miles to go there must only be fifty of us left in the lead pack. With eleven miles left there are perhaps forty. Soon Michael and I watch the strongest riders pull away from us, not dramatically but consistently, as if they were suddenly experiencing a milder gravitational force.

We stay with the small pack. My feet hurt from pushing on the pedals. My ass wants off the minimalist saddle. The legs, however, are still game to go. They don't feel too bad, especially considering my two competitions a day earlier.

With only a few miles left, Michael slows. Or maybe it's that I don't. At first the decline is barely palpable, just a little less energy given to each stroke of the pedals. Michael says nothing, but the fractional difference in speeds between our bikes is apparent. I don't blink, I don't consider. My ability to ride faster than him isn't personal, and I say nothing as I slowly ride away from my friend. The friend with more experience, more training, and often more ability. I try to think about nothing—friendship, trust, drugs, exhaustion—as I move one leg and then the other.

I crest the hill and ride alone toward the finish line, which is in a ski area parking lot. I ride around the lot in a giant circle, looking over my shoulder for Michael as I approach the finish line. I don't see him. I cross the line, tired but not exhausted. Innis, my riding pal from the Bay Area who has come to Oregon to help support a women's team, is one of the first people to greet me.

"You're already here?" he says in a surprised rather than praising tone. I've left behind some other riders who Innis and I both expected to finish ahead of me.

I straddle my bike frame and wait for Michael to appear. Thirty seconds, then sixty go by. Those are considerable chunks of time to put between you and another rider in the final miles of a bike race. Finally, almost ninety seconds after I finish, Mike crosses the line.

He stops short of me. I ride back to where he's standing, doubled over his handlebars. His upper body is heaving as he tries to catch his breath.

Maybe thirty seconds later he looks up. His glasses are stained with dried sweat droplets and his lips are scaly. He says nothing.

"Talk to me," I beg him.

"What am I supposed to say?" he finally replies. "Congratulations?"

THE NEXT MORNING, I wake up before Michael does in our Bend motel room. I rise and do some silent, easy stretching on the floor. After yesterday's huge effort I can feel fatigue in my quadriceps. My lower back is tight. Calves are sore. But I'm not tired to the point that I can't imagine racing again. In pro cycling, drug-free riders who experience deep exhaustion while facing doping competition are said to experience "passive doping"—the stronger the drugs make the cheaters, the more the clean athletes suffer in their attempts to keep up. That's not to say that I had my way with yesterday's competition.

Floyd Landis I'm not, at least in terms of my cycling abilities.

But I am interested to know how the other racers feel today. I'm interested to know how Michael feels.

I know how I feel. Excited.

Some ethicists say one emotion that I shouldn't feel is guilt. For nearly thirty years, Norman Fost, a professor and director of the program in medical ethics at the University of Wisconsin School of

Medicine in Madison, has spoken out against what he believes is a ridiculous outcry against performance-enhancing drugs. In a 1983 opinion story titled "Let 'Em Take Steroids" for *The New York Times*, Fost wrote, "The widespread use of anabolic steroids by athletes is upsetting to many people, but it is not clear why. The misgivings appear to be based more on vague, moralistic feelings than on rational analysis." Fost has argued that advances in training technology, gear, nutrition, and coaching already favor some competitors over others. Ball-sports athletes including Tiger Woods, for instance, have had Lasik laser eye surgery with hopes of making their visual acuity better than "natural" (20/20). Does that make medically achieved, 20/15 vision, which might give someone superior ability to pick up a baseball pitched at one hundred miles per hour, or read the way a green breaks, illegal? *Super*natural? Fost also insists that there's a lack of evidence proving steroids' health risks, and that athletes including boxers, skiers, football players, and cyclists volunteer to threaten their own well-being courtesy of the dangerous sports in which they compete. "It's illogical to criminalize these performance-enhancing substances," Fost would later say over the phone. And John Lantos, a professor and bioethicist at the University of Chicago whom I also ultimately reached by phone, echoed Fost and then some: "Does fairness mean you get to use your own genetic endowment, and if yours sucks you're screwed?" debated Lantos. "And if you're good, then you win?"

Stretching my hamstrings from a seated position in our Bend motel room, I survey the heaping piles of Michael's equipment. One of his bicycles is seven years newer than mine. It's lighter and more responsive than my bike. His other bicycle, designed only for use in time trials, offers superior aerodynamics, as does his goofy, time-trial-designated, cone-head helmet. Then I think about our upbringings. Mike's mother and father always encouraged him to play sports. My dad could've cared less if I knew a touchdown from a home run. He barely did.

Maybe I should tell Mike to quit crying into his steel-cut oats. I smoked him yesterday. His superior equipment and athletic breeding versus my drugs.

Mike's long body starts to move a bit under the sheets. He's always been a slow riser, but today his motions seem sluggish. His moving foot initiates a glacial rise and fall of the sheet. He elevates his head off the pillow and sees me on the floor.

"Hey," he says, his voice, unused since yesterday, is unusually deep. Then he lies back down and stares at the ceiling.

"Hi," I say. I'm still seated on the floor, bending my left leg underneath me to stretch my quadriceps muscles.

"How do you feel?" he asks.

Nope Mike, you go first. Because when I tell you that I feel pretty great, well, you're going to bring up the doping, and we'll start where we left off last night with you asking me again if I'm taking drugs to write a book or to become a better bike racer, and, again, I'll have to dismiss my actions and will feel weird. Let's hear how you're doing first.

"How do *you* feel?" I ask, unfolding my left leg and folding my right.

"Like I've been hit by a train. I don't know how I'm going to race today," he says. Digging his elbows into the motel mattress, he props up his torso and head to look at me.

"Tell me you feel the same," he says, slowly blinking and unblinking his eyes, as if he can't believe I'm already up and moving my limbs.

"Tell me that this is hard for you, too. That my old friend Andrew hasn't been wrapped up in some alien body."

"I'm still me," I say, twisting my torso. "Not the Terminator."

"So you're really sore too?" he says.

"Mike . . ."

"It's alright," he says, "I can suffer alone."

He climbs out of bed and walks stiffly toward the bathroom.

"I'll wade through the misery that we once knew together," he says, and shuts the bathroom door behind him.

MICHAEL IS CURRENTLY in forty-forth place overall in his category. I'm in eleventh, forty seconds out of tenth place. If I can make up that time on the rider placed just ahead of me, or finish far enough ahead of anyone above me in today's last race, I'll make the top ten.

Achievement! Prize money!

Scandal . . .

Michael and I don't talk much during breakfast, and then ready ourselves for the morning's sixty-seven-mile, four-lap circuit race. We ride from the motel to the start, winding our way over western Bend's perfectly paved streets, which are dotted with Porsche SUVs, Subarus equipped with bike racks, and a lot of muscular, tanned people out jogging and walking. Bend is a fitness-minded town, like Boulder, Colorado and Madison, Wisconsin.

Someone should market the T here.

Mike and I again line up together at the start line.

"Feeling any better?" I say to him, unthinkingly reaching toward my handlebar to reset the mileage counter on the power meter that isn't there. I reset the computer before every ride, but I've left it off the bike for today's race. Today I'll pay attention to the competition, not the watts. Holmes will understand.

"Better," he says, fastening the buckle on his helmet. "You?"

"I'm good," I say.

Michael finally cracks a smile. "Let's see what you can do."

Early in the hot and hilly race, Michael speeds ahead of the group of one-hundred-plus riders with a few other competitors. He's gambling that his small cluster of athletes can work together, taking turns battling the wind and riding fast, and perhaps hold off the larger (and at least, for one race, lazier) group for the entire race. Every once in a while such a banzai approach works.

I ride more conservatively, happy to stay close to the front of the main pack of riders. I complete one lap with the group and then a second, at one point passing Michael, who's by the side of the road and holds a wheel in his hand. Flat tire. His race is over. We soon catch the others from Mike's group.

The back half of each circuit through northwestern Bend is hilly and curvy, and the third time around I frantically ride around eight or ten other riders directly ahead of me who fall behind on the steepest part of the incline. I don't know if it's God or drive or the T, but I latch onto the back of what must be a sixty-rider bunch for the final lap of the event.

I suffer. There are no easy moments, and for seventeen miles I broker teeny tiny deals with myself to keep up with the group of strong competitors.

Ride with everyone to that tree. Pedal hard for thirty seconds. Catch up to the guy in the red and white kit. Stay in a bigger gear for twenty revolutions of the pedals. One, two, three, four, five . . .

At the top of the final climb, I am firmly anchored within the group of top riders. I am drooling.

I am so tired that I want my mommy.

Something inside of my cerebral cortex keeps me upright and aware enough to stay with the main group on a flat stretch of road toward the finish. I no longer have the energy left to shift gears or drink. I don't care anymore about nose snot, burning eyes, or tingling in my numb toes. I am only one of twelve riders from my category to ride in with the strongest cyclists from Michael's group.

At the finish area, I'm not exactly hoisted onto anyone's shoulders. Nobody sticks a camera or microphone in front of my face. I am nothing but a forty-three-year-old, category 4 bicycle racer, with a best friend by my side who shrugs instead of smiles. I'm lost in a crowd of sweaty riders with quivering legs. But, as it turns out, I am also a top-ten competitor at the 2008 Cascade Cycling Classic. A rider who's successfully employed his chosen technologies—a titanium bike, a power meter, lightweight wheels, and practically seven months worth of testosterone—to shove almost all of my competition beneath me.

LATE THE FOLLOWING AFTERNOON, Michael pulls up in front of my house, and I don't have time for the hero's welcome that hasn't been planned for me anyway. A couple weeks earlier, immediately after Dr. Patil had warned me to be diligent about not exposing my family to my testosterone cream, I'd found a woman on the Internet who lived in the northwest and had reluctantly agreed to talk to me over the phone about the experience of her husband's supplemental T "contaminating" her child. I scheduled the interview for late today, thinking Mike and I would be back in the Bay Area hours earlier. I was due on the phone in fifteen minutes.

I open the door of the minivan and walk up to the wood fence that separates our driveway from the garden. Juliana and the kids are in the dirt, pulling yellow weeds. Until recently those weeds were green, and in my mind a decent and easily maintained alternative to ground cover. Justification for riding instead of gardening.

Juliana waves and smiles. They're all wearing shorts and T-shirts. They're my beautiful family. It's a sunny day.

"Welcome back. Hey, can you grab me the rake?" she asks, standing up, slapping together her gloved hands.

"Hi," I say, and I walk into the garage and fetch the rake. I return to the fence and hand it to Juliana. Mike starts pulling my bags from his vehicle.

"Hi Daddy," says Benjamin with his sweet and high voice, looking over his shoulder at me while he continues to pull on one weed. "Did you win?"

"Hi Dada," says Sophie. She gives up on a weed and starts kicking dirt.

"Hello little ones!" I say. "Ben, I came in tenth."

"Oh," he says, and turns back around.

"That's actually good," I add.

"Oh! Good," says Benjamin, still concentrating on the weed.

I turn to the minivan and help Mike remove all of my stuff. We move everything as far as the washer and dryer in the garage.

I give Mike a big hug and he tells me that we need to talk some more. He'd spent a while during the drive home warning me that I could get hooked on the T, physically and emotionally. He wants to know where I'm headed with the drugs. I promise him that we'll talk.

Then Mike goes one way, and I go the other. As he pulls out of the driveway, I apologize to Juliana and the kids for having to disappear so quickly after returning home and then I walk up the stairs from the garage to the house. I grab my laptop and quickly shuffle downstairs and into our office.

I pick up the phone and call this woman, a forty-seven-year-old mother of one, who made me promise that I wouldn't make her identity public. She explains to me that, back in 2004, her then sixty-six-year-old partner was using a topical testosterone supplement. She says her partner was highly disciplined about making sure that his testosterone application had been fully absorbed before handling their baby son.

Sounds familiar. How many times have I rubbed on the stuff, fanned myself for three minutes, washed my hands, and then tried— somewhat carefully, anyway—to cover up with sweats, or at least the boxers I wear to bed.

Her partner, says the woman, was also careless about washing his clothes independently of everyone else's.

Never even thought of doing that.

"Then something started to look different on my two-year-old," she says. "I thought I saw this peach fuzz above his penis, but it was something more than peach fuzz."

"What was it?" I ask.

"It looked like pubic hair," she says.

"Really," I say. "He was two?"

Oh my God. Benjamin and Sophie.

"Two-and-a-half," she says.

"What made it look like pubic hair?" I ask.

"It was dark," she replies.

Pubic hair on a two-and-a-half-year-old? Steady.

The woman's nightmare continued. The boy's penis enlarged. He grew armpit hair. The woman's father was also on a topical testosterone supplement. Maybe he was an exception, she says, in terms of how readily his body absorbed the T. Soon, her son, she says, was "humping pillows."

We talk longer. She tells me that she took her son to a pediatric endocrinologist who discovered that the toddler's testosterone levels were very high, and that anyone on supplemental T needed to be extremely careful with it—the substance can cause unnatural maturation of little boys or girls. The ultimate solution for her partner and father, she explains, was testosterone via injection instead of a topical solution.

The woman is quite chatty, and has a lot to say about hormone replacement therapy. But after a while, I become so preoccupied with the plight of my family that I ask her if we can talk again another day.

We hang up, and I immediately walk upstairs and into our tiny bathroom. My bath towel is hanging low enough on a towel rack that the kids could use it to dry their hands or wipe their faces. I grab it.

Ugh.

I look at our bed. Lola is sleeping, sphinx-style, atop our sheets.

Arggh.

I lift Lola off the bed the way that I'd likely handle plutonium. Is she contaminated?

I strip our bed, wash my hands, and go into the kids' bathroom. I grab their towels. I strip their beds. I empty the hamper. I look around.

Who or what else has the T touched?

I carefully put the kids' towels, sheets, and clothes in one laundry pile in the garage (hopefully not contaminated). I put Juliana's and my sheets in another (could very well be contaminated). I make a third pile for Juliana's clothing (I don't know). Then I make a fourth pile consisting of my bath towel and clothing, and all the dirty laundry from my trip to Oregon (code red). I survey all the piles.

Kind of like a Superfund site.

I grab my pile first, and shove everything—whites, darks, all my delicate cycling clothing—into the washing machine. I press every available button. "Heavy Duty." "Hot." "Second rinse."

I turn to go back upstairs to wash my hands yet again when Juliana walks into the open garage with too many gardening tools in her hands. The rake is slipping from her the crook of her right arm.

"Can you grab this from me?" she says.

"I can't right now," I say. My hands are empty.

The rake falls to the floor. Juliana looks at me, and then her eyes scan all the piles.

"Are you okay?" she asks.

"I wanted to do laundry," I say with what I hope is an innocuous looking shrug. "Had a lot of my own stuff, and kind of gathered momentum. Thought I'd wash everything. You know, get it all clean."

getting in the habit

Sweaty and happy, Juliana walks through the front door. Right along, I fear, with the newest member of the Tilin family, the substance that may have left its syringes the way a genie escapes from the bottle.

For starters, I'm unquestionably paranoid that I've "contaminated" Juliana and perhaps the kids with my supplemental hormones.

"And I'm free, free fallin' . . ." she loudly sings, presumably so that she can hear herself over the Tom Petty tune playing on her iPod. Headphones in her ears, an hour-long run now behind her, Juliana lies face-up on the living room rug and starts into a series of abdominal exercises: crunches, twists, and V-type sit-ups where she raises her straightened arms and legs simultaneously.

"I feel really good," she says, beaming. "I ran all the way up Tres Sendas. I could've gone farther."

Juliana takes hour-long runs with regularity. And, like me, she goes through stretches of time where she's disciplined about doing sit-ups and the like. But I don't recall her ever saying that she's run all the way up Tres Sendas. Tres Sendas is a beautiful, redwood-tree-lined, approximately mile-long trail in the parkland near our home. It's frequently steep, and to my knowledge the trail has always reduced Juliana to a walk. Until now.

Your wife is officially T-powered.

Let's think this through. I may very well have *not* contaminated my wife. She's physically strong, and has run a lot this summer. She could just be in great shape. Or Juliana might be experiencing an influx of testosterone courtesy of her own hormone-replacement therapy. Wiley would later tell me that the hormone DHEA, which Juliana takes, can convert into the T. Wiley would also say that she'd heard few tales of her creams contaminating those who come in close contact with Wiley Protocol users. Patil, however, told me she'd encountered a number of such occurrences with her patients.

But maybe my wife is simply energized because she's in a better place in her life. The heaviness and sad feelings around last month's pregnancy and its difficult termination have begun to fade, and she seems like her old self again—genuinely joyful. Only about two weeks earlier, before I'd gone to Oregon for the bike race, we'd hosted some friends with a nice dinner party. I barbecued steak, Juliana made corn on the cob and a tasty arugula salad. We enjoyed sharing our home. The next morning we lingered in bed and made love while the kids sat in front of the telly.

Plus, today is a travel day for Juliana and the kids. Travel always makes Juliana happy. Her desire to experience life away from home is limitless. There was that trip years ago to Southeast Asia, of course. With and without kids, we've also been to places like Costa Rica, India twice, various spots in Mexico, and all over the western United States. We've slept in palaces as well as the floors of miserable Third World airports, and ridden on camels through the desert and in jeeps through the jungle. Today Juliana is upbeat even if she's only going as far as Austin for a nearly annual pilgrimage so the Tilins can spend a week with my wife's tribe. I'll join Juliana and the kids in a couple weeks, and spend over a week with them. For me that's plenty of time in the Texas heat.

I watch Juliana do more V-ups.

Those hormones could be in her veins.

After speaking days ago to that woman who had been so upset about her baby being contaminated by his dad's testosterone, I went through a mental checklist of preventative measures I can take to prevent the 'roids from spreading: Keep my bathing towels separate; keep my laundry separate for the rest of the laundry; allow the T cream that I apply to dry thoroughly before I come in contact with my family. Also, I decided that I wouldn't immediately tell Juliana that she and the kids may have absorbed some of the supplemental testosterone meant for me. If supplemental testosterone is indeed in all of our lives, then there's no better time for Juliana, Benjamin, and Sophie to put 1,700 miles between themselves and our dope-infested domicile. They can leave me to try and beat back the T.

Their flight leaves in less than three hours.

"Why don't I bathe the kids?" I say loudly to Juliana, whose torso seems to be coming off the carpet as if she and the floor were magnets of the same polarity. Smiling and rocking out, she nods.

Sophie is in her room.

"Time to shower, girlfriend," I say. Sophie is holding up a blue and white summer dress in front of her pink nightgown, and looking in the mirror.

Sophie's whole body shakes with resistance.

"Daddy, I'll shower when I get to Texas," she says. "I don't need to shower."

I knew I'd encounter resistance with Sophie. She's still at that age where she hates the shower. Sophie doesn't like the feeling of water pouring down over her, of something literally washing over her. These days I can identify.

"How about you get in the tub?" I say, and she nods.

"Can Benjamin join you?" I ask. She shrugs. I take that to mean she won't fight me, and she'll go retrieve her brother.

Neither of the kids is particularly dirty. But I want more than to freshen them for their trip. Ever since hearing about that contaminated little boy, I'd been sneaking peeks at the children's bodies. At every available chance, I've scanned their limbs and torsos for anything irregular. Lousy as this sounds, I've looked at Ben's shorts: Any erections? Thankfully, no. Every part of Sophie's little body looked normal. I hate that I'm looking.

What hath I wrought?

My concerns were only fueled by further research. I found a disconcerting medical paper published in 2005 in the *European Journal of Pediatrics*. Belgian researchers documented three cases of "exogenous testosterone intoxification," which is a fancy way of saying that the three studied children all had fathers whose topical steroids had made contact with their skin and been absorbed. The transfer likely occurred via skin-to-skin or fabric-to-skin contact. The subjects' symptoms freaked me out: a two-and-a-half-year-old girl who had been growing pubic hair for seven months, and frequently played with herself. An eighteen-month-old girl who had an enlarged clitoris, a condition known as *clitoromegaly*. A thirty-two-month-old boy with an enlarged penis. The bones of all three subjects, says the paper, were maturing too fast.

Gawd!!!

The water out of the faucet is hot, and I ask a naked Sophie and Benjamin to get into the tub. They both stand in the bath water until it's about ankle-deep, and then they both slowly and somewhat hesitantly sit down. It's been a while since they've taken a bath together. Maybe two years.

"This is about saving time," I fib, grabbing a bar of soap. They don't need to know that I want to inspect their bodies. "Don't want to be late for the flight," I add.

I look over the children while turning the bar of soap in my hands to create lather. Their little sloping shoulders, straight arms, and flat chests. No sex-hormone overload!

You hope. What the hell would clitoromegaly look like anyway?

"Dad, what are you doing with that soap?" asks Benjamin, looking at my hands. They're covered in a foamy lather.

"Oh. Sorry," I say.

"I can wash myself," he says, sticking out his hand.

I give Ben the soap and continue to look at their bodies. I notice some dark hair on Benjamin's back. And hair on Sophie's lower legs. Was all of that there before I started using testosterone?

Why weren't you more disciplined with the T? Why weren't you more careful with your clothes?

But I can't find much else, and decide that Benjamin and Sophie look fine. Perfect, really—not a nick on either of them. Plus, neither child is displaying any aberrant behavior.

The paper from the *European Journal of Pediatrics* also reported that, once the subjects' exposure to the T ceased, that the children's curious actions diminished. The boy's testosterone level normalized, as did the size of one little girl's clitoris. The scientists believed that potential dangers to children of long-term exposure to exogenous testosterone could cause premature puberty and "reduced final height" from unnatural maturation of bones.

But I feel increasingly confident that I haven't bathed Ben and Sophie in steroids. I occasionally slacked in my efforts to cover up like a nun, and/or allow the cream to absorb, before lying down with one or the other of my kids at bedtime. I never, however, directly exposed them to my back or groin. Plus the guilty fathers in the research paper had been taking the T for years.

Dodged some bullets!

I'd later discover that kids weren't the only sobering cases of what's called *exogenous hormone intoxification*. Pets have been victims, too. Veterinarians chatting over the Web realized that a small but notable number of curious failures to effectively spay cats and dogs weren't really coincidental cases of poorly executed procedures. The affected female pets, which seemed to go into heat even after their ovaries had been removed, were actually displaying sexual behavior courtesy of being contaminated by their age-battling owners. The masters had applied hormone creams to themselves and then held their pets, or let the animals lick the very hands and body spots that had recently been in contact with the supplemental hormones.

I'd ultimately give our cat Lola a once-over. I declared her no more hirsute than before my experiment began.

I flip the drain lever on the bathtub and wrap Benjamin and Sophie in towels. I'm now left to focus on Juliana's apparently increasing brawn.

"How are you two coming along?" she says when the three of us emerge from the bathroom. Juliana is showered, dressed, and walking through the hallway carrying her huge suitcase toward our bedroom. Juliana always over-packs, and her bags regularly verge on being so heavy that the airlines charge us for excess weight.

"You want a hand?" I ask.

"No, I'm fine," she says. "Forgot to pack a bag of toiletries."

I'd researched women and testosterone. Women's bodies naturally contain *some* testosterone, just like men produce low levels of estrogen and progesterone. But women who have unnaturally high levels of the T display telltale symptoms including aggressive behavior, enlarged clitorises, and either hair loss that can resemble male-pattern baldness or excessive hair growth on their limbs or chests, among other places. Tammy Thomas, an elite cyclist who was once busted for steroids-related charges, was believed to shave her face.

We load up my car with suitcases and the kids. We drive south on Highway 13 and then east on Highway 580 toward Oakland's airport.

"We won't go everywhere without you. As soon as you arrive we'll go to Barton Springs, and Amy's too," says Juliana, reaching over to hold my right hand. She knows that I crave cold swimming holes, as well as Amy's excellent, locally made ice cream, on Austin's ridiculously hot summer days.

"Two weeks feels long. We'll miss you," she says with a smile.

I steal glances at Juliana.

Still looks like my wife. No mustache. No bald spot. Not funny.

"You three will be so involved the minute you arrive. Nonstop action, I'm sure," I say while driving. "Time will fly. Have a blast."

Get away from Oozing Hormone Man.

At the departures terminal, Juliana and I unload the car. I lean over and give Benjamin a long hug.

"I love you, Daddy," he says, his smile full of oversized permanent teeth. "Dee Dee loves you, too," and he holds up Dee Dee the cat doll—the same Dee Dee he had as a baby—for me to hug.

Ben, you and Sophie are the last people in the world that I want growing up too fast.

As I watch the three of them walk into the airport, I seriously debate the idea of ending the experiment early. The next thought I have is more troublesome. I wonder if I'll be able to end the experiment at all.

I'M NOT THE ONLY one thinking that the drugs have a hold of my life.

"I can imagine what's on tomorrow's schedule for you. A seven-hour ride followed by a thousand push-ups and then a twelve-mile run," says Michael, unloading the sarcasm as he takes the napkin from his place setting and puts it on his lap. We're in a Chinese restaurant near Mike's South Bay apartment, fresh from showers after a four-hour ride. The kids and Juliana have been away in Texas for over a week. In their absence I've successfully turned away from my work long enough to spend a day with my old friend.

Mike looks at me with a grin that's crooked and uncertain. "I'm thinking I've seen the last of Old Andrew for a while. Guess I'll get used to this new you."

"Don't bother. I'm entering the homestretch of my drug test," I say, taking a sip of hot tea. "Been on the T since January, it's almost August. A few more months, a few more experiences. Then I'll wean myself off the drugs."

"Hmm. Ever thought that going off them could be the hardest part?" he says, opening the menu, and still smiling. But the grin doesn't hide his concern. "What with all of your newfound strength and success."

"Yes. Falling in love with the dope has more than crossed my mind. I'll admit it. But I try not to dwell on the notion of addiction. I remind myself that doping doesn't automatically make life fun," I say from behind the menu. "I'm not always reveling in my strength and swagger. It's definitely not enjoyable when I'm at the gynecologist with Juliana, or washing every last towel in the house."

"Are you ready to order?"

Michael and I look up from our menus. A young and very cute, dark-skinned Asian waitress, with her brown hair gathered in a bun and wearing jeans and a V-neck, aquamarine T-shirt, stands at the side of the table. Her hips tilt sexily to the left. She holds a pad and pen.

Yes, I'd like to order off the menu. You, naked, under soft sheets.

"We'd like some sizzling-rice soup," says Mike slowly, and she nods. Then, in a benign tone I've heard a million times, a tone that he hopes engenders sympathy and even attraction, he asks for a medium size bowl.

"We'd . . . enjoy . . . that," he says, drawing out the words suggestively.

I roll my eyes.

Mike's never nailed down the flirting thing. Always erring on the side of formality.

"How many pot stickers come in an order?" I ask.

"Six," she says politely.

"Can we get an order and a half?" I ask. She shrugs her shoulders, her small breasts moving up with them. Then she shakes her head.

"How about an order and three-quarters. Or five-sixths?" I banter.

She smiles. Her mouth is small, and yet her lips are deliciously plump. Her smooth face doesn't have one seam. She shakes her head again.

"What if we get two orders but send back three pot stickers that we say don't taste right?"

"Oh come on," says Michael. "Puhleeze."

The waitress looks me straight in the eye. This time her smile is broad. Her teeth are straight and perfect and white.

"Go ahead with just one order," I say, also smiling.

"Okay," she says, her eyes returning to her pad. "I'll get your soup and dumplings going. I'll return in a moment to see what else you'll want." The waitress looks at her two graying customers, flashes another quick smile, and turns to leave.

Check that out, she digs me! Or was she only humoring an obnoxiously chatty perv?

"Nice pooper," I say, watching her walk away.

"She was into my shit," says Michael. "At least until you opened your mouth. Don't tell me that's not fun."

"It's fun," I say. "Sometimes I feel more like a pig than a forty-something given a second chance at youth. The sex with Juliana is wonderful, but the novelty isn't there anymore. We're not having sex so often. Sometimes when I get an erection out of nowhere I want to swat it like a fly. I wish it would go away. The horniness I feel isn't, you know, terribly soulful. Sometimes I wish I could come off the T for a few days. Act my age. I think what I've really become is a dirty old man with this chemical toy that is a twenty-year-old's virility," I add. "No toy holds its shine forever."

"The day will come when you fantasize about the good times as a dirty old man," says Michael, pouring us both second cups of tea. "You could go off the drugs and then want back what they give you. Or more. Have you thought of those outcomes?"

I don't want to have this discussion right now. At this very moment, the doping isn't bringing me overwhelming amounts of happiness. The testosterone didn't dramatically alter my performance on the training ride that Michael and I took earlier today, when we climbed Old La Honda Road and ended up on Skyline Boulevard. I was more taken with the sunshine, hills, and views than my own fabulous strength. My current restaurant experience wouldn't be that much worse if an ugly old man had just taken our order.

I'm here because I'm counting on Mike to keep my spirits up, not give me grief. Whenever Juliana and the kids leave on a vacation without me I become unmoored. At home alone, instead of making the best use of my time, catching up on sleep, going for long bike rides, and eating healthy meals instead of grazing off the kids' buttery pasta, I become discombobulated. I write late into the night, often skip workouts, and sleep fitfully. The house feels vacant, and at some point during my days of relative solitude I'm humbled by the realization that I'm not some lone wolf that functions better on my own. Testosterone can't turn me into some clichéd drifter whose fulfillment comes from self-reliance. Juliana and the kids fuel me. And friends like Michael. When he isn't bugging me.

"Can you become addicted to the testosterone?" Mike asks after passing an ice cube from his mouth back into his water glass.

"Apparently so," I say dutifully.

"Tell me more," he says.

I roll my eyes. Second time tonight.

"Come on," he says. "What do you know?"

I tell him that I've researched steroids and addiction. Scientists estimate that up to thirty percent of anabolic-androgenic steroids users develop some type of unhealthy bond with their 'roids, and that, according to some experts, dependence can initiate after only nine months of use.

"You know how they say models can't be too thin?" I ask Michael while I try to hold the chopsticks properly in my right hand (I'm left-handed).

He nods.

"Some steroid addicts, at least at first, can't be too big," I say.

I tell him that steroids aren't like other addictive drugs, such as heroin or cocaine. There's no quick high. Instead there's the belief that you're becoming bigger and stronger, or at least not shrinking.

"You're not getting much bigger," Mike says.

"Well that's one reason, I hope and believe, that I'm not a prime candidate for addiction," I say. "I don't want to look like Hulk Hogan."

I tell him more. Scientists are still unclear on the mechanisms and reasons, but they believe that steroids might also do a number on a user's brain. One study, conducted in 2004, permitted some hamsters to "self-administer" until they'd repeatedly dosed themselves on relatively high levels of testosterone.

"What happened?" says Mike.

"Seventy percent of the hamsters dosed up until their nervous systems short-circuited," I reply. "They ODed. They died."

"And, I must add, I'm not a hamster. Or Ben Affleck. What was that horrible movie where he played a high school kid addicted to steroids?"

Mike shakes his head, and I Google it on my iPhone. *A Body to Die For: The Aaron Henry Story.*

I'm very tired of the topic.

"Let's discuss eating instead of doping. What should we order?"

Mike isn't done.

"I'm more than curious about this addiction research. I think maybe you should be concerned," he says.

He'd said something along these lines when we drove home from Oregon.

"I'm very aware that I'm visiting Testosterone Island, Mike. Or should I call you *Dad*," I joke, putting down the menu. "I have a return flight."

"Listen to you, talking with such confidence," he says. "*I know what I'm doing. It's under control.* Really, it's beyond me what you're doing. You don't know if you're getting hooked," he says. "Forget about the youth and sex. You're doing well in races, having your way, and getting some good results. That's a lot of fun, I'd imagine.

Personally, if I relied on results to motivate me to race my bike, then I would've been out of the sport a long time ago. I think about quitting because cycling is time consuming. Not because I can't win."

"I haven't won," I say.

"You're up there," he says. "What happens if you go off the testosterone and decide to try something new?"

"You're right. I'm thinking of pureeing mu-shu pork and putting it into syringes," I say. "I'll shoot it up, and then lose my shit, throwing chopsticks and soy sauce packets in Chinese restaurants across the Bay Area. I'll blame everything on MSG. I can see the film now. *Mu-Shu Madness! Confessions of a Take-Out Addict.*"

Michael doesn't laugh.

"Mike, I hear you. I appreciate your concern," I say, sitting back in my chair. "I must respect the power of these drugs, you're right. I'm not above anyone else. I don't know what I'll feel like when it's time to come off them. But there's nothing I can do right now, except maybe die of hunger."

"You do have that manic streak," he says. "Remember the Omni on Broadway Street?"

Mike *loves* to remind me of the time when we were both twenty years old and I drove a tinny, black, souped-up Dodge Omni. It was a terrible car with a very willing motor. One day when I was behind the wheel and Michael was my passenger, I became very impatient with a slow driver about to take a blind curve that leads to a short but steep hill in San Francisco's fancy Pacific Heights neighborhood. I passed the driver on the curve, and with no ability to see over the rise. We could've died any number of ways.

The whole experience was a rush.

"I remember," I say with a smile. "'Roid rage without the syringes. That was when I was young and au naturel.

"Mike, growth hormone is out," I say. "Did the recreational drugs in high school and college. No more."

"There's always EPO," he says.

"Man!" I say. "I won't take erythropoietin. That's hard-core. Black market."

Our server shows up, interrupting the conversation. She sets down an oval plate containing six beautiful pot stickers. They're doughy and glistening in a thin layer of grease. One side of each fried dumpling is tawny. They're perfect.

Neither of us acknowledges the hot waitress for long. Mike stares at me as I grab the serving spoon and put two pot stickers on his plate.

He says nothing.

"What?" I say, serving myself a couple of pot stickers. "You don't believe me about walking away from the drugs?" I add, grabbing the glass dispenser of hot oil. "Fine. Don't."

EPO AND POT STICKERS. During one notable week of my life, years earlier, such seemingly disparate yet nearly habit-forming elements also nearly converged. Unfortunately, my youthful (and creative) vision—for my mom to become an erythropoietin user, join me in a grand Chinese meal, and see a baseball game live at San Francisco's new ballpark—fell short. And in the days and weeks surrounding that failure, I was dogged again by the kinds of losses around identity and innocence that were first triggered by my father's demise in 1989. This time around, however, it was my mother forcing me to tamp down thoughts about being young, free, and who I wanted to be. This time around, eleven years after my dad passed away, my mom was dying.

It's a Friday in the middle of August 2000, and Juliana and I, along with seven-month-old Benjamin, are visiting the Bay Area. We've come for a number of reasons, the most important of them being to see my mom. She has terminal breast cancer.

"Hi, Bennie," my mother says, dressed in a pretty white night-gown, sitting up in bed and lightly grabbing Benjamin's bare left foot. Her voice is strangely light and faint. "Have you learned to count these precious sweet toes yet?" she asks Juliana's and my little boy.

Benjamin, a kinetic blob of humanity who's dressed in a green onesie and lying on top of Mom's bed sheets, stares into the nothing-ness of the white ceiling in my mother's first-class condo. She lives near San Francisco's pier-lined northern waterfront, in a one-bedroom place that, of course, required the services of decorators, contractors, painters, and sound-and-light specialists before she declared the envi-ronment inhabitable. In my mom's condo, the dishwasher talks to you. The litter box cleans itself. Marble countertops glisten.

But today, with my mother so compromised, and Ben in her arms, I find my way past the years' worth of resentment that I've accumu-lated for Mom's extravagance. For her behaving like a child instead of my parent. The past decade in particular had delivered struggle like it was a daily paper landing on Mom's doorstep. Soon after I'd left the Bay Area—and my mother, sister, and father's parents—for Colorado in 1990, Mom had entered a short-lived marriage, and then was broke, alone, and sleeping on a couch when she was diagnosed with her first round of breast cancer in 1993. While she fought the disease she also landed money via loans, gifts, and work as a medical transcriptionist, but was soon forced out of several apartments that she couldn't afford. Most memorable was the couple of months or so that she spent in an apartment on one of San Francisco's most acclaimed pieces of real estate: a one block stretch of Lombard Street consisting of brick hairpin turns that attracts tons of tourists and has been called "the crookedest street in the world." Mom liked the novelty. I remember visiting her there and telling her that I was concerned about her finances. I was sympathetic but also furious for having to tell her to be responsible. I don't think she unpacked half of her boxes before moving somewhere else.

Despite the evictions, disease, and near bankruptcy of those years, my mother retained her optimism. I was always amazed and impressed. She regularly wanted to talk Giants baseball, the possibilities of grandchildren, when Juliana and I could join her for pot stickers (I inherited her addiction), and, with zero self-consciousness, enjoying the good life.

"Come on Tilin, live a little!" she'd say when Juliana and I would fly out to San Francisco for a visit, using the same battle cry that she'd used when I was a teenager. All these years later, the comment still had bite. Mom continued to push for my masculinity, albeit in a way that an aging, materialistic mother wants as confirmation that her son is successful. Nice clothes and an imported car. A fancy bottle of wine with dinner. Swank vacations, and shiny jewelry for Juliana. While I was an endurance athlete and a modestly compensated editor and journalist, not the tennis-playing doctor she'd envisioned, she still wanted me to enjoy the good life she'd dreamed up for her son. Sometimes I did enjoy that life, too, either to please her or, unwittingly, to satisfy myself. I am my mother's son.

In 1999, Mom was months short of proclaiming herself cancer-free for five years when the disease returned, as telegraphed by swollen lymph nodes in her left armpit. Incredibly, she would re-marry the man who had left her after a week of wedlock back in 1991, and while my sister Tracy and I disliked him to the point of frequently avoiding him, he did move my sick mother to a nice San Francisco zip code. He put her inside of four luxurious walls.

Now on this summer day in 2000, I want to make some peace with Mom. I hope to treat her to what I envision as a perfect mother-son date.

"Join me weekend after next for the Giants game, and some Chinese food, too," I say to her as she picks up Benjamin to stroke his head of thin hair. My mom has hair, too—the chemotherapy hadn't done away with her mouse-gray, soft, and curly hair. She was no longer a bleached blonde, and never wore makeup. This was Mom unplugged. Fine by me.

"I'm waiting to hear from the doctor," she says, using a free hand to adjust the nasal cannula which feeds her supplemental oxygen from a small tank beside her bed. "I need some strength back."

"I really hope you can go, Angela," says Juliana, sitting next to me at the end of my mother's bed. "We'd hate for you to miss this game."

This was not just another Giants home game. These are seats at the team's brand new downtown stadium, Pacific Bell Park. Tickets are expensive and difficult to find, and a friend in publishing has invited me to join him in his company's luxury suite. He told me I could bring my mother, who hasn't yet been to the park in its four months of existence.

Watching baseball with the swells! Perfect views!

Much as she frustrates me, as clichéd as her visions for me are, I want to show my dying mother that I know how to live a little. For one afternoon and evening, I'll go out of my way to be whomever she wants me to be.

"Mom, how can the doctor help?" I ask, watching Benjamin's baby face scrunch up. He looks like he's about to cry.

"He's considering a blood transfusion. Or giving me erythropoietin."

"What do those things do?" I ask. "What's . . ." I couldn't repeat the word erythropoietin. It was far from being in my everyday vocabulary.

My mother explained that the chemotherapy she was receiving to fight her cancer tumors suppressed her body's ability to produce red blood cells. The low levels of red blood cells have made her anemic— weak and tired. Blood transfusions or EPO will, one way or another, put more red blood cells in her body.

"If I can feel better," she says, "I'll go."

Come on, modern medicine, get my mother's butt to one lousy ballgame.

Benjamin begins to whimper, and my mother hands him to me and says that she wants to rest. Mom's husband is, fortunately, out. Juliana and I tend to Benjamin in the living room, and wait for the doctor to call back. And wait some more. The day goes by, and then the weekend, and then Monday.

"Any word?" I ask my mother on Tuesday, five days before the Giants game.

Give her the drugs!

"I'll call him later today," she says, turning down the television. She sits quietly, without complaining. I can see her chest move up and down with relatively quick, shallow breaths. She's watching *Titanic*.

How perfect is that? Leo DiCaprio pretending to be a rich guy.

I knew nothing about blood transfusions, or erythropoietin, like I know now. How the transfusions, which have been around for centuries, can occasionally cause infections. As for the protein and hormone erythropoietin, it's primarily produced in the kidneys, and was successfully synthesized in a lab and patented only in 1987. (The search to isolate it lasted two decades before a purified form of the protein was successfully extracted from the dried concentrate of approximately 670 gallons of human urine.) The beauty of recombinant (synthesized) EPO, which triggers the production of oxygen-carrying red blood cells in the bone marrow, is that it has few side effects, although EPO can trigger the *growth* of cancer tumors, and too much of it causes the dangerous thickening of one's blood. I also wasn't fully aware that, by the year 2000, many of the best professional cyclists in the world were already well versed in the finer points of doping with EPO. They knew how the hormone was key in boosting their blood's hematocrit, or red blood cells, and how to time and titrate their doses so that their blood became rich but not syrupy. If the cyclists used EPO properly, their performances could leap by a reported fifteen to twenty percent. The EPO delivered more oxygen to their tired muscles, so they suffered less. Really, that's all I want for my mother, too: suffer less, and feel stronger. *I want her on the Mom-enhancing drug.*

But she doesn't go on it.

A couple days before the game, Mom calls me. I can hear her labored breathing.

"The answer is no, Andrew," she says, and then takes a short breath. "I'm sorry." Another breath. "The doctor doesn't want me receiving a blood transfusion or erythropoietin right now . . . And I'm just not feeling well enough to go to the game, sweetheart . . . Enjoy yourself."

Later I would find out that my mother likely knew something else about EPO that, at the time, I didn't know. EPO requires weeks or even months to kick in. I'm not sure that, in the end, it was the doctor who decided that my mother shouldn't get a transfusion or the erythropoietin. Maybe she opted out because she was tired of hospitals, surgeries, and physicians. Perhaps she couldn't bear the thought of yet another needle poke. Multiple tumors, I thought, would have to keep Mom from walking, along with her son, down the proverbial red carpet and into a Giants game. I think she knew that she was that sick, because a month later she would die.

On August 19, 2000, I sit in a luxury suite at brand new Pacific Bell Park. The stadium is beautiful, a drug trip in its own right with a gigantic mitt and Coke bottle decorating the area behind the left-field bleachers, and San Francisco Bay waters just beyond right field. I look out at Giants superstar Barry Bonds in left. Only a few months in the future, prosecutors will later claim, Bonds will test positive for steroids for the very first time.

Watching the Giants beat the Atlanta Braves 12–3, the EPO comes to mind. What if that magic hormone had transformed my mother? Mom would've been the happiest mom-kid in the stadium, and her son would've had a far better time with his mother at the game than he did without her. Even if he would've had to pretend for nine innings to be the bon vivant, the man with the title "esquire," the doctor, the confident and self-indulgent Mom's man that he's never really been.

I GET A WILD HAIR and, on a Saturday afternoon in late July 2008, I line up for the start of the Berkeley Bicycle Club Criterium in the East Bay town of Albany. A "criterium," like the one I'd raced in Bend, is a particular kind of cycling competition that frequently involves a hill-free, short, turn-filled course that one races around many times. Combine flat terrain, which makes it difficult for any individual racer to escape a hard-charging peloton, with all of those people navigating high-speed corners together, and you have the parts in place for crashes. Roller derby meets cycling kinds of crashes, which would be slapstick comedy—Bent wheels! Airborne bikes! Launched riders!—if those accidents didn't also result in broken bones, body-length scrapes, deep gashes, and unwieldy ER bills. I almost never enter *crits*. But now that I'm making my power meter sing—Coach Holmes says he's impressed because my lactate threshold remains around 300 watts, and is surprised that my power hasn't peaked during the season so much as it has plateaued, at a level somewhere in the clouds—I consider a weekend without racing to be a waste of good T.

"Shouldn't you start with less air in your tires?" asks Luke, standing next to me near the start line and also straddling his bike. "Given the circumstances, I think that's only just."

I stare at him cross-eyed.

Just announce my doping to the world, fool!

I look around to make sure nobody else is listening to our conversation. Nobody is. Our competition, like us, is nervous. Most of them fidget with their accessories and equipment, making sure that shoes are tight, glasses are straight, and wheels are perfectly centered between brake pads. Luke and I cope via sarcasm.

"The rest of us could benefit from you voluntarily offsetting your advantage," he says, giving me a sardonic grin from underneath his white helmet. "Why don't you carry my kid on your handlebars?"

He points over to the sidewalk about thirty feet away, where his blonde wife holds his sixteen-month-old son. The best thing about criteriums is that they're run over a small area instead of dozens of miles of open road. This race, for instance, navigates closed, residential, tree-dotted streets, and goes round and round Albany High School, its playing fields, and a small park. Luke's family will have the opportunity to cheer for him every half-mile-long lap.

I wave to his sweet wife. She waves back.

"Where are Juliana and the kids?" asks Luke, tilting his torso, which is wrapped in a white and rich blue team jersey, to one side and then the other in a half-hearted attempt to stretch. "They decide to stay home and clean closets?"

It's good to see Luke. Funny, quirky Luke, who rides hard, and loves to race and talk about *echeloning* and *pacelining* and *bridging* and all matter of race strategy, but still never takes the sport or himself too seriously. I wish more of us were like him. Many amateur racers (myself and Michael included) forget that bike racing is a hobby, just like stamp collecting and salsa dancing. Too often my spare time revolves around fitting in my workouts, cleaning the teeth on my bicycle gears, shaving my legs, and looking at my power output downloads. The argument can be made that a midlife crisis tempered by bike racing only swaps one set of mundane preoccupations (work and commuting) with another (hard training and driving hundreds of miles to a race). All I need to do is look at Luke, long and lean Luke, wearing those dorky knit red gloves of his, to laugh at him, and then at myself.

"They are in Texas," I say. "This isn't a family-friendly event, anyway, what with monsters like me competing," I joke.

I look up and spot Innis, a couple rows of racers ahead of us. He looks sufficiently nervous, resetting his bike computer and fumbling with his helmet straps.

Innis and I had talked race strategy before showing up for the competition. Unlike Luke, who likes mixing with everyone in crits, Innis and I agree that we're intimidated by these types of events. So if the race slows down with perhaps a half-dozen laps to go, we plan to attack, or sprint as far ahead of the main pack as possible. We think that all of our competition might figure that we'll exhaust ourselves and be caught. But working together, frequently switching who rides in the lead and who "drafts" in the other's slipstream, Innis and I think that we might be able to run away with the race.

Sounds heroic, anyway.

To my mind, Innis's and my strategy is the only kind that can give either of us a chance at finishing in one of the race's top spots. Criteriums often come down to giant sprints for the finish line, with several if not a dozen people riding elbow to elbow. I'm terrified of those pack sprints.

Days earlier, Coach Holmes had agreed that I should attempt such a strategy.

"See if you can catch those clowns sleeping," he wrote in an email. "You've got all the power these days."

Dust off the podium for me!

The criterium starts as such races often do—fast, with some of the most determined riders attempting to rid the race quickly of its weakest competition. A smaller peloton is easier to navigate. And the fewer the people, the less chances one has of crashing.

I am quickly in survival mode. I don't feel strong. My legs feel fatigued, and I'm breathing hard. Everyone else is riding with their mouths closed—are they breathing at all?—and I'm wondering what all my earlier confidence was about. Perhaps the difficulty of Cascade has caught up with me. Or the balloon finally popped on my testosterone boost. I have already entered what could be called the five stages of crit-racing grief. I'm in the middle of "depression."

I'm a lousy bike racer. I don't know what I'm doing here.

I ride what to me feels very fast to keep up with the group. Many of the other riders are not built like me. They're beefier, with legs like firewood and torsos and arms that, unlike mine, fill their jerseys.

I search for lifelines in the forms of Luke or Innis and their blue jerseys. Just past the race's second of four right-hand turns I spot Luke, maybe seven riders ahead of me in a loose cluster. For a moment there is an opening and an opportunity for me to move right behind him. I want to ride "on his wheel," which means directly behind him, and in his slipstream. But as I come within two bike lengths of him another rider comes around me and positions himself directly behind Luke. Totally legal. But for a split second, I tighten up and ride into the street's gutter, and nearly brush my wheels against the curb.

Avoid crashing. Preserve all flesh.

I back off ever so slightly and my trepidation nearly causes me to crash. Like driving a video-game race car too slowly, as soon as I ease up on my pedals, competition from behind rushes past me in a wave.

Suddenly Luke is fifteen riders ahead of me, and Innis, too. Again I methodically pick my way past racers in pursuit of my friends, and at one point my front wheel barely misses the rear wheel of a rider ahead of me who had turned too sharply through one of the course's corners. He cut me off.

Stay upright. Remember the insurance salesman? The one who said he couldn't get disability insurance for you because freelance writers are considered big, flaky risks who feign illness and hardship? The one who said being a freelance writer was maybe enough of a challenge to the stability of a family, and that maybe I shouldn't be a bike racer too? The one who basically told me to grow-the-fuck-up, do the responsible thing, go jog a few miles a day?

My cycling friends and I, we all know the pain and repercussions of crashing. Luke's wife essentially had to care for two little boys by herself after, back in April, a pair of racers fell right in front of Luke and, riding straight into the pileup, he rushed over his handlebars like water spilling in a grand trajectory over falls, and on impact he broke his left hand and suffered a hairline fracture of his pelvis. Innis had to call his wife from a distant emergency room in June after crashing in a race when his tire went flat. A year earlier, Michael's body slammed to the pavement in a criterium outside of Sacramento. He'd had to crawl out of the way of the onrushing racers, collapsed lung and all, and his mother and I tended to him in the hospital where he was kept for a week. In January 2006, I was on a training ride in the Berkeley hills, on a road I'd ridden probably a hundred times before. But on that particular day, in the middle of a turn and moving at twenty-five miles per hour, something was somehow different, and I crashed onto my left side, breaking my collarbone and scapula, destroying my helmet, and running my body over what felt like a two-lane, asphalt skin grater.

At least, I think to myself as I finally reach Innis and slip into a small slot between two other rides and directly behind my friend, I won't crash with a bunch of erythropoietin in my veins. That same type of EPO that could've made my mom's life a little better for a little longer was once clogging the veins of doping pro cyclist Joe Papp when he crashed. Papp actually had taken so much EPO (and who knows what else) that by the time of his crash in the summer of 2006, his blood had practically become concentrated enough to resemble raspberry Slurpee. Surgeons had to drain him like he was a car ridiculously overdue for an oil change. Doctors later said the muck in his veins could've killed him.

A bit more than halfway through the Berkeley Bicycle Club Criterium, the pace slows, which is what I've been waiting for. It's the criterium lull that sometimes comes after the initial rush and before some crescendo of a finish. I find that my muscles and lungs, now plenty accustomed to the race's earlier hard efforts, don't want to slow down. After all my training, racing, and *testosteroning*, my body doesn't feel the need to recover, and suddenly I become antsy.

On the flattest length of the course, with twenty-five riders strung out in a skinny, long cluster, I ride up beside Innis. As a rider, I'd always considered him the mighty Innis.

"The plan," I murmur, not wanting any other riders to hear. "You ready?"

"Not sure," says Innis, flicking his handlebar lever to shift into an easier gear. "You're up for this?"

I look at him and smile. I feel really strong, which is one of the lasting mysteries of endurance sports competition. For any given stretch of a race you can feel terrible and become preoccupied with quitting. Then suddenly, with all the drama of a solar eclipse, everything changes, and you've found your inner bullet train. Psychologists, coaches, and drug dealers have all made livings promising consistent ways to deliver this beautiful moment.

"Apparently you're ready," says Innis, catching my grin, his Midwestern twang subdued.

"I can wait one more lap," I say.

A lap that only takes minutes feels much longer. Along the grass island on Key Route Boulevard. Up the slight incline of Thousand Oaks. Into the headwind on Carmel Avenue, and past Luke's wife and kid sitting on the grass of Memorial Park. Down Portland Avenue.

The peloton lazily turns back onto Key Route, and I say nothing as I slowly steer my bike outside of the pack of cyclists and begin to accelerate, into the wind, passing Innis, and up the left flank of the group. I figure that Innis is now right behind me, and shortly after making the turn onto Thousand Oaks, I am alongside the race's leaders as we begin the slight climb back up to Carmel. I only look straight ahead as I focus all of my energies into a beautiful explosion made of power, steroids, and conviction. I stand up and sprint, ten pedal strokes, twenty. Then I sit back down and continue to pedal with all of my strength. I catch glimpses of numbers on my power meter, 620, 200, 415, 295. But this key moment isn't so much about data. I want to ride as fast as I can, for as long as I can, to surprise and then demoralize the others.

Crush their hopes and fantasies. Distance yourself from the pack by a full city block. Disappear. Make them think it's a race for the rest of the podium.

I hammer at the pedals on Carmel Avenue when I finally look back for the first time. It's Innis's turn to lead so that I can get a couple dozen seconds' rest while riding in his slipstream.

Innis is not right behind me.

He is twenty yards back, pedaling furiously, trying to catch up. The peloton, a twenty-rider monster, is 150 yards behind him.

I slow down slightly, giving away some of my hard-won advantage, in order to let Innis catch up. When he does, his thin chest is heaving. His mouth is open to help gather air.

"Come on," I yell to Innis, wanting him to tuck in as close to my rear wheel as he can, and then I look forward to what's ahead of us and slowly increase my effort to try and regain some of our advantage. Innis and I go past the thirty or so spectators at the start-finish line and then make another right onto Key Route. I finally let up on the pedals, and Innis rides by me to take his turn at the front. Fifteen seconds later he motions with his left elbow for me to come around him.

"Can't maintain this," he says as I go by. "Going back into the group."

"Try," I say. "You'll surprise yourself."

"No," he says. "Too much."

I'm at a crossroads. I've already expended a lot of effort to create our advantage. If I let the peloton catch up now, my race to win is over. I won't win a sprint. But to ride out in front alone, without anyone to spell me, is probably a suicide mission. The only way I'll hold off the entire group will be if a crash slows them down.

Suicide mission.

I again stand up and pour gobs of energy into my pedaling. My quadriceps feel like they're standing next to a roaring fire. The balls of my feet burn as I press down, hard as I can, on the pedals. I turn around. I'm maybe 100 yards ahead of a fading Innis and 150 yards ahead of the monster.

I turn again up Thousand Oaks and look back. I've put a little more distance between myself and the peloton. I ride past Luke's wife and kid. I can hear them cheer for me.

"Go Andrew, go!" she yells.

I ride down Portland, again past the start-finish line and past some sort of emcee talking into a speaker.

"And that rider is Andrew Tilin, gapping the group . . ."

Moi!

I am energized, into the first half of the course I go, and then around the backside and past the park, where I hear Luke's wife yell for me again, and now a couple more people cheer. I look over my shoulder. The monster is no farther away, and yet no closer.

"Annnndrewwwww Tilinnnn . . ." says the announcer as I ride past the finish area.

My legs have now become ridiculously heavy as I complete a third lap alone. I savor every moment.

I feel no remorse, no. Not when I'm leading the race. The thrill! The air is so clean, the riding so uncomplicated. Nobody's pedal or wheel to get in my way. I'm number one!

This is my most triumphant—or is it my saddest—moment as a doping cyclist. I'm living the most stereotypical of jock dreams. I have left Innis—the great Innis, the Innis who always surges ahead of me and whom I know so well from behind—in my wake. All of the big and strong cyclists trail me. They are not just today's competition but yesteryear's bullies, the same people who as bigger kids called little-boy Andrew "Tater" and "Shrimp," the taller and stronger boys who always landed the hottest girls and did everything better than me. Now I'm showing them, and although I hate to say that I encounter such hopelessly predictable emotions . . . I do.

And while many bike racers in countries around the world have done what I've done—break far, far away from the field—a million times before me, I have never experienced it. It is freedom, and that freedom is a huge high, and all you want is for the feeling to go on, and that even if you're in front because you've trained hard enough or because the others are slow, the reasons really don't matter, you're a forty-something dad living a *Sports Illustrated*–cover dream. And perhaps your best friend is right—that I really do *love* this stuff, these steroids, and fuck if I'm ever going off them, because I'll take whatever I need to always ride in front because this is such a hoot. And there's Luke's wife and kid again and I wave at them in the middle of the race, I'm the one to beat, this is glory, this is so pathetic and delicious, like chocolate pudding going down, grown men who race bikes shouldn't enjoy pudding because it's fattening but there right in front of me is the win, the redemption, the forever elusive domination.

Then after several laps of glory I'm transported again, but this time to the shores of the Amazon River, where I'm in quicksand, and the dream ends because the many-wheeled beast behind me knew this would happen, that the lactic acid inside my meticulously shaven but slightly saggy legs will no longer dissipate, and that I am now, officially, physically unable to perform. I can barely push the pedals, and I'm caught with less than two laps remaining. Luke spins by me. Innis passes me on my left. There goes everyone.

Like I say, I'm not a great bike racer. But my ever-supportive coach will later tell me that he is proud, that I "animaaaated" the race, which means I dictated the race instead of vice-versa, and he'll tell me that's what champions do, and that I learned about pacing, and that maybe I can better exploit my strength and abilities next time and actually win the race, or finish top-five instead of twenty-third out of thirty. Luke and Innis both finished in the top-fifteen.

After the great Berkeley Bicycle Club Criterium of 2008 ends I watch the awards ceremonies. The winners, still dressed in their multicolored kits but now walking in tennis shoes or flip-flops instead of cycling shoes, and wearing beanie style hats with printed brims advertising obscure bike-culture brands and phrases like "Campagnolo" and "Dopers Suck," are invited to speak into the microphone and address the tiny audience. Before the winners of my race are announced, my name is unexpectedly called. I walk up to the microphone and I'm recognized as the "Most Aggressive Rider" in my particular race. The skinny emcee hands me a bottle of red wine and asks me some canned sports question about what it was like riding so far out in front of the pack, for so long.

I don't know what to say.

"It was sort of intimate out there," I declare, looking at Luke, who's holding his son not ten feet from me. He's smiling his funny big grin. My friend is highly amused that his doping buddy has center stage. He loves all the irony and twists and bizarreness of the moment. He loves them more than I do. In fact I'm not really enjoying the spot-light. I feel small, and really dishonest.

"Intimate? How so? In terms of you being far out in front and by yourself?" asks the announcer. He's confused.

I look down at the ground. I am nervous, and extremely tired. My whole body really wants a cushy chair that's far away from here. My brain is misfiring.

This is what it's like to be Floyd Landis, on drugs and on the podium. Living a lie.

Then I look up, and scan the scene to see who's paying attention to this interview besides Luke and the announcer. There are a few of the other racers, their jerseys splotched with dried sweat stains that they wear as proudly as a soldier wears his stripes. Everyone else is in the middle of something—a conversation, a post-race stupor, or the slow walk with their bikes this way or that. I don't see Innis.

"It was addictive being out ahead like that," I finally say into the microphone. "Habit-forming."

I FEEL FUNKY.

Habit-forming.

I said that, so naturally, and to an audience of strangers no less— bike-racing strangers.

Practically spilled the beans.

Come on, half of those folks had to be at least as spacey as I was.

But you *heard it.*

Dang Michael, putting notions of addiction in my mind. His thoughts were now piggybacking my thoughts, just as they had been before I began doping, when he asked me whether this odyssey was about a story or self-enhancement. His concerns are weighty enough that the "addiction" word bubbles up right from my subconscious, while I talk, for chrissakes, into a microphone. Forget about the idea of flying high on EPO. The notion exists that I won't be able to walk away from the T.

Maybe it really is time to abort the mission.

Hello, that criterium was a huge blast. Months remain on your experiment. The erections and swagger have done you some good. Farewell, T?

Time to weigh my options. Dumping the drugs might be a hasty move. My bike racing season is coming to a close—what could improve upon Cascade, and the swell taste of a top-ten finish, *top-ten*, at a multi-day event!—but there's still plenty of riding ahead of me. The sex with Juliana could break through its new ceiling, the one that's established a couple of weekly lovemaking sessions as the norm. A lot better than the old standard of a few times a month. Maybe more months on the T, perhaps years, and my biceps will erupt from my arms instead of just curve atop them.

But taking the drugs with no end in sight raises the notion of that word, *addiction*, again—such a crappy word. Addicts are walking manifestations of what one might see as the anti-T: weak, vulnerable, and depressed. I don't want to join that club. Addiction makes me think of Nicholas Cage as a drunk in a movie that I could barely sit through, *Leaving Las Vegas*.

Alert! Hollywood fiction, just like Sly Stallone's Rocky Balboa or John Rambo. Are your feet touching the ground? You're not in a movie. You aren't a rider in the Tour de France. You're not on the cover of Men's Health, *or a poster child for the anti-aging community. This is your life, bud. Layering testosterone onto your body for months on end may at times seem as innocuous as a bong hit, as amusing as a tequila shot, just a convenient tool for adding size, strength, and masculinity. But it's often more. The T is about coming to terms with middle age, marriage, virility, decades worth of little-man issues, your dad's homosexuality. Complicated stuff!*

Alright, so when I *really* wrap humanity around addiction, I think of Juliana's West Texas grandfather coming home from work drunk, staggering past the family, and for decades going to bed every night right at dinnertime. His enormous absence was also, sadly, his presence. I myself never saw him drunk, nor did I really get to know her grandfather. By the time I entered the family he was sober, slow moving, and quiet. He watched a ton of TV while unknowingly dropping cigarette ashes everywhere. One time he pointed at Jerry Seinfeld on-screen and bellowed to me, in his deep yet hollow voice, "That's you!" because, apparently, he didn't know too many smart-alecky Jewish guys. Juliana, her cousins, and I had a good laugh.

Another time, I rubbed her grandfather's bare and twisted feet with lotion because he asked me to, straight up, and because I loved his granddaughter so much. We touched but never truly spoke, and certainly not about his addiction's persistent stain on a sweet and well-meaning family. His alcoholism, however, stuffed human emotions into corners of musty West Texas closets. Her grandfather's addiction unquestionably fueled Juliana's departure from Texas, and pushed her to become outspoken, and informed her hooking up with a remotely Seinfeldian guy from California, a man that never failed to say what was on his mind. Juliana and I would create our own happinesses, and our own dysfunctions, too, and they wouldn't have to do with substance addiction. At least not yet.

The Tilins have enough hurdles without a steroid problem. I desperately want to avoid becoming a drug addict.

Could that really happen? Maybe I can take baby steps to avoid it. A compromise solution: Cut down my dose.

Lowering my daily dose of the T sounds, in theory, like an excellent plan. Enjoy some of testosterone's benefits without abandoning it entirely. Potentially reduce the instances of irritability, and the risk of contaminating my wife and children with the residue from my testosterone cream. And perhaps best of all, lower the dose in order to prove to myself that I don't *need* what the T gives me. I don't have to dictate bike races or have hard-ons all the time to feel complete. Like I told Michael, sometimes I want a break from the testosterone anyway.

But my proposed solution has a glaring problem. I'm unsure how to approach cutting back on the protocol. Should I continue to take the T daily, and only take less? Skip the T every few days? Every other day?

Susie Wiley doesn't like patients tinkering with her hormone replacement therapies. I'd first become aware of this back in February, when I attended the Wiley Protocol user's group meeting in San Francisco. One of the women in the group said that she was worried about developing breast fibroids (breast tissue that's rubbery and/or lumpy, although also benign), or even breast cancer, and considered cutting her dosages of the Wiley Protocol for Women in half. She'd said that her husband, who is a physician, wondered aloud about the WP's large estrogen doses taken by his wife, and how many studies back up Wiley's research. Wiley hadn't held back in her response.

"Last time I checked, two people were not endocrinologists," she'd snapped over the speakerphone. "Did you read *Sex, Lies, and Menopause?* This is all laid out. I didn't just make this up."

Never mind that Wiley's conclusions about her women's protocol, which she often admits butts up against mainstream science and has yet to be comprehensively tested, largely remain unproven. Or that Wiley's self proclaimed professional title—"medical theorist"— isn't particularly reassuring to a lot of people suffering from what are very serious health issues. In the ensuing six months following my attendance at the San Francisco user meeting, I'd learn of an infamous past occupied by Wiley and her female detractors. I'd come to decide that using the Wiley Protocol for Women puts people into one of two camps: You're either with Wiley, or you're in the shower, trying like mad to scrub off any possible trace of her hormone-filled creams. The latter camp believes that, yes, Susie Wiley's protocol requires serious tinkering, if not complete re-thinking, because basically, they insist, she has made it up.

I discover that Suzanne Somers is among what Wiley estimates are many thousands of women, like most of the women I met at the user meeting, who are very faithful to Wiley's rhythmic-style protocol. Somers's adulation, however, agitates Wiley's enemies. In the month after Somers's pro-Wiley book, *Ageless*, reached bookstores in the fall of 2006, the blonde celebrity and Susie Wiley appeared on CNN's *Larry King Live*. King wasn't as interested in hormone replacement therapy as he was in an angry letter that had already been written to the publisher of *Ageless*, Crown Publishing, from "Dr. Erika" Schwartz. Dr. Erika is an anti-aging doctor who herself seems to covet the media spotlight, with her own book as well as morning-show appearances. Dr. Erika and other anti-aging physicians, including endocrinologist Diana Schwarzbein, have signed the letter.

"Wiley has no medical or clinical qualifications," wrote Dr. Erika in the letter. " . . . [She] dispenses gratuitous advice on significant medical issues, including the use of bioidentical hormone therapies."

The conflict only worsened. During King's show, Somers, Wiley, Schwarzbein, and Dr. Erika sparred as if they were in a sandbox looking to pull lots of hair. A core sample of the exchange:

SOMERS: *Here [Dr. Erika] is, writing a complaint letter about the fact that I am writing about rhythmic cycling, which is one of the ways that you can take it [hormone therapy]. And she has been prescribing T. S. Wiley's protocol . . . this woman is a hypocrite.*

DR. ERIKA: *I prescribed [the Wiley Protocol] to one patient.*

SOMERS: *Not true.*

SCHWARZBEIN: *[Wiley] is not a doctor. What I'm saying is, if you read the chapter on T. S. Wiley, what you come away with is that her protocol has been thoroughly researched . . . and that is not true.*

WILEY: *We hold meetings in Santa Barbara once a month for fifty to eighty people on the Wiley Protocol. It is remarkable how many of them are your ex-patients, Diana.*

Ugh! Bam! Ouch!

If only King could've called a timeout. Instead, after a commercial break, he looped in another guest, Dr. Wulf Utian, who was the executive director of the North American Menopause Society. He stated what millions of dubious viewers had to be thinking: Who would trust any of these people?

"The whole group as I heard it are all off base," says Utian. "They sound more like a cult. This whole bioidentical thing is really merchandising under the guise of medical practice."

Whomp!

Websites are equally determined to claw at the Wiley Protocol for Women. The site wileywatch.org "scrutinizes the Wiley Protocol and its stakeholders. Both have proven deserving."

Sure enough, the website dissects Wiley's credentials (she'd initially lied about earning her college degree); debates her research (citing a bioethicist who published a piece stating that one of Wiley's proposed Wiley Protocol studies "does not meet criteria for regulated or ethical research"); and calls out Wiley's husband for sending clearly frustrated but also harassing correspondence (even cloaked as holiday well-wishes) to critics of the protocol. Another website, Rhythmic Living, runs an interview between the website's creator, Laurel McCubbin, and Bent Formby, the molecular biologist who co-wrote *Sex, Lies, and Menopause*. In the interview, Formby explains, "I said [to Susie] I don't think you can use these protocols you are using for yourself for other people without having tested them first. And then she said well, I'll do what I want, if you don't want to get involved that's fine with me."

Today Formby has nothing to do with the Wiley Protocol, although Susie Wiley herself insists that Formby had plenty to do with the science. The two no longer communicate, Wiley says, for personal reasons.

In summer 2008, I have the chance to interview the forty-seven-year-old McCubbin, who's in the midst of a trip away from her home in the Pacific Northwest, at a restaurant near my Berkeley office. McCubbin recalls one terrible experience after another on the Wiley Protocol, which she began in fall 2004 and followed for about seven months. The protocol's supplemental estrogen, McCubbin explains, did her a lot of good. The gobs of progesterone did not. She suffered from profuse menstrual bleeding, as well as pronounced hair loss. Wiley, however, wouldn't budge in her guidance. "Whenever I was experiencing some side effect, Susie said my thyroid was out of whack," says McCubbin, "or that I was going to sleep at the wrong time."

Of course I have sympathy for McCubbin, and all the other women who felt physically and emotionally betrayed by Wiley's protocol. But honestly, for months, the issues were somebody else's problems.

Now they are mine. Again I ask myself if I should cut back on the T.

In hindsight, I should've called Wiley or Patil. But I thought Wiley might become resentful or put off, in a relationship already shadowed by my journalistic endeavor, if I suggested changing my protocol. And Patil had already told me that if anything, Wiley wants men upping their testosterone supplementation during the summer months. My doctor had also suggested that when applying the fluctuating protocol's peak dosages, I should try to apply less T more frequently so that my body might be required to absorb less of the hormone at once. Or, she suggested, perhaps reduce the dosage on one day and increase it the next. But she never told me to lower the overall amounts of testosterone. To Patil's credit, nothing in my blood work suggested that I should take less T.

Instead, I seek advice from a doper's oft-trusted resource: a peer. Wiley's people had, over the past couple of months, helped put me in touch with other men on Wiley's male protocol. Among them were a seventy-two-year-old painter, a fifty-five-year-old bus driver, a fifty-two-year-old building contractor, and a fifty-four-year-old physicist. Collectively, their strongest impressions of life on the T were a lot like mine: increased libido, added strength, and greater overall vitality. The contractor raved about how he tired less frequently while outrigger canoe racing. Everyone had also said that the T had made them more edgy, if not aggressive. The seventy-two-year-old painter from Southern California told me, "My wife says when I first started that I was like the Hulk."

But only one of these steroid users became concerned like me that perhaps the testosterone was having too much influence on his life. Fifty-four-year-old physicist Van McComas, who hailed from Virginia, told me that one of the first things to improve on the T was his sex drive. He also soon noticed mood swings—feeling depressed one day, angry on another day.

Not long before leaving Oakland to join my family in Austin at the end of July, I receive a message from McComas.

"I'm tired of this sine wave of emotions, so I'm doing something about it," he wrote, and attached a schedule that, like Patil had recommended, smoothed out the month's worth of dosages without changing the amount of testosterone he'd take each month. Ironically enough, in an earlier message McComas had been concerned that altering Wiley's math might get him "kicked off the protocol." Months later, after McComas also experimented with another chemical substance in his program (called *chrysin*), Wiley's people threatened to give him the boot.

But at the end of July I thought I'd take McComas's and Patil's suggestions, and monkey with the dosages ever so slightly.

The tweak might mellow you out. Maybe you're not an addict. You're just neurotic.

I pack five full syringes in my suitcase and head for the airport.

JULIANA ALWAYS HAS A PLAN for my visits to Texas. The plan is to make Andrew happy. I'm not proud of this. But Texas and I are not an easy fit, and Juliana, bless her heart, is hyperaware of what I perceive as vast differences between Austin's welcoming yet bipolar southern/progressive culture and my Type A disposition mixed with a heavy dose of Nor Cal provincialism. She knows that I struggle with Austin's summer heat, so Juliana puts swimming on the schedule. She's also great about me leaving her, Benjamin, Sophie, and my in-laws behind for hours at a time so that I can ride a bike with some of Austin's many strong racers through the pretty Texas Hill Country. And she picks out restaurants that I might enjoy, including Mexican places that go easy on the queso and heavy on the fresh ingredients. The only thing Juliana doesn't anticipate for my ten-day visit to her homeland is my steroid sidekick making me as combustible as Habanero peppers.

My first morning in Austin, I'm up early and in the bathroom of the vacation house we're renting, dutifully applying enough Wiley cream onto my thighs to get a 70-milligram boost of testosterone instead of what the schedule calls for—90 milligrams. I'll make up the difference in the next phase of the protocol, rubbing on 60 milligrams worth of T in the morning when the directions call for 40.

Soon, Benjamin, Juliana, and I begin to make our way west out of town in our rental car on the four-lane, highway-like Bee Caves Road. We're expected later at the comfortable, waterside home of one of Juliana's aunts, who has a place about sixty miles away on Lake Lyndon B. Johnson, or Lake LBJ. Sophie is already out there. She'd spent the night, which no doubt made my little girl very happy. Her great aunt and uncle have a home unlike ours—big TVs, the pool table, a fridge full of brisket and homemade tortillas, motorized watercraft of various dimensions, and lots of girl clothes that Sophie can use for playing dress-up. So far in Texas, you'd think, so good: tasty enchiladas last night with the in-laws at Güero's on South Congress Ave., and now we're headed straight for tepid but welcome water on a windless, hot, and humid summer day.

But somewhere inside my head, while I drive down the road, is the edgy equivalent of a tickle in my throat.

You feelin' the T?

Juliana is on the phone, laughing in conversation with Tina, who is one of her oldest friends, and who still lives in Texas. Ben is behind us, strapped into his car seat, looking around at all the vehicles. He loves cars just the same way I did as a kid, and points out a blue Ford F-150 pickup as it passes us going the other direction.

"Did you see those wheels, Daddy?" he asks.

"Chrome," I say.

"Sweet Cadillac," says Benjamin, pointing at a black and gold SUV. Juliana giggles into the phone.

A happy family vacation, and I am . . . clenching my jaw.

What is the problem?

Maybe I still need to let go of my life-stresses. Writing a magazine story, I'd nearly pulled an all-nighter before leaving for Austin. I'd also bloodied my knuckles while trying to loosen a pedal from my bicycle.

You're just frazzled.

Didn't help that, before I'd left, I found our kitchen at home to be crawling with ants.

You need this downtime.

Benjamin points out a bright red Mustang. Juliana's conversation with Tina grows louder. My wife's short torso shakes with her laughs.

Juliana and the kids have already been on vacation for nearly two weeks. Relax your shoulders. Chips, salsa, and a cold beer await.

"Tina, that will stir up a hornet's nest," says Juliana, looking sideways at me with a big smile on her face while she speaks into the phone.

What are they talking about?

"No. I'm not going there," Juliana says in an upbeat voice.

Oh, I know what this is about. Tina. That woman wrote the book on persistence.

"We've already settled it," Juliana says into the phone. "I'm not spending the night with you and Barb."

Days ago, Juliana had asked if I'd be okay with her having a girls' day and night out with Tina and her other close friend Barbara only forty-eight hours after I'd arrive in Austin. Even while asking, Juliana had apologized because she knew that the timing was bad. She knew that I'd like more opportunity to decompress before going solo with the kids, my in-laws, and the not entirely familiar streets of Austin. I'd told Juliana that I wasn't comfortable with the idea. I was reasonable in how I said no.

Juliana reminded me: Scheduling-wise, the dates represented the only window that the three women could find to spend an extended stretch of time together.

In my most mature and even-tempered voice, I'd replied again that I'd prefer if she didn't.

Juliana didn't argue, and the issue went away.

Apparently Tina wants us to return to the negotiating table.

"All right," says Juliana into her phone, smiling as she looks straight out the windshield as I drive. "You speak to him."

Juliana extends her left arm and mobile phone toward me.

"Tina wants to talk to you," she says.

Now I'm not particularly proud that my wife feels compelled to ensure my soft landing in Texas, or that I'm not encouraging her to wander off for a day and a half because I need time to settle into Lone Star State rhythms. (Austin is, in many ways, a very cool town, with lots of funky people and places. A lot funkier than I am. Though I sometimes struggle with the malls and *y'alls*.)

But agitation is in my DNA. There's eleven-year-old Andrew, wound up enough to throw real punches (why I don't remember) at my friends after watching Sylvester Stallone—my eternal homeboy, Sly!—in *Rocky*. There's twenty-four-year-old Andrew, pissed off at Michael about our chosen bike route and accelerating away from him as we ride over Teton Pass at the Idaho-Wyoming border. Now as a fortysomething, I'm taking angry swings again, at least in my head, at deadlines, insect problems, and my wife's stubborn friends.

Stay cool, bro.

"I don't want to talk to Tina," I say in a low voice.

"Just for a sec," says Juliana, her expression changing slightly. "Please?"

"I really don't want to talk to her," I say.

"Just say hi," says Juliana, the phone still outstreched toward me.

We have a situation!

"Juliana, get the phone away from me!"

Iccchhh.

"Daddy?" I hear Benjamin say tentatively from over my right shoulder. "Is everything okay?"

"Let me call you back," Juliana says into the phone, and then hangs up.

"Don't talk to me like that," she says. "In that awful voice."

"Then don't push me. We've discussed this issue, your girls' night out. My earlier response was a polite no. Now it's an irritated no. Why make me go there again?" I shout. "No, no way, never, not, nix!"

"You are such a jerk!" says Juliana, shaking her head. "You're a—"

"I don't need this," I scream. "Screw Lake LBJ. Forget Lake LBJ," I yell. "I'll go back to the house and work, and you can spend two nights with your friends. Three nights! Five!"

"Daddy!" Benjamin yelps. He starts to cry.

"You're scaring him," says Juliana, reaching back to hold Benjamin's hand. "You're out of your mind."

And then my T-fueled fury takes me where even I've never gone before.

"*Aaaaaaaaaahhhhhhhh!*" I yell, and pull on the steering wheel, turning left across two lanes of Bee Caves Road and into the empty parking lot of some business office that's closed for the weekend. I bring our silver Suzuki rental car to an abrupt halt.

I glare at Juliana and then look at Benjamin. His brown eyes are bugged out in fear. In a matter of seconds I'm full of remorse.

What have I done?

Juliana and Benjamin both get out of the car, while I remain in the driver's seat, my forearms resting on the wheel, my head resting face down on my forearms. Juliana sits down on the curb, and Benjamin climbs into her lap. I can hear them bawling. I am deeply sorry for my outburst and for ruining the plan. My vacation is not going according to the plan. In fact, it's off to a terrible start.

"I don't know you," says Juliana. I look up, and her face is all creases and wetness. "You're not yourself. Not on that stuff."

I wish she were right. According to at least a couple of scientists, I am, at this moment I'd love to forget, in fact very me. Robert M. Sapolsky, a professor of neuroscience and biology at Stanford University, argues that supplemental testosterone can turn someone who's already irritable into someone downright nasty. Sapolsky says that if the pathway between two emotion-related portions of the brain, the amygdala and hypothalamus, is already primed with aggression-inducing signals, that more testosterone intensifies those signals. "[Testosterone's] not turning on the pathway, it's increasing the volume of signaling if it is already turned on," Sapolsky writes in his book, *The Trouble With Testosterone: and Other Essays on the Biology of the Human Predicament.* "It's not causing aggression, it's exaggerating the preexisting pattern of it."

Harrison Pope, a professor of psychiatry at Harvard Medical School who has researched psychology and steroids for years, doesn't necessarily agree with Sapolsky that personality and disposition determines levels of aggressiveness. But Pope later told me that studies where subjects use 500 milligrams or more of testosterone per week "can produce aggressiveness, although it's in the minority. The majority shows little or no change."

Just my luck. Born with a temper, dosing up with anywhere from 500 to 1,200 grams of testosterone per week, and apparently the rare, unlucky recipient in some aggro-dude genetic lottery.

Maybe it's good the T and I are not in a long-term relationship.

I TAKE BENJAMIN to the altar. The morning after losing my temper with Ben and Juliana in the car, my son and I pull up in front of Mellow Johnny's bike shop in downtown Austin. Everything

I've heard is that Mellow Johnny's, which is housed in a completely redone, old brick building and been open for less than three months, is one of the coolest bike shops on the planet. It's apparently spacious, light, and decorated with artwork and photography, making it as much a museum and ode to cycling as a store where you can buy a simple bike.

However, I'm not nearly as excited as Benjamin is about the visit. He tugs at my hand as we walk up the steps from the parking lot, through the glass doors, and into the polished and perfectly climate-controlled shop. Benjamin is drawn to Mellow Johnny's because it's co-owned by the legendary former professional cyclist, Lance Armstrong. Armstrong is one of his heroes. Ben already wants to ride Lance's bike, wear Lance's kit, and read my old, well-worn copy of Lance's autobiography, *It's Not About the Bike,* which chronicles Armstrong's incredible comeback from cancer patient to world-beating bike racer. But because of Lance Armstrong, I have my own feelings about visiting Mellow Johnny's. They're mixed. Fair or otherwise, I'm preoccupied with the notion that—to this doper, anyway—the place could feel like it sits underneath a syringe shaped cloud.

"Daddy, over here," says Benjamin. He's standing at a wall displaying cycling helmets of every color and silhouette. Above the helmets are some of the old bikes that Armstrong rode on his way to winning races all over Europe in the 1990s and 2000s, which of course included his record seven Tours de France. But through much of Armstrong's impressive cycling career, and even into retirement, he's been—we all know—accused of doping. Just about every great cyclist that Lance Armstrong ever defeated has been busted for taking performance-enhancing drugs. Is it possible, Michael and I have asked each other many times, that a natural Lance Armstrong could be better than *all* of his chemically enhanced competition?

Was he born on Mars?

"What's this helmet for?" asks Ben, and he grabs a tapered and elongated, red helmet off the wall that's about as contoured and aerodynamic as a Ferrari. He tries it on. The helmet looks ridiculous, like a giant bird beak that he's wearing backwards.

Benjamin returns the helmet to the display, and something else catches his eye.

"Ohhh," he says, walking in another direction. "Livestrong bracelets."

Benjamin seemingly let go of Juliana's and my miserable altercation in the car about two hours after it ended. At that point he was in his swimsuit and skimming along Lake LBJ on some giant floatation device that his great aunt pulled behind her Jet Ski–style machine. Despite my apologies, hurt feelings remained between Juliana and me for the remainder of that day, and though I didn't know it yet, we'd both feel somewhat raw for the rest of the vacation. Juliana lived with a certain amount of trepidation that my fury would resurface. Honestly, so did I.

Still, twenty-four hours after the episode, I'm determined to make sure that things are copacetic between Ben and me. I don't want him having any lingering feelings that my outburst, and Juliana's and my argument, are in some way his fault. My therapist had told me eons ago that kids can blame themselves for their parents' relationship struggles. More significantly, I believe, is my yearning for Ben to look up to me. Does he have to see all my flaws? He's my boy—and entitled to a father he can trust, and who will be a role model. Someone who makes the world safe. Someone who's a hero instead of a disappointment.

Lofty goals.

"Dad, check out this tricycle," says Benjamin, atop a brand new and overbuilt blue trike with big knobby tires. He's borrowed a shop helmet.

"A guy told me I could ride it around the store," he says. I wave him on.

While Benjamin rides laps, I look up at the framed yellow jerseys on the wall. The yellow jersey, which is worn by the leader of the race during the Tour de France, is the most prestigious piece of clothing in pro cycling. The yellow jersey is also synonymous with Armstrong.

Lord knows how many millions of milligrams of testosterone have been burned to keep riders in that top.

Benjamin comes to a stop in front of me.

"Can we buy this?" he says, slowly pedaling the tricycle back and forth in front of me. "Please?"

"No, buddy," I say. "How would we get that thing home? You already have a bicycle."

"But . . ."

"Benjamin, come on," I say. He bows his head, but only for a second.

"I like this helmet," he says, tapping the blue lid on his head.

"Yours is fine," I say.

This time he bows his head a little longer. He resumes riding, and I look around. Benjamin already has a lot of water bottles. The Mellow Johnny's hats are too big for him. Then Armstrong's framed yellow jerseys catch my eye again.

I stop Ben after he laps part of the store again.

"How about this," I say, leaning over to look straight into his face. "Why don't I buy you a kid-size version of Lance's yellow jersey? I think I saw some."

"Really?" says Ben. His face lights up.

"Special treat," I say, and we head over to the kids' clothes. The small yellow jerseys are expensive—$75 each.

I'll be lucky if Ben doesn't outgrow it in four months.

I don't flinch.

"Try a couple on," I say, and Ben excitedly lifts himself off the trike and takes off his T-shirt right next to the clothes rack. He holds up the expensive garb to his chest. I'm enjoying watching him.

Folks who want to be heroes do all sorts of things. Maybe they build beautiful stores, or buy their kids fancy sports clothes, or race in famous bike races, or even take mysterious potions. Perhaps along the way, these people who want to be heroes aren't even sure what kinds of heroes they might become, and the routes they take to becoming heroes aren't obvious, either. Maybe someone will slap down some money in a bike shop to become a hero. That same person might also take performance-enhancing drugs just for the experience, thinking that there's some celebrity, something heroic, something compelling, in the endeavor. Others might take PEDs too. Maybe someone who owns a bike shop has taken them. Perhaps such a person is a different kind of hero.

While Benjamin busily tries on jerseys, I don't resent my doping self more, and I resent the idea of Lance Armstrong taking such drugs less. Because in some microscopic way, I think I understand that while the desire to become a hero is pervasive, arriving at such a triumphant moment can be full of unexpected turns, and maybe mistakes, and ugliness. Then when you become a hero, if you're so fortunate, dwelling on the mistakes seems like an energy suck, and time poorly spent. The value is in being the hero, the sun that emanates light and power and heat. Heroes make the world a better place.

Right?

"How does this look, Daddy?" says Benjamin, beaming in a jersey that's actually plenty big for him. It's bright yellow, and shines like the sun indeed.

"Awesome, buddy," I say. "Let's buy it."

new old me

Weeks after we return from Austin, the scores arrive in the mail: Andrew, 759. Juliana, 129. We'd each had blood work done and received our results. We're both full up on the T, but relatively speaking, Juliana is king. My total testosterone number (in nanograms per deciliter) is still well within the recommended range for an adult male. Juliana's, measured in picograms per milliliter, is more than twice as high as the highest figure in the lab's suggested reference range for that particular hormone. Half a year earlier, Juliana's testosterone levels were approximately twenty percent of what they are now. Her T is on steroids.

My nightmares regarding contamination have been realized, at least in my own mind.

"You called the doctor, didn't you?" I ask Juliana as soon as I get home from work the day the results arrive. "What did she say? Should we take you to the ER? How do we de-T you?"

"She said—"

"Do you feel sick?" I interrupt. "Or strange in any way?"

"Andrew, she just said—"

"Will there be any permanent damage? Juliana, I'm so sorry—"

"Andrew, stop! I'm going to be fine," says my wife. "I spoke to the doctor and she told me we can definitely bring my levels down safely. She said, 'Honey, be more careful. Keep him away longer. Make sure he's dry and that the cream has been completely absorbed before he gets in bed. And wash the sheets regularly,'" says Juliana.

"Maybe I ought to live next door," I say.

"Stop stressing, everything is all right. She wasn't alarmed, and I'm going to be fine."

We decide to get some fresh air and take a neighborhood walk with the kids, who run a few steps ahead of us and busy themselves tossing a tennis ball. Sophie doesn't have the throwing motion down, despite my obsessive coaching. I always tell her to "squish the bug" with her back foot—that is, to rotate on the ball of that trailing foot—as she makes the throw. Forgive me, but I'm determined that my little girl learns to throw like—yes, here it comes—a *boy*. At this very moment, however, I realize that my desire is particularly warped. The last thing the Tilin house needs is another female becoming more male.

"She also said that in terms of excess testosterone, I'm not sprouting chest hair, or encountering other symptoms like acne or a deep voice," says Juliana. "It's not like I'm on my way to becoming a man."

"Thank heavens," I say.

Juliana grabs my hand. She doesn't always do that anymore. Nice when she does.

Despite her calm, I know that Juliana is feeling real relief over my growing readiness to end the Great Tilin Hormone Experiment. We've already agreed that it's time to wind down the project. Without a doubt, such closure means farewell to excitement and fun for Juliana, and to her zipping up the forest trails in her running shoes (Wiley will later emphatically tell me that Juliana's high T scores may be a result of her own hormone-replacement therapy and not contamination from my Wiley Protocol creams; in the end I can't be sure what caused Juliana's dramatic rise in T, which did occur in step with my time on the 'roids). But right now sharing a life containing *less* intensity, power, and sexuality seems appealing to her. To us, I should say.

"It's nice not to be in a rush," says Juliana as we meander up a sidewalk-less street. She's right. It's beautiful outside: a still and warm, mid-September, Indian summer evening. Birds sound off in the tall pine, redwood, and oak trees that neighbor the homes on our street. The cloudless sky is a black-blue, and the light, coming from a low sun that is farther south on the horizon, is sharp and warm, but also somehow feels vulnerable. There is the slightest hint of transition in the air. Summer is clearly impermanent. Cooler air is coming.

Juliana's bright paisley blouse shows enough of her flesh and shape to remind me of the body just underneath.

We could screw right now, in that little flat opening in the mini-grove of redwoods just up the rise. I could throw the tennis ball over Benjamin's outstretched, small, and puffy hands, and he and Sophie could chase after it, far down a hill, and Juliana and I could scamper to that little opening, and I could sit on one of those old Adirondack chairs and she could put all that Yoga Friday flexibility to use.

Ah yes, the Jekyll-like, T-infused, sudden thoughts. Will I miss those? I'm accustomed to them now, all these months of steroid use have turned me into a doper's perfect "10." Really, I'm a *759*, as in total testosterone, which takes me beyond Patil's and Wiley's hopes of my male hormone levels someday cracking the 600s. Earlier today I'd emailed the news of my T score to Van McComas, the Virginia physicist and fellow Wiley Protocol for Men user.

"Congrats on making the 700 Club," he wrote. "Hope to be there in a few months."

That's right. I'm on the summit of Mount T. Planting the flag!

And yet, as the Tilins walk up the rise, I look at the Adirondack chairs but do not hurl the tennis ball past Ben and Sophie. I don't grab Juliana and head for the opening in the redwoods. The four of us are having a sweet family outing and enjoying each other's company. It's a rare but precious instance where testosterone doesn't have a say in the action. I should try to get used to such moments.

I pull three more tennis balls out of my pockets and tell Juliana, Benjamin, and Sophie to form a square with me in the street.

I hand Juliana and Sophie balls and keep one for myself. Ben already has one.

"Throw your ball to the person on your left and catch the ball from the person on your right," I say. "Simultaneously. Don't let a ball touch the ground."

As a team we fail almost immediately. We all laugh. Sophie's smile shows her Chiclet teeth. Juliana's dimples form. Benjamin airs his sweet, high-pitched chuckle. The pleasures derived of a benign and simple game. Maybe all of that testosterone has allowed me to better acknowledge—and hopefully appreciate—a life without it.

"Why don't you put some muscle behind that toss?" Juliana teases as the children run in different directions to field the balls. "You know, maybe the bigger achievement is that you can throw it softly."

I chuckle.

But why can't I have it all? The power and the control over it?

I can easily go to a place, right here, right now, with my happy wife and kids, on this quiet street, and believe that there's at least a nanogram of proof that I can be an upstanding member of the 700 Club *and* not the out-of-control jerk that I was in Austin. Time and experience have allowed me to discover that maintaining equanimity is key—benign, serene, or at the very least even-tempered feelings seem to beget more of the same for me. If I'm upset, the T only amplifies my unhappiness or anger.

Still, even though science hasn't confirmed that there is anything such as 'roid rage, what did that one guy say on the DVD of the 2008 steroid documentary *Bigger Stronger Faster**? That one freakish gym rat, who so unscientifically put it: "'Roids will take a little asshole and make him into a big asshole. You just become a bigger asshole."

Even at only 147 pounds dripping wet, I wondered, as did Juliana, if the 'roids were making me stronger, sexier, and, at times, just a little-big asshole.

Tennis balls. Chiclet teeth. Family. No more T.

Walking back to our house, I remember that day back in Austin, after Juliana and I fought in our rental car on Bee Caves Road, how long it took us to get back on track. Our relationship misfired in a mall, on a run, and on our one date night, where a pretty sunset and dancing couldn't get us past lingering feelings. Sad, and I know much of the blame is mine. Then, on the plane ride home, when she and I were both calm and the children were watching a movie, we made a pact. The time had come to wind down what at the point was about an eight-month drug-test. Coming to that agreement alone made both of us feel better.

The decision has been made. Move toward that agreement, and aspire to have a quiet head, as well as a life that doesn't build on the hyperbolic results that the last three-quarters of a year have provided.

BEFORE I KICK THE T, I have to address two pieces of unfinished business. The first is a face-to-face farewell to Susie Wiley. She's granted me access to an annual medical seminar that she hosts, which introduces and educates doctors and others primarily in the medical field to her hormone-replacement therapy programs. The seminar is scheduled for a mid-September weekend in Southern California, and when I'd signed up for the event three months earlier, I'd decided to travel by car. I love to drive. I love solo road trips—I can play my music, speed to my own satisfaction, and do some thinking. But the significance of my chosen travel day hadn't occurred to me until, on that very departure day, I load my suitcase into the trunk and look at my watch. It's September 19. The anniversary of my mother's death.

As another phase of my life winds down, it's fate that I drive the bare and empty Interstate 5 to Southern California on this day.

On September 19, 2000, in a cold Bay Area fog, I stood in a cemetery with Tracy, Juliana, baby Benjamin, and plenty of family and friends who had stood in the same place with my sister and me one decade earlier. In 1989, Tracy and I numbly watched as my father's casket slid into the same tall and blocky, slab-surfaced, multi-tenant marble crypt where my mother's remains were headed in 2000.

On the day we said goodbye to Mom, and said a sad "Hello" to my neighboring dad, I remember only wanting to feel young again. *Where's my bike? Where's the fun? Screw pneumocystis pneumonia and AIDS and God's Will against gays and stage 47 breast cancer and oncologists and executors and attorneys and tax ramifications and weird, subdued staffers in the mortuary business.*

I hate my last visions of my mom. The doctors had given her just about every pill and potion except EPO, literally burned her with chemicals from the inside out. They'd rearranged her tissue—they called it reconstruction—in an attempt to provide her with a girlish figure to match her girlish demeanor. But in the end, she was so *not* Angela, physically or mentally, not the mom-kid at all. She fought to stay aware and awake, to touch blob-Benjamin, to beat back the narcotic effects of the morphine, to eat a pot sticker. I watched her chest heave, and her breath progressively slow like she was some garage-sale metronome. *Screw this!*

At that cemetery in the dank city of Colma, I was so pissed at becoming a thirty-five-year-old orphan. How dare both my parents leave Tracy and me to figure out the rest of our lives. They wouldn't be there through my relationship challenges, career uncertainties, kid raising. And we wouldn't have the moments of happy reflection when we would totally get each other. Doesn't that happen, isn't there even an instance in a long parent-child relationship of *bilateral-dysfunction-disarmament*, where the children are old enough and the parents aren't too old and there's détente and flavorful food, and nobody yet has to stand up with a walker or go to the bathroom a bunch?

Maybe that's only a fantasy. Tracy and I would never know the truth. Our children won't know their paternal grandparents, never smell their funky old-person stink, or see their recessed gum lines. No elders to take them to Giants home games, or shopping—on nearly maxed-out credit cards—for pint-sized finery in downtown San Francisco. No mustachioed grandfather, with his ability to play almost anything by ear, to idolize at the piano, his long, veiny hands skimming the keys as he produces lively versions of *Tie A Yellow Ribbon Round the Old Oak Tree*, or *I Will Survive*, or, I don't know, Coldplay. The man could make a piano sing. Why couldn't he have stuck around?

Why did you both have to go?

But eight years and about 25,000 milligrams of exogenous testosterone later, I want to stop being angry. I've gone back in time, relived my youth, marveled at the biceps and increased power at lactate threshold. The added edge—the aggression—however, I don't want.

The longer I'm on the drugs, the more I realize that even the benefits of being a doper next door are peripheral. The anti-aging "before" and "after" shots? Where's the performance bump in intimacy, sentiments, and care? The drugs don't do squat for your soul.

Of course, who needs love to win the Tour de France? Hit the baseball to the stars? Performance-enhancing drugs are fantastic tools for sports, where scores matter, technology and science already have so much of a say in terms of training and equipment, and there are winners and losers. My kids and wife don't hold up scorecards to tell me how I'm doing. There's no sports ticker running along our hardwood floors. Maybe it's the dopers next door who need drug testing. Maybe they're the ones who desperately need to be kept off the juice.

And maybe I'm just championing different myths, but I'm giving myself some leash: Months and months into my experiment, I find myself wanting wisdom and perspective. I yearn for some serenity that I believe comes from maturation. In these years in which I still know youth and yet can now imagine growing old, I see the merit in slow moments like walking through neighborhoods, watching Sophie plunk keys on the piano, lying quietly in bed next to Juliana and hearing birds and seeing sunlight, and sticking to the athletic sidelines as I watch Benjamin muscle up and learn to snag line drives. Six-pack abs won't help me give guidance to growing children, and while Juliana likes that the T takes me out of my head, it doesn't necessarily put me in my heart. To say that steroids provided me with a life-changing epiphany would be silly hyperbole, but they've delivered an ironic lesson. Perhaps what I really want isn't to be younger. I want to be able-bodied of course, but also insightful and caring, and a have a quiet mind. Maybe I want to be *older*.

At least that's what I think for a few moments on a September 2008 day while I drive down I-5.

Boyo, you're still doing ninety-plus down the Interstate in a sweet old BMW, sliding past the stodgy Corollas and slo-mo minivans. Good times! Give up this fun, too? Why? Remember that Mom left you with a legacy: Live a little, Tilin!

Hey—will this thing do a hundred and thirty?

I'VE COME TO WILEY'S seminar seeking doping closure, as well as specific hormone-related advice. As I walk up to the Glendale Community College Planetarium, however, I'm not sure how I'll

initiate a conversation about what is my final doping-related conun-
drum, which is getting off the 'roids.

I feel as if I can't easily ask for such advice. The fifty or so casually dressed people mostly from the medical industry who are gathered here in the GCC Planetarium on a Saturday morning have come
seeking Wiley's wisdom (as well as "Continuing Medical Education"
credits from the American Medical Association). No nagging hecklers
from the Rhythmic Living chat group, or rival anti-aging "experts"
will make it through the door. The seminar's ambitious course descrip-
tion says the gathering will "provide up to date information on envi-
ronmental endocrinology . . . and present approaches to such common
problems as insomnia, menopause, osteoporosis, thyroid function,
sexual dysfunction, cancer, GI problems, Type 2 diabetes, endocrine
effects on HIV infection, as well as a broad spectrum of other clinical
problems in endocrinology."

No cure for world hunger?

Not only is this meeting bound to be Hormonapalooza. It's sure
to be quirky. From my seat near the front, I look around at what is,
well, a planetarium: domed ceiling, stadium-style seating for about
fifty people, and muted lighting.

*It's a planetarium, all right, for a seminar called "Two Days Back
on Earth." A medical seminar, no less.*

We take our seats, and Susie Wiley, who is truly one of her
industry's supernovas, walks through the door at the bottom of the
planetarium.

"Good morning doctors and almost doctors, and pharmacists and
nurse practitioners and agents and everybody who's here," says Wiley
in a voice that I've come to understand is naturally coarse—perfect

for someone going against the grain of conventional medicine. She's dressed in black and white Chanel high heels, a low-cut black dress, four strands of pearls encircling her neck, and a long white jacket that isn't a physician's coat but resembles one.

Perfect for an almost *doctor.*

Wiley tucks her hands into the pockets of her coat and shifts her weight onto her right heel as she scans the full facility. "I feel so important," she says with a genuine smile.

She asks everyone in the audience to introduce themselves, and in turn most people are more than happy to validate Wiley.

"I'm currently regional sales director for a large publishing company," says one woman at the back of the planetarium. "Thank you for your protocol. I've been on it for about eight months. It's the best thing ever."

"I'm a general surgeon, and a busy surgeon, in a little town," says another woman. "It's a very long story how I came to this. But it's my opinion that everyone should have their hormones balanced before you get treated for any disease."

"You know my practice has always been more of the spiritual," says a psychiatrist. "I do energetic medicine as well. And I'm thinking—I'm seeing intuitively that patients' hormones are off, but I don't know how to fix them. So I've learned how to do a little bit of the static dosing and have a few people on that. But when I learned about the Wiley, I thought, oh, this really makes intuitive sense to me just from just reading it energetically."

There's a women's health specialist and a naturopath, several pharmacists and plenty of MDs, including an orthopedic surgeon. Patil is here, too.

"Susie has basically rekindled my love of learning, because she is the biggest picture person that I've ever seen," says my doc, sounding unusually cheerful, and looking the part, in a pair of jeans and a cotton shirt. "I keep coming back to learn more."

Eventually it's my turn.

Go ahead, announce that you're not like the rest of them. Tell them that you're giving up the juice.

"I'm Andrew Tilin. I'm a writer," I say.

"I know you," says Wiley.

"A little less than two years ago, I had this idea to write about men on hormone-replacement therapy. But I couldn't find the right one to talk to me. You know, men who take testosterone are called cheaters."

"Dopers," says someone in the audience.

"Dopers, right," I say. "I wanted to explore that, so I kept looking for someone who would let me into their life and write about their experiences. But I couldn't find that person. So I became him. Now I've been on Wiley's Men's Protocol for nearly nine months."

"Feel any different?" asks Wiley.

Ohhhhhh. Big question. How you gonna handle that?

"My wife loves it," I say.

Nice sidestep. Juliana takes one for the team!

"Too bad you didn't bring her," says Wiley.

With that I sit down, and the moment moves past me. Soon the lights dim. What comes next is a one-hour planetarium show that, like Wiley's book, is heavy on science and concepts that aren't terribly easy to grasp.

"The only thing I need you to remember is that man is an emergent property of the universe," she says right before the theme song from

2001: A Space Odyssey cues up. "If you can keep that in mind while you're watching this, everything that's said will not seem random."

Uh, yeah, okay.

Six computers generate myriad infinity-and-beyond images on the dome above us, and a guy from the planetarium begins to narrate. He tells the audience that space is fluid and dynamic, and he describes how space has moved from the Big Bang to baryons and quarks, and then to hydrogen and helium, and then to stars and modern galaxies, and stuff has formed like gravitationally repulsive dark energy, and supermassive black holes.

Wiley interrupts.

"Anybody have any questions?" she asks, an omniscient voice coming from the darkness. "Everything in space is moving. When you cease to move, you cease to be. And that's how it works in medicine. And that's why you're confused about when your patients aren't well. What's happening? What's happening is so external, you can't even imagine. It becomes internal."

Uh huh . . .

The narrator resumes our space tour only for Wiley to repeatedly interrupt. She can't help herself. *Circannual rhythms* and *synchronization, Pythagoras* and *musica universalis.*

"We hear the cosmic tunes. That's *entrainment,*" she says. "And what it means is estrogen, progesterone, cortisol, insulin, melatonin, HGH all play like the keys of a big grand piano to be sheet music of the cosmos. That's what hormones do. That's endocrinology. It's astronomy. It's astrology. It's physics. It's everything."

The lights finally come on and everyone blinks.

"Did you follow all of that?" I ask the naturopath from Portland who's sitting next to me. She nods unconvincingly.

I look around the room, and people are in quiet conversation with those around them, the way folks talk in low voices in a movie theater after watching some movie with a complicated plot.

But Wiley doesn't let the audience chatter go on for long, because she's feeling it, the music, the endocrinology, the astronomy, and for that matter the anthropology and the oncology. She slips out of her Chanel pumps and launches into a rambling discussion of in-vitro babies who'd started out as "freezer-burned Franken-fetuses," and we move onto circadian rhythms, and when a physician in the audience asks her if hormones arrive at cell receptors in "waves" as Wiley claims that they do, she stumbles a bit. Then she says that she doubts that anyone with an electron microscope has ever seen "a hormone come rolling into the beach as a wave."

From that little hiccup, Wiley transitions beautifully into causes for Type II diabetes, and it seems that a lot of the audience is impressed like I was when I first met her, if not by the contrast between her strong convictions and her unusual credentials, than by Wiley's charm, wit, curiosity, and enormous passion. Many of the MDs in the crowd, who are open-minded enough to show up at a medical seminar in a planetarium, genuinely want to believe that Wiley somehow has this whole hormone thing figured out, and before the seminar ends she'll argue her case in part by scribbling about a thousand authoritative looking, wave-type diagrams on the planetarium's white boards.

And yet, just when you want to believe that she's dead serious about turning her innovative medicine into mainstream science, Wiley will get a huge hug from a hulking, deep-voiced transgender female gynecologist whom Wiley helped through "the journey," and call on a member of the audience who proclaims that Wiley is "awakening the poet in everyone that went to medical school." And then Wiley will go on and on about how incredibly famous rock stars are on the WP (but remember, she'll say with a wink, their names don't leave the planetarium's confines), and how one such superstar "just wrote us a check" for one of Wiley's modest studies. At that point Wiley and her whole hypey endeavor seem discomforting.

I don't know if her science is wrong or right, good or bad. Nobody does. I'm also unsure whether Susie "T. S." Wiley will continue to deliver humanity, or at least her clients, hormone by hormone, to a better life. But I no longer feel the need to find out. I'm ready to let someone else be a guinea pig.

Lived on the edge plenty long.

During one of the meeting breaks, I walk up to Dr. Patil, who's sitting by herself in one of the planetarium's seats. She hasn't been terribly warm to me down here in Glendale, not that she's under any obligation. Patil is here as a student, not as my physician. Then again, Patil has never been warm, although she's always been honest and professional.

So it's appropriate that I approach her seeking only advice, and a sliver of advice at that. I want to know how to go off the T.

"Hi," I say, approaching her seat. "Can I talk to you for a minute?"

"HEYYYY, THERE HE IS," says Holmes, seated at a café's outdoor table and nursing an espresso. I roll straight up to him on my bike. Holmes is dressed in his gray-and-orange cycling kit.

"The day we've been waiting for, huh Coach?" I say, taking my foot out of the pedal and putting it on the ground. I look into the brown eyes of Roman Holmes. "Finally see who's faster."

And who's a liar.

This late September Saturday is clear and cool—as good a day as any to claw at your lungs and dip your muscles into an acid bath. That is, to bike race. Today is the Mt. Tamalpais Hill Climb, a 12.5-mile competition starting at Northern California's Stinson Beach and ending, 2,200 vertical feet of climbing later, near the top of Mt. Tam.

Seeing Holmes is bittersweet. We meet outside of the restaurant in the perfectly coiffed Marin County town of Mill Valley, where racks on car rooftops hold multi-thousand-dollar bikes, and trunks are filled with burgeoning Whole Foods grocery bags. Holmes straightens his long and thin body—he's built a lot like Michael—to get on his feet and shake my hand. Immediately I feel his good vibrations. From his deep but warm voice to his soft manner, he's that much more of a wonderful, positive guy in person than he is on the phone. If only I hadn't felt the need to dodge his multiple invitations for us to ride together over the last seven months. The doping undermined what might have been a real friendship.

"You'll do great today," says Holmes as we pedal away from Mill Valley's cozy downtown. Not long before today, Holmes had sent me some analysis of one of the workouts that I'd downloaded from my power meter and then uploaded to him. My lactate threshold for a twenty-minute interval was holding steady at 287 watts, and Holmes was impressed. Over the course of a grinding, seven-month racing season I'd experienced almost no drop-off in my peak power, which is a phenomenon unknown to most mortals.

But I'm not mortal. At least until sometime after this race.

The Mt. Tam event will be my last competition of the year.

"You'll do well, too," I say stiffly. Despite our many phone conversations and a multitude of email exchanges, Holmes and I aren't that familiar with each other.

Exactly how I wanted it.

"I don't know. The constant changes in gradient really mess with my legs," he says. "We'll see."

Holmes and I ride about forty-five minutes from Mill Valley up the opposite side of Mt. Tam from which we'll be racing. It counts as our pre-race warm-up, and when I think about how we're climbing a mountain in order to prepare our muscles and lungs to re-climb a mountain, I'm reminded just how ridiculously fit I am.

We descend from a shoulder of Mt. Tam into the tiny town of Stinson Beach. The beach's public parking lot is filled with cars, bicycles, athletes, and a couple ambulances on standby. Holmes and I are sweaty and hot, and we rush to register and pin our race numbers to our jerseys.

"Go get 'em, Coach!" I yell to Holmes as he rides toward the start line for his heat.

My race begins moments later, and about forty of us crowd into one lane on coastal Highway 1, riding the four miles northwest toward Bolinas Fairfax Road in a very tight and fast-moving cluster. I watch the shoulders and backs of the riders in front of me to anticipate what's happening ahead. Tempting as it is to stare at the rear wheel of the rider only inches in front of you, a racer is better off looking well beyond, as the leading edge of the group is where any abrupt changes in the peloton often begin, and then like a moving ripple eventually affect you. I ride as close to the front as possible to stay out of potential harm's way, and to wait for the right turn that represents the start of the eight-mile climb to the finish line. Eight miles is a long climb.

For once I feel good from the start. Shoulders and back are loose. Lungs feel cool and expansive. And the legs want to go harder. Credit goes to Holmes's and my long warm-up. And my fitness, and the T.

The group turns onto the smaller and rougher Bolinas Fairfax Road and several riders around me accelerate dramatically.

Knew this was coming!

Two riders in blue jerseys, another few in red and yellow kit, a sixth in gold, black, and white, and a seventh rider in blue and red, start to scamper up the lower, steeper sections of the climb that take us away from the Pacific Ocean.

Stay with your peeps.

The strongest riders want to distance themselves from everyone else as rapidly as possible. Their goal is to demoralize the group. Convince the athletes toward the middle and back of the field that they are hopelessly slower—nothing but posers and weekend blowhards in shiny shorts. Make them feel so inferior that, even with lots of racing left to go, they virtually give up on winning.

That's not me. I didn't dope and train and leave Juliana alone with the kids all those mornings, weeknights, and weekends to fall behind this group. I have the watts and stamina, the training miles and race experience to stay with these guys. Perhaps to have my way with them.

I latch onto the back of the lead group, and for maybe a mile we ride together, in silence. When the curving road steepens, I stand up on the pedals to keep apace. Standing feels good on my back and legs. I'm working different muscles. But I notice that none of the others stand. Not necessarily a bad sign. Some riders never stand up as they ride.

I'm fine. I could win this thing. Hell of a way to go out, to end my era of creams and syringes.

We round a couple more bends. One rider in the group falls a bit behind us, and when I look back seconds later he's twenty bike lengths in arrears, dropping like a bird falling out of the sky.

Completely demoralized. Hopes crushed.

Again none of the others come up off their saddles, and this time my six remaining opponents surge ahead of *me*, and I have to stand up again and work to catch up to them.

Hard.

I sit down to get comfortable on the saddle and a small gap almost immediately forms between me and the others. This time I ride almost as fast as I can, with a burst of energy lasting maybe five or seven seconds, in order to rejoin the group. The sweat finds my eyes, and pawing at them with my gloved right hand provides no relief.

Don't be left behind. Persevere!

None of the other riders look at each other, but there is a sense among the group that someone is weak. The road again steepens, and this time I don't stand up for fear that the others will notice that I am uncomfortable, or that even one of them will notice that I'm not feeling great and accelerate while I cannot.

This is where champions are made, forged out of flesh, determination, synthetic cycling-short chamois, and steroids. Don't give in!

But my opponents needn't accelerate. Each time the pedals go around, the other six riders pull a little ways ahead of me, and a gap of two feet becomes four, and then six. Six feet grows into twelve, and I stand again but my legs can't move the bike faster. The six men are half a bend ahead of me.

More effort!

I'm fading, like the exhausted guy who falls off the lifeboat in stormy seas and gets pulled inexorably in a different direction than the dinghy. The leaders are three quarters of a bend in front of me, and then a full turn ahead. And then they disappear.

I've been in this situation before. Many times. But this race, this moment, feels different. It feels *good.*

Oh, I've beat myself up before for being left behind in a bike race: *Why didn't you hang on a little longer?*

Why did you listen to the pain?

You were better than the competition!

But as I ride alone up part of the mountain, and still plenty fast— I'm in seventh!—there's a drop in my internal pressure. Not just the relief of avoiding head-to-head competition with the other top racers. But some unexpected consolation that the T, which for plenty of guys is as accessible as saying "Andrewpause," isn't an automatic game-changer. Even with all of my dedicated training and doping, I can't rely on my drugs to put me at the front of races. As far as I've traveled in my steroid odyssey, there's some satisfaction in knowing that my testosterone can't pedal, steer, and push a rider across the finish line.

Kind of a weird revelation for a doper. A doper, I guess, who *at times* loves the drugs yet *always* loves his sport. Someone who, in a perfect world, really wants bike races and baseball games and discus throws decided by other factors than drugs, even if those other factors still include true chemistry in the form of better training and equipment technologies. Why *not* toss in the drugs? Are we really making sport more fair, compelling, and safe by not acquiescing, by not saying WTF, syringes for all?

Sport reflects society. A subset of athletes will always cheat. But if we don't attempt to forbid drugs, which can wreak havoc not only on a sport or on a life but on lives, then where should we draw a line?

I know, this profound message comes from someone who is completely clear on the hypocrisy of his statements, who is pulling a stunt that essentially shoots gasoline from a hose at a drugs-in-sports issue that already burns bigger than a five-alarm fire. But this citizen doper can tell you that he's looked at the argument from a strange but different perspective: He is lab rat, athlete, father, journalist, fan, and mortal rolled into one. He's seen the drugs change some very precious lives.

One more contradiction comes to me as the sweat runs down my back: not winning is okay. As I move my legs round and round, I think about how there is happiness to be found in not leading the race. Because what I lose in vanity and glory, I gain in authenticity. Out of the running for the win, what I feel is truth—at least the truth that I'm supposed to be somewhere other than the front.

Those dope-fueled, exhilarating, catch-me-if-you-can moments at Berkeley Hills and the Berkeley Bicycle Club Criterium, as well as similar moments at Wards Ferry and the Cascade Classic, were a total blast. But those instances were so impermanent. When I was (sort of) crushing the competition, I never felt completely convinced that I was where I should be. And after the glory rides ended, and my preoccupations with victory subsided, I'd feel empty if not bad.

In retrospect, those infamous instances, even while I was in them, felt how one might feel to borrow someone else's Ferrari. Go fast, get some attention, and give back the keys. I felt removed. Those aren't my wheels, or my perfect body. That's not my *motor*.

I've never wondered where I'd put trophies in my house. Juliana and the kids forget what little I tell them about races five minutes after I deliver the news. Maybe I'd feel less ambivalent—more addicted—if I'd *won* every race. Perhaps if I took *more* drugs, and trained harder on them, and could always smell victory, I'd keep taking the stuff and maybe seek out more. I can imagine a professional cyclist falling prey to that dynamic. The number of times I considered taking my project to another level!

But now, riding alone up this ridiculously long climb, I'm sufficiently sobered.

Is there more to life than riding at the front of a fifty-man race held in the boonies? Cheating in order to do it?

I believe so.

THE FINAL SEVERAL MILES of the race up Mt. Tam ascend on rolling Ridgecrest Road, and its short but nagging grades are known as the "Seven Sisters." I ride up the first sister with several racers closing in on me, but now I'm relatively rested. Just when my competition thinks that it will pull alongside me, I accelerate on a steep section of the grade. I can practically hear the hope being sucked from their psyches.

Still the devil, you!

I continue to tease the others until I start to tire on what is, I don't know, maybe the fourth sister. That's when I receive my final boost of the 2008 cycling season. It's a drug that can't be found on any governing athletic body's list of prohibited substances.

"Come on Tilin! Keep it going!" yells Michael, who's standing on a grassy knoll, right next to the road. He's watching me roll very slowly up the grade. He's clapping hard, and then jogs alongside me. "You're top-ten!"

"I think I'm seventh," I gasp. "How many more Sisters?"

"Almost there," Michael yells. He's wearing his typical three-day beard, and a pair of baggy gray sweats. "Maintain that gap. Nearly home!"

"You don't need to yell Mike," I say. "I'm right next to you."

I'm hardly mad. What a guy! It's a pretty day, and from various stretches of Ridgecrest you can enjoy incredible views of the Pacific Ocean, coastline, and hills. But if I weren't racing today (Michael doesn't particularly like hill climbs) I'd be doing something besides watching a bunch of bulky-legged, big-lunged athletes crawl up the side of a mountain. Maybe I'd clean rain gutters on my roof. Road racing has to be one of the world's least satisfying sports to watch live. Spectators wait forever to see ten seconds of action.

But Michael didn't hesitate to make the long drive from the Silicon Valley to offer me his support. He traded the better part of his day just to yell three sentences of encouragement at a friend who's just as crazy—actually, crazier—than he is. That's Mike. Three decades of friendship, and while he'd rather his closest pal not be a doper, for me he's willing to look past the rules of a sport that for many years has consumed him. Somehow, in the straightforward ride-eat-sleep world according to Mike, where bike racing is supposed to be a simple and pure passion, he's tolerated me making the endeavor thoroughly complex. Maybe at some level, Michael knew that this crazy year provided me with the closure I needed for a sport that he and I wouldn't compete in for too much longer. I could be wrong. Whatever the case,

I believe that Mike is the kind of friend who would give me his highly developed left leg.

In that last stretch of the race, Michael makes my heart happy, and my legs a little bit stronger.

I cross the line six seconds ahead of the eighth place finisher and look at my power meter: 47 minutes, 43 seconds. When I find Coach Holmes in the finishing area, he informs me that he finished minutes behind me.

"I beat you by a little," I say, kicking my cleated shoes out of my pedals, getting off my bike, and sitting down on the pavement. I'm flattened.

Anything else to report?

"Just a little?" he asks with nothing but warmth in his voice.

"Okay, a bit," I say, taking off my glasses.

Nail your hands to the cross, doper! Speak up!

"Guess we finally arrived at the truth about who's a strong rider," he says cheerfully. He's wearing a proud grin.

"Yes," I reply, looking down at the ground. "I guess."

I'm too ashamed to say anything more.

"THE MOMENT, HAS COME," I announce to Juliana soon after pulling my car up to the house after returning home from the race up Mt. Tamalpais. "The experiment is over. Starting tomorrow, I quit the drugs."

She's sitting at her desk, holding up a camera lens to the light in our downstairs home office. "So this is it. You're sure?" she asks, grabbing another lens and holding it up to the light. "You're ready?"

"Last race is finished. Been chasing and taking the drugs for a year."

"I knew decision-day was coming," she says, setting down the second lens and bending over at the waist to rummage through a camera bag that's on the floor. "But you know, I don't know if *I'm* ready."

This is not something I expect. "Really? I don't get it."

"You're a different Andrew," she says, straightening, with a lens polishing cloth in hand.

"No kidding," I say, grimacing. I can feel the encrusted salt on my upper cheek. I hadn't washed my face since I'd raced. My entire body is covered in a film of dried sweat.

"You're not the only one who's thought twice about saying goodbye to the new you," she says. "The person you are now has some great qualities," Juliana continues. "Aggro and intense, yes. But there's also a certain lightness that comes from you being more in your body and less in your head."

"I know, that's true." I say. "But what am I supposed to do? Keep doping?"

"No. Do what you say you're going to do," she says, arranging a bunch of camera batteries. "Off the testosterone, you're going to be whoever you'll be. Maybe you'll be the same, maybe you'll be someone entirely new—not the old Andrew, not the T Andrew. Maybe someone new will emerge." She smiles and begins to pack her camera bags.

A whole new Andrew. There's something to think about.

Juliana finishes packing for a photo shoot she has later. A family portrait. Juliana's job will be to make sure everyone looks good for the camera, although that doesn't always mean she wants everyone smiling. She likes photographs that are more interesting and revealing than they are adamantly happy. Her sensibility isn't universally liked, but I appreciate it. Our home's walls have long hosted Tilin family shots that are candid, or barely staged. They feel real to me. There's Benjamin holding Dee Dee close, a vulnerable look on my son's face. There's Sophie walking across the sand of a beach, looking haunting and waif-like rather than cute. There's Andrew with a furrowed brow. Smiling a lot would be great, and I like to smile. But I don't always smile. No one does.

Real moments in real lives.

Maybe that's what the doping has been all about. An attempted escape from me. From my life. Not only from my head, but from my maturing relationship, and the mundaneness that is the same blue shovel I've always picked up to clean Lola's litter box, the same gas station that I always visit, and the same, skinny and bored, Safeway cashier lady looking straight through me every time she asks, "You need help out to your car?"

The bike alone used to represent escape. Days filled with sun! Speed! Mountains! But after Benjamin and Sophie were born, the bike rides shortened, the opportunities to explore new roads, or trails on my mountain bike, were largely history, and time was a huge factor. Juliana and I raised babies.

Then the kids graduated from diapers and naps, and the bike beckoned again. If the rides couldn't be all-day excursions, at least they could be intense, and if they were intense than why not race, like your buddy Mike? Join him on the Nor Cal circuit, and use the races as levers to travel, and to be gone again for a day or days at a time. Freedom returns! But then organize your intense and derailed workouts, truly systematize them, put them on a calendar, and before you know it, you're an upload/download/workout-data human hamster on a wheel, complete with a twenty-pack of razor blades for your legs.

I've done this to myself, I know. This binge-purge bicycling exis-tence. Something inside me likes all of the control and discipline required in a racer's daily life. But not all of me likes it.

That's where the T comes in. As complicated as the Wiley Protocol is, the T helps me bring the *riding* into focus. The essence of cycling, which is moving your legs. That's what you want to do on the drugs—ride, not obsess and plan and dwell.

Indeed, at one level the T is this fitness geek's recreational drug. I seldom drink more than a beer or glass of wine, and haven't smoked much pot for decades. What better way to escape reality than while *on* my bike? The freshness comes in sizing up the competition through steroid-tinted lenses, the physiologic/psychological disposition that magically lets me change the dynamics of a weekend group ride or a piddly-ass bike race with a few angry, high-wattage strokes of the ped-als. Oh, the sweet rush! The drugs helping me fly over life's otherwise mundane roads!

Hey Safeway lady, look at me. I'm leading a bike race. Does it look like I need help out to my fucking car?

One minute I bid the T a thoroughly thought out farewell. The next I don't want a life without it.

There are the bedroom issues too, and the swagger. Cast another vote for the new Andrew. The masculinity factor plays a huge role in why I juiced for so long. Really: Wasn't the very first indication of morning wood enough to get the point? Did I really need the 89th erection? The 173rd?

But all that sex . . .

"All" is a relative term, dude.

Quiet!

But all that sex did not create true intimacy between Juliana and me. Hearts don't necessarily touch along with those other parts, and on occasion, when the relations were bad and the sex was good, the feeling was hollow. As if Juliana and I, two decades into a relationship, were using each other. Marriage sluts. Juiced marriage sluts, living under a roof built over a house of T.

It's a strange sensation to be a man in the middle of his life, contemplating the notion of walking away from the person that he is.

THE NIGHT FOLLOWING my race up Mt. Tam, Juliana and I crawl into bed, beat after a busy day. I move closer to my wife, spooning her, and I'm confident that she feels all of me. While Juliana doesn't turn around, and I don't push to turn closeness into sex, she does draw her right leg back and, using her foot, hooks that leg around my right leg. Two smooth, muscular legs, intertwined.

"Sure you want to go off that stuff?" she teases.

The next day I wake up early, ready to end the party, to quit the T. I am on drugs. I want to be off drugs.

At Wiley's seminar, Patil's reply to my inquiry about how to quit the protocol boiled down to two words: cold turkey. She didn't smile as she said it, or offer any more guidance. Could be that she saw me as a traitor, or a dilettante.

I shuffle in my slippers, on a Sunday morning and in a quiet house, toward the stairs, and the laptop that awaits me in our home office.

I sit down at my desk, turn on my computer, and do something inadvisable. I surf the Web.

Many of the steroid- and bodybuilding-related websites have pages and pages dedicated to advice and chat-site exchanges about coming off steroids. They warn that depression and loss of motivation can go hand in hand with deflating muscles. Steroid.com recommends a nine-part termination, including a slow wean from certain substances, taking multiple drugs to avoid "an estrogen surplus," and other drugs still to increase the body's own testosterone production, which according to Wiley can slow down by as much as seventy-five percent when exogenous testosterone is used consistently.

"The cortisone receptors will be free," reads a passage of the website's page titled "Coming Off Steroids." "In combination with the low testosterone and androgen levels a considerable loss of strength and mass, and an increase of fat and water, and often gynecomastia will occur."

I understand enough of what I read to feel very uncomfortable. Gynecomastia is the sometimes significant enlargement of men's breasts, otherwise known as "bitch tits," which can occur in certain unlucky steroid users when their bodies convert hormones like testosterone to estrogen.

Wiley had previously told me that her rhythmic dosing protocol is specifically designed to avoid any excessive conversion of testosterone to estrogen. She said that her system is essentially bitch-tit-proof. I sure hope she's right. I don't want to go from the 'roids to a bra. Or to take more drugs to get off the testosterone and DHEA that I'm already on.

Still worried, I email Juliana's women's health care doctor. I'm grateful when she soon writes back. She cautions that while she doesn't know my exact situation, I could consider weaning myself off the hormones by cutting my doses in half for the first week and then in half for another week before stopping the treatments entirely. She says that Patil may have given me her advice because, in terms of mature women on supplemental hormones, the medical literature doesn't recommend one method of discontinuing HRT protocols over another.

"Slower weans are less shocking for the body," the doctor writes.

But I'm spooked. I take no action for two weeks. I remain on the protocol, and just for old time's sake I sign up for a fitness assessment at a local gym. As part of the assessment I ride a stationary bike until I can't ride any harder. I equal my personal record for sustainable power: 310 watts.

"You were in there for a long time," Juliana says to me a couple mornings after my fitness assessment, as I open our bathroom door. "Have you reduced your dosages at all?"

I shake my head. "I'm scared, Juliana," I say with a sigh, and sit down at the edge of our bed.

"Oh," she says, and walks right up to me. Then she hugs my head against her warm belly. It's smooth and reassuring. I feel calm.

"What are you afraid of?" she asks quietly.

"I don't know. I guess change. Something new. Old-new," I say.

"I'll still love you," she says. "You're going to be the man I've known for almost twenty years. The person I married. Not the man I've known for less than a year."

"I know we've already been through all of this," I say. "But will you miss the new me?"

"Some things," she says.

"It's hard for me to say goodbye."

"I can imagine."

"Will you love me if my boobs get bigger than yours?" I ask. That's funny, and we laugh. It's also not funny.

"Andrew, have some faith," says Juliana, and she looks down at me, appearing calm and wise behind her librarian glasses. She lightly touches my forehead where it folds together when I think hard. The creases are permanent. I know.

"Maybe you can look forward to less turmoil," she says. "Being more peaceful."

Peaceful.

That'll work.

I NEVER PUSH ANOTHER full dose of the T out of a gray Wiley Protocol for Men syringe. The week of half doses goes by uneventfully. My chest doesn't metamorphose. The small but real biceps remain. Ditto the nocturnal penile tumescence.

By the eighth day, not much has changed, and I grow impatient. I'm intolerant of the syringes, the cream, and all the ceremony and caution required of a doper. I'm ready to be divorced from strength in a tube. But I apply the quarter dose as planned.

On the tenth day I'm done. I can't wait the full fourteen days, I just can't. I stop applying supplemental hormones.

On the twelfth day, I feel like I have the flu, and have little strength. The testosterone production machinery in my brain and balls is no longer accustomed to working very hard. My own body might not produce pre-Wiley levels of testosterone, Wiley had once informed me, for approximately three to six months.

"Look at that," I say to Juliana on the first morning my body is truly out of whack.

I'm standing by my side of the bed, woozy but insistent that we make it. We always make the bed.

The top sheet is pulled back. There's a big stain where I sleep. Night sweats.

"I think I'm hormonal," I say. Juliana grins.

In the coming weeks, I don't feel tip-top or terrible—just kind of puny. I work. Juliana and I occasionally make love. I ride my bike some, but not a lot. It's hard to know if I don't ride because I'm depressed about life without syringes, burnt out on riding, or feeling funky about my year as a doper. Lots of racers can't get on their bikes for a month or more after the season ends. Maybe I'm just tired—from the hard racing, or the emotional energy spent on my project, or the loss of the super fuel. Or all of the above.

I take the time away from my bike to do anything that doesn't resemble cycling or doping. I cook the occasional dinner, and give Juliana the green light to take on heaps of photography work. *Good for her*, I think, and my weekends quickly fill with soccer dad chores. I drive Benjamin and Sophie all over Oakland for their weekend games, and it's a big change to have the car filled with the smell of someone else's sweat. It's Indian Summer in the Bay Area, and two or three or four Tilins often eat ice cream on Sundays courtesy of the ice cream man who always magically appears at the soccer fields when the kids' games end.

I'm not the only one who's trying new things. Mike starts dating a sweet brainiac of a biologist, and he calls often to talk about her, and how his priorities are shifting along with mine.

"If she and I are a solid *we* then I have zero problem missing a race, even a big one," he tells me one day in the fall of 2008. "That's the value of a good relationship, no?"

I'm happy to hear him happy and tell him yes, he's right.

"By the way," he adds. "How's the detox?"

Wiley's assistant calls, too. Wiley had heard—maybe from Dr. Patil, or the pharmacist—that I had gone off the protocol, and she wanted to know why. I explain to her assistant about the book, and that turning away from the supplemental hormones is part of my year's experience. She tells me that if I ever want to go back, Wiley herself will help put the HRT machinery in motion again. I reply that maybe someday I'll consider it. Then I hang up as quickly as politeness allows, the way I would with a telemarketer.

For now, what I really want is some distance from the doping. I want to live on a non–hormone planet for some time, to feel normal and do normal things. I'm starting to feel better physically, but I'm still detoxing mentally. It's hard to explain this to other people.

Innis phones me one day. "Want to go for a ride?" he asks.

"No thanks. I'm not in the mood. Another time," I tell him.

"Hey, can I tell Scott about your doping?" he asks. "Your performance at Cascade still has him tied up in knots." Scott is another cycling friend of ours, but I hadn't let him in on the secret. Scott is a good guy, but I just didn't want too many people to know. He's also a very good rider. I'd finished ahead of him at Cascade.

"Don't tell him yet," I say. "I'm not ready to talk about it."

"Okay, that's cool, I can hold off. Let him stew a while longer," he jokes. "How is the writing going?" he asks.

I tell him the truth, that I haven't started writing yet. I'm still working through everything that's happened in my mind. I take walks or runs instead of rides, and while my body is in motion, my thoughts inevitably creep toward my doping odyssey. I think about the entire year. About what it is to put a face on the act of taking performance-enhancing drugs. I wonder what it's like to be a professional athlete who dopes, and spends perhaps years experiencing some of the things that I've felt—and maybe a lot more—without the ability to ever tell many people, if not to keep it a secret from the entire world. I think such a pledge of silence could drive someone crazy. My job as a doper, in comparison, wasn't nearly as difficult. I had Michael and Juliana, Tracy and Luke and Innis, to act as sounding boards. I could always turn to Benjamin and Sophie for hugs and love. My career didn't depend on PEDs landing me on a podium.

All the drugs had to give me, I decide, was an experience. Fast or slow, happy or pissed, horny or not in the mood, the outcomes mattered a whole lot less than the 3D, surround-sound process.

One day, some time after the drugs have left my body, I return home from one of my runs and look in the mirror before stepping into the shower. I measure up what I see. For sure, there is a man with smaller biceps and narrower shoulders than the guy I spotted in the same place months earlier.

Boyo, those chemicals did some wondrous things.

But the person I see is okay, too. I like him. My life is incredibly full, and further enriched by the drug-taking experience. As for the return of my skinny-ass body, I'm happy to have it back. It's what I needed to worm my way out of one deep hole.

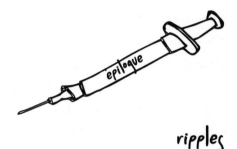

ripples

M y supplemental testosterone stopped flowing in 2008. But the drugs and doping, in ways large and small, continued to cause repercussions—and not just in my own life.

IN LATE 2008 I inform my cycling coach, Roman Holmes, that I no longer require his coaching services. I explain that I want to spend more time with Juliana and the children, and to focus on my work. The commitment to compete, I explain, is huge, and I never can successfully stick to the life schedules suggested in those fitness-training books.

I still feel crappy about my secret. But I don't confess to my sins, even when Holmes temporarily relocates to the Bay Area for most of 2009 to oversee operations of a bicycle touring company. He's a forty-five-minute drive from my house. Despite his attempts to get together, we do not see each other. I don't want to be reminded of the dynamic that I created.

Then in October 2010, I enter a hill-climb-style bike race that ends atop the East Bay's 3,900-foot Mt. Diablo. I train modestly and sporadically for the event, and my goal is to finish in under one hour. I feel slow during the race, and as many people pass me as I seem to pass. Two-thirds of the way up, a guy in familiar gray and orange kit rolls by me very quickly. It's Roman Holmes.

At the top of the mountain I find Holmes. We shake hands—I'm genuinely happy to see him, and thrilled to be competing, even at a modest level. I couldn't care less that he beat me. I apologize to him for having been in such poor contact, explaining that I was working on a big project. Holmes now lives back in the Pacific Northwest, and remains his easygoing self. "Everybody in California is so busy," he says matter-of-factly.

Again I say nothing about the doping or the book, but tell him that we should talk and that I'll call soon. Adding to the day's unsettling feel, I finish the race in one hour and twenty-five friggin' seconds.

It's not until January 2011 that I decide I can't put it off any longer. My book is already available for pre-order on Amazon, and I'm afraid that Holmes will soon get wind of what I've done from another source. I want to be the one to inform him. I call Holmes and disclose everything.

"I have to say, this is hilarious," he says when I tell him. "I can't wait to read it. Will you sign my copy?"

"You're not mad?" I ask.

Mellow as ever, Holmes wonders whether or not the T should receive a lot of credit for my improvements. He also thinks that my experience might do the sport some good.

"If you expose what might be going on at the amateur level in cycling, it'll open people's eyes," he says. "That's the funny thing about the truth. It's not something you want to hide or something that you want to get out. But in the end it's all we have. It's what we have to move forward in this world."

I love this guy.

I ONLY RACE my bicycle once in 2009, the year after my doping experiment, in a two-person "team" time trial in early March. Many factors play into one's result in a team time trial. Lack of strength certainly plays into mine. I finish almost two-and-a-half minutes slower than I had one year earlier, and am confronted with a sort of drug-free athletic mortality: *I'll never again be as fast as I was in 2008.* That is a really unhappy thought.

I'm not the only one to quit racing. Innis, with two small children, stops in early 2009. Michael races all of 2009 and then gears up for a 2010 campaign, only to quit before the year is half over. He stops in part to spend more time with his girlfriend, the biologist. She buys her own racing bike so they can spin together, but she only rides for fun.

My buddy Luke races to this day. Innis vows to return sometime in 2011. Michael and I still talk about competing all the time.

IN EARLY 2009, Harvard Medical School associate clinical professor of urology Abraham Morgentaler publishes *Testosterone for Life.* Morgentaler has performed years' worth of testosterone-related research, resulting in him frequently championing the prescribing and use of supplemental testosterone. Morgentaler's book makes many compelling arguments for men with naturally low testosterone to take the T. It claims, for instance, that such men will experience improved health, in regards to muscular strength, bone density, and perhaps a reduction in the chances of developing prostate cancer. (Morgentaler and Patil are two of a growing number of physicians and scientists debating assorted connections between the likes of testosterone, dihydrotestosterone, and prostate health. Both doctors told me, for example, that higher levels of DHT and testosterone found in the blood are not indications of higher T inside the prostate, where they can trigger enlargement.) "After six decades of use," Morgentaler writes, "T therapy appears to be safe, with appropriate medical monitoring."

When I attempt to explain Wiley's fluctuating dosing schedule to the same Dr. Morgentaler during a 2011 telephone interview, he remarks, "This rhythm method makes no sense to me." When I characterize Wiley as a researcher but not a physician, he says, "The idea that someone would get medical care from someone who's not an MD? That blows my mind."

Wiley doesn't exactly revere Morgentaler either, whom she says receives credit for unearthing information about testosterone that's been around for years. "Guys like him are not big hitters. They're idiots who got publicity," she tells me over the phone in 2011. "Do you want someone who holds your penis all day to tell you about hormones?"

As for Wiley herself, citing "seasonal changes in terms of breeding" and physiology related to testosterone hormones coupling with a sufficient number of cellular "receptors," in 2009 she dramatically raises the testosterone dosages in her Wiley Protocol for Men for certain times of the year. In the fall, for example, Wiley now suggests that men take seventy-five percent more testosterone than what I used. I wonder whether or not such high levels of the T could make an already edgy guy like me touchier still.

IN MAY 2009, the United States Food and Drug Administration requires that the manufacturers of two leading testosterone gel products modify the labels on their packaging. The labels for the topical testosterone, instructs the FDA, must include boxed warnings that alert users of the gels' potential for "secondary exposure." The catalyst behind such changes is a collection of "adverse event reports" fielded by the FDA indicating problems stemming from children coming into contact with their fathers' topical testosterone. Those affected range in ages from two-and-a-half to five years old, and they each display signs of virilization that range from five-inch growth spurts (over six months) to the emergence of hair on an upper lip to enlarged genitalia. One government expert wrote, "It is a concern of this reviewer that transfer through commonly used household items such as towels and bed linens may occur."

I'm reminded that testosterone—which some people might shrug off as an almost clichéd performance-enhancing drug—is very powerful. I do not miss living with the worry that what I add to my body could potentially change the bodies of my wife and/or kids. Anyone using such a drug should proceed with real caution. Heed those labels.

IN LATE 2009, a six-month, double-blind clinical trial of older men on testosterone gel treatment is halted because of "adverse cardiovascular events," including heart attacks and elevated blood pressure. During the National Institute on Aging–backed "Testosterone in Older Men Trial," five of the 103 men who receive a placebo suffer some sort of cardiovascular event. Meanwhile, twenty-three of the 106 who receive daily testosterone supplements encounter a similar fate. The average age of the subjects, all of whom have low testosterone and are not in great health to begin with, is seventy-four years old. They're not exactly fit men in their forties. But a halted clinical trial meant to answer questions about the long-term effects of supplemental testosterone should give any potential T user reason to stop and think before taking the plunge.

I SEE MY primary care physician, Regina Vu, in April 2010. My medical checkup is uneventful, and we're both glad that I'm in seemingly excellent physical health following my year of doping. She listens to me complain about the ebbing of my sex drive, and what I feel is my loss of swagger. Vu orders a complete work up of my blood, and tells me that she'll have a copy of the results sent to me, and that she'll call me if the numbers show cause for concern. My total testosterone is 254 nanograms per deciliter, or basically one-third of what it had been at its highest measured point during my year on the T. I am barely within the lab's suggested reference range for testosterone (250 to 1,100 ng/dl). Vu doesn't call me. Apparently she thinks I'm fine.

I visit my urologist in January 2011. I'm freaked out because I often feel a great urgency to pee, and I urinate with increasing frequency. Is my prostate enlarged? Do I have cancer? Was my experiment completely reckless? Am I going to die?

He looks unconcerned, snaps on a rubber glove, and feels my prostate gland.

"Large, but not hard or bumpy," he says. "You're fine."

He tells me that I'm middle aged, and so is my prostate. He tells me to dial back the coffee. Caffeine might be irritating my bladder.

The urologist also sees the results of my last blood test, and asks if I'm interested in going back on the T. I take a sample box of Testim, a testosterone gel. It remains unused.

AROUND CHRISTMASTIME OF 2010, with Juliana standing by my side and in our home's living room, I tell Benjamin and Sophie that I'm in the middle of writing a book that's interesting but not necessarily a happy tale. Both kids are lying on the couch.

"In fact, it's kind of a weird story. It's called *The Doper Next Door*," I say. Benjamin is now almost eleven years old, and has an older and bigger face that better match his permanent teeth. He also already has an air of teenage self-consciousness about him. His eyes dart about.

"Wow, Dad," he says. "I guess that's cool. You cheated? Why?"

I tell him it was partially in the name of writing about doping in a way that hadn't been written.

"It was an experiment," I say. "I don't know if it was right or wrong. I think some people might be mad at me when they find out that I cheated. I feel badly for lying to folks and some athletes. I'll apologize," I say.

"Oh, okay," says Benjamin, looking confused. "You did something knowing you'd have to apologize?"

Good question.

"Yes, Benjamin. I did," I finally say.

"Oh, okay, cool," he says.

He's bewildered.

"I like cheese!" announces eight-year-old Sophie, who's clearly bored, and hanging upside-down off the side of the couch.

Hopefully, by the time my children are old enough to understand the book, *I'll* fully comprehend what I've done, too, in putting my family and me potentially in harm's way to experience PEDs.

I pray that Ben and Sophie judge me kindly.

BELIEVE IT OR NOT, we're moving to Austin in July 2011. Soon after I told the kids about the doping, Juliana and I made the huge and difficult decision to move—a decision that's based on finances, lifestyle, and Juliana's longtime desire to live near her family. The week I finish writing this book is the week our house goes on the market (so much for returning to post-doping normalcy). The move is the next Tilin odyssey.

EX-PRO CYCLIST JOE PAPP, who is scheduled to be sentenced for dealing performance-enhancing drugs sometime around the release date of this book, responds schizophrenically to my telling him about the project. "I'd be willing to consider writing the foreword, if that's something you want to pursue," Papp tells me over the phone in January 2011. But soon thereafter, he helps launch a minor flurry of Web-generated bile about my upcoming work. "Wonder how aggressively @usantidoping will come out against the author of this filth," he tweets soon after our conversation. I can't tell whether he's writing to help me promote my book, raise his own profile, or because he's truly disgusted by my behavior. Papp and I have a decent relationship. But he's a complicated guy, and difficult to read.

However, I'm not the only one in the business of distributing filth. Papp had distributed drugs through the website www.eposino. com, and in March 2011 I catch up with Neal Schubel, a 46-year-old,

ANDREW TILIN 365

former amateur bike racer from Saginaw, Michigan who had once been an eposino.com customer. Schubel, it turns out, had purchased the performance-enhancing drug EPO approximately five years earlier. The United States Anti-Doping Agency, a national sports-policing foundation, busted him near the end of 2010.

"I shouldn't have been online buying illicit things. But I kind of wanted to know the dark side," Schubel, who wasn't a top competitor, told me over the phone. "I didn't even race on the drugs. I just wanted to see what they would do from a performance standpoint." Schubel believes Papp ratted on him. Papp and USADA don't discuss the case.

"I was just some Joe Schmuck on Papp's list," a resigned Schubel told me. "I'm the low-hanging fruit."

Apparently a doper never knows when the call may come.

IN JANUARY 2011, I call USADA. I have multiple motivations for making contact. I want to be forthcoming about my doping odyssey. I don't want the folks at USADA to be surprised by my stunt when the book gains notice—I'm not out to show up the agency. And I want closure on my project. What does it feel like, metaphorically speaking, to have the 'cuffs slapped on your wrists? I knew I'd be suspended. At least I thought I knew that.

I play phone tag for a week with someone in USADA's communications department, and when we finally connect he says he'll ask his superiors to call me. Six weeks later, I make contact with him again.

"The situation is unique," the communications man says.

This is taking forever, and I'm confessing to my sins. Will the doping cops look the other way? Never bust me? Whassup?

I go online and buy myself a 2011 USA Cycling racing license, because I can. I consider entering a race, even though the book project has anchored me to my desk for months. I'm out of shape.

On March 4, I receive a call from USADA CEO Travis Tygart. He tells me his agency takes very seriously what I've done. He laughs in an irritated way more than once, I think because he's bothered by the thought of me gaming the system for the purpose of selling a book.

I understand.

"Do you think you get special treatment?" he asks.

"No, I don't," I reply.

"We're obligated to stop whoever breaks the rules. You don't get forgiveness," says Tygart.

Two weeks later, I receive a call from Stephen Starks. Starks is USADA's legal affairs director.

"I don't want to make this adversarial," he says. "I think your book can be very useful."

For what? Fueling USADA bonfires? As a cautionary tale?

Starks asks me some basic questions about when I first took PEDs and what substances I took. He asks me if I trafficked in the drugs.

"No."

Starks explains that, if I promptly accept a two-year sanction from USADA, I'll avoid the possibility of a four-year sanction for "aggravating circumstances," which includes me doping with multiple substances on multiple occasions. The ban will make me ineligible to compete at events authorized by USA Cycling (among other sports-governing bodies), and I'll also be banned from, ahem, participation on any U.S. Olympic team. I can request a hearing, too, and opt to mount a legal defense.

I also must return all race winnings, but that is a non-issue. I never cashed the check I received for twenty-five dollars for my tenth-place finish at the July 2008 Cascade Cycling Classic.

"That's where we are," says Starks. "Nobody's telling you not to write your story, or how to report it."

I decide to accept the two-year sanction. The next day, Starks sends me the boilerplate, three-page contract.

Within days I sign the document, and watch it feed through the fax machine. As the pages move, I feel shame and confusion. Gone are my race results, as I'm officially disqualified from every event that I'd entered while on the drugs. I'm also giving the drug agency permission to have me pee into a cup, under the naked eye of a doping cop, whenever USADA wants to test me. The faxed pages are like sad, flattened memories of what had been a fun year of competing, and I want to say that I'm truly sorry to my fellow racers, cycling's organizers, and its governing bodies for my misdeeds. You didn't deserve my lies. No matter how curious or interesting the story may be, nobody deserved my lies.

All of this darkness, however, also comes with a strange epiphany.

For better or worse, heading to the doping penalty box is only one more chapter in the experience of some of society's most visible—daresay most modern—men: chemically enhanced, clock (and stopwatch) defying, attention-grabbing, crush-the-competition, successful, twenty-first century men. Stallone. McGwire. Schwarzenegger. And the rumors, of course, won't stop swirling around huge names like Bonds and Armstrong anytime soon. I'm being penalized, yes, as well as initiated into an exclusive club, although the highbrow members will never acknowledge me. Others eventually might. In the coming years, I wonder, how many guys like me will join.

acknowledgments

Thank you, body. You did it. You pulled through. I'm looking forward to many great years together. I love you.

I also want to thank other people's bodies, particularly their fabulous brains. Laura Mazer, Charlie Winton, Jack Shoemaker, and all the great folks at Counterpoint, who saw much more than syringes and biceps in this project. I'm grateful for their faith, vision, and patience. Laura deserves a second (and third and fourth) bow, as she's everything a writer could want in an editor: positive, energetic, and extremely sharp. Joy Tutela, a member of the fantastic group at the David Black Literary Agency, is more tenacious than the grittiest bike racer. Joy only knows one direction: forward.

Susan and Alex Heard, who have been my mentors, editors, friends, researchers, and cheerleaders now for about two decades.

Other publishing-business pals and peers were also key in making this book. Andy Raskin for his fantastic early guidance. Gretchen

Reynolds, a great friend and one of the most thorough journalists I know, for unselfishly sharing all sorts of information. Mark Bryant, who always listened and stuck up for me. Adam Horowitz, who consistently asked nicely if I was done yet. Chris Keyes and *Outside* magazine's staff for giving me the chance to tell my story in magazine form.

Publicists Gregg Sullivan and Jesica Church, who helped me spread the word. Jen Colton buoyed me with her enthusiasm and friendship. And a shout out to Marlene Saritzky for her encouragement and friendship.

Readers and super-close amigos Kate Hartley, Karen Donald, Adam Willner, Stephen Myers, Courtney Weaver, Robin Strawbridge, Phillip Kelloff, Alison Biggar, Jeff "Padre" Kunkel, Sally Small, Joe Anastazi, Sandy Bails, Bob Howells, Lilian Carswell, Stuart Stevens, and Jim Feeley. I didn't do it. WE did it!

Fabulous assists and information from Al Johnson, Sara Gottfried, John Hoberman, John Amory, Margery Gass, Arlene Weintraub, Brian Alexander, and Susan Cohen.

Maude Foster, who gave me courage and, in front of the mirror, x-ray vision.

Transcriptionist Vanessa Barth, who's heard more about endocrinology than some endocrinologists.

Friends who kept in touch and sent positive vibes long after I'd turned into a writing hermit: Dana Wiltsek, Michelle Wilson, David and Mary Rosenthal, Andy and Inga Sweet, Doug and Amy Boxer, Evan and Laura Marquit, Graham and Hilary Cooper, Mark Kenward and Megan Armstrong, Gia Laverne, and Gary Theut.

Everyone who makes amateur bike racing run, from USA Cycling to race directors to all of the racers. My inner circle of riding buddies, who hopefully will bring me back up to speed, or some fraction thereof. Of course a big nod to the open-minded Coach Holmes. I'm in awe of your dedication to the sport—all of you. My sentiments are similar for the fearless practitioners, supporters, and patients of anti-aging medicine. Thanks for letting me through so many doors.

Joe Papp, whom I wish well.

Tracy Tilin McKendell, who is my big sis and a ridiculously enthusiastic fan. I don't know how, but you still laugh at what I say. And you make sure that Larry and Alec are never too far away. Don't ever stop bringing the hugs and humor. I love you all.

Michael, wow. You're just so dang faithful.

My dear sweet children, whom I'm lucky enough to see every single day. And my wife, who wants nothing more for me than happiness. You've given me every opportunity to chase visions. How wonderful you are.